AND PARTY
EVERY DAY

AND PARTY EVERY DAY

The Inside Story of

Larry Harris

with Curt Gooch and Jeff Suhs

An Imprint of Hal Leonard Corporation
New York

Published in 2009 by Backbeat Books
An Imprint of Hal Leonard Corporation
7777 West Bluemound Road
Milwaukee, WI 53213

Trade Book Division Editorial Offices
19 West 21st Street, New York, NY 10010

CASABLANCA is a trademark of the Universal Music Group family of companies and is being used under license.

Printed in the United States of America

Book design by Lynn Bergesen
Typography by UB Communications

Library of Congress Cataloging-in-Publication Data

Harris, Larry Alan, 1947-
    And party every day : the inside story of Casablanca Records / Larry Harris, with Curt Gooch and Jeff Suhs.
        p. cm.
    Includes bibliographical references, discography, filmography, and index.
    ISBN 978-0-87930-982-4 (alk. paper)
    1. Casablanca Records—History. 2. Sound recording industry—United States—History. 3. Scott, Neil, 1943-1982. 4. Popular music—United States—History and criticism. I. Gooch, Curt. II. Suhs, Jeff. III. Title.
    ML3792.C37H37 2009
    781.640973'09047—dc22
                        2009032038

www.backbeatbooks.com

To Neil Bogart, my mentor, friend, and second cousin
(once removed, whatever that means)—
a true creative force in the entertainment industry,
whose energy and gutsy approach to everything
from music and film to philanthropy
made the world a better place.

While, like the rest of us, he wasn't perfect,
he certainly made his mark
on the lives of countless millions.

Contents

Preface

A long time ago, I met a man who was painting a building. It was a small building, and he asked me to help him paint it, so I did. As we were painting, people would walk by. A few of them looked a bit crazy, just like us, so we asked them to help, and they did.

And then the building started growing. The more we painted, the more the place grew. The more it grew, the more crazy people showed up to help us paint it.

The building was becoming a palace, but it wasn't necessarily a "nice" palace. Soon, it was filled with things you wanted so desperately you could taste them. Things that you got and ended up wishing you didn't have. Money. Cocaine. Weed. Booze. Sex and mountains of Quaaludes. Success and excess at every level. And, worst of all, the promise of more. Within five years, the palace took up an entire city block, and the sign out front read "Casablanca Records."

My boss, my cousin, my mentor—a complete fucking genius named Neil Bogart—was the guy who started us all painting. "Painting the building" was his mantra, his way of saying that if you looked successful, you *were* successful. Perception was reality. He was right.

But the story of Casablanca was about more than just Neil. It was about the 1970s. I take that back—it wasn't about the 1970s, it *was* the 1970s. It was the story of the music industry in the go-for-broke Me Decade. In those five years, we built our beloved Casablanca from a four-person, one-act outfit into a corporation with 175 employees, more than 140 artists, and an Academy Award–winning motion picture division.

I was along for the ride, sometimes serving as the train's engineer, but for the most part, I was the one in charge of stoking the fire and clearing the tracks so that the unstoppable steam engine called Casablanca could keep chugging up the hill. We all believed in that bedtime story about the little engine, and, no matter the odds, we always knew we could, we knew we could, we knew we could . . .

Larry Harris
July 2009

Prologue

"Even in the bacchanal of 1970s Los Angeles, the drug and promotional excesses of Casablanca Records stood out. In a period when cocaine use was probably at its peak in the music business, Casablanca set the pace . . ."
—Encyclopedia Britannica

July 21, 1978
Casablanca Record & FilmWorks Headquarters
8255 Sunset Boulevard
Los Angeles, California

"You stupid fucking idiot!"

I was pissed. I was so pissed I was shaking. I was on the phone with Bill Wardlow, the head of *Billboard* magazine's chart department, holder of one of the most powerful positions in the music business. I had just called him a stupid fucking idiot. And I wasn't even close to being done.

"You can't do that! We had an agreement! I don't care if their record is selling better than ours—that has nothing to do with it! Give them No. 1 next week. We discussed this yesterday, and you told me we would have No. 1! You have to change it back. I already told Neil that we would be No. 1."

I wasn't just pissed, I was scared. I had promised to deliver *Billboard*'s No. 1 album in the country to Casablanca, and now a done deal had been yanked from me—from us—at the eleventh hour.

I was intimately familiar with all the steps that had to be taken to get the top album in the country, and screaming at the head of *Billboard*'s chart department was way, way down the list. Yet it was a step I was taking. I knew that they weren't going to let out the chart information for another two hours. They could still change it. I wasn't going to stop screaming until they went to press.

"I couldn't care less if Al Coury already knows about the numbers! Did he pay you off in cash? I helped you out where no one else could, and this is how you pay me back? You are a complete asshole to put me in this position!"

People were beginning to congregate outside my office to watch the meltdown. Neil Bogart walked in through our adjoining office door, clearly surprised at my outburst, and attempted to talk me off the ledge. No one had ever heard me yell with such venom and hatred. And they certainly had never heard me yell at Bill Wardlow.

Bill had promised me that our three-disc soundtrack LP for *Thank God It's Friday* would be No. 1. Now he was reneging and giving the top slot to *Saturday Night Fever*. In truth, *Saturday Night Fever* deserved it. It was outselling us ten to one—easily—and I knew it. RSO, the label that had released *Saturday Night Fever*, shared a distributor with Casablanca, and I had access to their sales figures. The movie was doing much bigger box office than ours, too, but I didn't care. Not only did I want to end *Saturday Night's* impressive twenty-plus-week run at No. 1, but I also wanted the image enhancement that went along with being No. 1 and the increased sales for our picture and album.

For the past two years, I had had control over the *Billboard* charts and was able to significantly affect the positions of our records to help establish a perception that our company, Casablanca Records, and our artists—among them, KISS, Donna Summer, the Village People, and Parliament—were the hottest in the music industry. I was not going to accept a broken promise. This guy had screwed with the charts for years and years, and now he was screwing with me.

Casablanca was our child. We gave birth to it, we nurtured it, we fought many battles to keep it alive, and to have someone not give it the respect I felt it deserved was unacceptable. But this story begins long before I even knew who Bill Wardlow was, when Neil Bogart was not king of the hottest label in the record biz but just Neil Bogart, my second cousin from Brooklyn.

1

The Beginning of a Beautiful Friendship

**An Introduction: Neil and Bobby—Cameo-Parkway—
Art Kass and Buddah**

**Summer 1961
5620 231st Street
Bayside, Queens**

The first time I met Neil Bogart—in fact, the first time I became aware he existed—we were in my parents' living room in Bayside. Neil and his parents were introduced as relatives, but beyond that no explanation was given. They stayed for about five minutes and left me a copy of a single, titled "Bobby," by some guy I'd never heard of named Neil Scott.

Turns out Neil Scott and Neil Bogart were the same person, and "Bobby" had been something of a hit, reaching No. 58 on the *Cashbox* and *Billboard* charts in June 1961. I had a relative who had recorded a song! I was fourteen years old and had never met anyone who had recorded a single, to say nothing of a hit—and to have him be a relative, no less, sent my head spinning.

As I would learn, Neil was a gambler—the kind of guy who would bet a hundred dollars on when the cheese in the fridge was going to go moldy—and he had wanted to be in entertainment for as long as he could remember. He was born Neil Bogatz in Brooklyn in 1943, and when he was young, his mother, Ruth, sent him for singing, dancing, and acting lessons (among his teachers was TV's Archie Bunker, the late Carroll O'Connor). Family was always the center of the Bogatz's world, and the generosity of spirit shared by Ruth and Neil's father, Al, was apparent in every aspect of their lives. The family's house doubled as a foster home, and at a very early age Neil acquired a larger sense of family that extended beyond bloodlines. It would shape his world, professionally and personally, throughout his life. Feeding and tending to such a large and ever-changing brood was expensive, and on Al's postal service salary, the Bogatzes could scarcely afford luxuries like Neil's acting lessons. As he always would, Neil persevered, and by the mid-1950s, he had become a performer at summer-stock-type camps in the Catskills; by nineteen, he was part of a song-and-dance team working Bermuda cruise ships. A year later, he was playing a club in New York City when Bill Darnell (a singer of some note in the 1940s and 1950s) saw him and said, "Your voice is bad enough to sound good on this song that we have." That song was "Bobby."

- February 9, 1961: The Beatles give their debut performance, at the Cavern Club in Liverpool.
- April 12, 1961: Yuri Gagarin, a Soviet cosmonaut, becomes the first human in space.
- November 18, 1961: US president John F. Kennedy sends eighteen thousand military personnel to South Vietnam.

Neil was a born entrepreneur, and his promotional skills were often dazzling, even at a young age. When his single "Bobby" was pressed, he managed to get it played on the wildly popular Murray the K show on WINS-FM in New York. The radio show was hosted by Murray Kaufman, a pioneer in the radio business who more or less invented the concept of the fast-talking, high-energy DJ. On his show each day, two songs were paired in a competition. The one that received the most calls won. "Bobby" was pitted against an Elvis Presley tune—pretty tough competition. But Neil had one thing going for him that Presley didn't. The afternoon of the contest, Neil organized a large group of old school friends to file into the candy store near PS 251 in Brooklyn. Using the store's phone, Neil's friends bombarded Murray the K with calls, eventually propelling "Bobby" to victory—this was likely the impetus that would push the song to hit status.

As are so many other skyrocket-to-stardom stories, Neil's entrance into showbiz was due to a moment of blind luck and ballsy confidence. While working at an employment agency in Manhattan in 1965, he fielded a phone call from a representative of *Cashbox*, a powerful music industry magazine, who wanted to advertise a position in the magazine's chart department. Rather than process the request and file the ad, Neil shelved it, went directly to *Cashbox*'s offices, and applied for the job himself. He secured the position and quickly worked his way up the company ladder, eventually landing a gig as assistant national promotion director with MGM Records, then one of the biggest labels in the industry. A year later, in early 1966, Neil parlayed his upward mobility into yet another choice gig when his former boss at *Cashbox* (who had since moved to Cameo-Parkway Records) offered him a job as national promotion director and eventually vice president and head of operations at Cameo. Neil thereby became the youngest person ever (at that point) to helm a major record label.

One of Neil's first accomplishments at Cameo was discovering and marketing the group ? & the Mysterians, who had a hit record with "96 Tears" in 1966. "That's a very strange name for a song," I thought. Neil later told me that the original title was "69 Tears," a reference to the sexual position, but it was changed to make it marketable. Though, given Neil's ability to sell a story, this may have been apocryphal.

In March 1967, early in Neil's tenure as Cameo's vice president, a controlling interest in the company was bought by Allen Klein (of Rolling Stones and Beatles fame). His view of what the label should be was at the opposite end of the universe from Neil's, and it was clear that the relationship wasn't long for this world. Fortunately for Neil, despite being a neophyte in an industry of emerging giants, his success was highly visible, and it left him with many opportunities. There was some speculation that Neil was pushed out of Cameo by Allen Klein, but that was not the case. Klein soon came under investigation and was eventually jailed when the company's stock exploded overnight, attracting the attention of the SEC. Neil had seen the writing on the wall.

Not long after Klein bought Cameo-Parkway, Art Kass offered Neil a position as general manager of Kama Sutra Records and its newly formed sister label, Buddah. Timing is everything, especially in the go-for-broke music business, and with Cameo-Parkway's future suddenly darkening, Neil jumped at Kass's offer. Art was a former accountant at MGM Records (where he had first met Neil), and he had been brought in by Kama Sutra founders Hy Mizrahi, Artie Ripp, and Phil Steinberg to help establish the new company.

Kass had started Buddah in March 1967 as a way to get out of a distribution arrangement that existed between Kama Sutra and MGM, and he felt Neil was the perfect choice to help jump-start the new label. Kass, wisely, had the foresight to bring in Neil's entire promotion staff (most notably, Marty Thau and Cecil Holmes) from Cameo-Parkway as well—why mess with a winning team? They did what they had done at Cameo: Marty handled the rock singles for radio, and Cecil promoted the R&B product. While Cecil would stay with Neil through the Casablanca days and be a major asset to the label, Marty would go on to become the original manager of the New York Dolls.

In contrast to the oppositional relationship he'd had with Allen Klein, Neil's working relationship with Kass was amicable, and in the years to come it would bring great success to the company, spawning bubblegum music, a genre Neil once told me was about falling in love and sunshine—about enjoying pure entertainment and the good things in life.

2

Woodstock (No, Really, I Was There)

Life in Queens—A big event—Traffic jam—Stars everywhere—Caught by security—The rain and mud— Three sleepless days

July 1969
5620 231st Street
Bayside, Queens

The summer of 1969 is probably the only time in American history where you can say the season and the year and people just know—Oh yeah, *that* summer. Neil Armstrong, hippies, the amazin' Mets, and a landmark mud bath called Woodstock.

I was twenty-two and invincible then, or at least young enough to think I was. My days were filled with work, going to the beach, smoking dope, hanging out with friends, admiring our cars in the parking lots at the Queens Boulevard White Castle or the Bay Terrace Shopping Center. I was living with my parents, and I held down a job at a deli and worked as a salesman/delivery person for my dad's sanitary supply business, where we sold toilet paper and cleaning products. Like most guys I knew, I wasn't much interested in career planning. I was just too busy enjoying life to worry about what I was going to do with it.

One weekday in early July, a friend mentioned that a big concert—a three-day happening—was being planned in August somewhere in upstate New York, and maybe a bunch of us should go. Sounded good to me, so a few of us purchased tickets at a Queens record store, and we were set.

Never one to forgo comfort when it was available, I insisted that we book hotel rooms. Roughing it had never been high on my list of life choices, so the prospect of camping out for three days with no showers or fresh clothes wasn't exactly appealing. We were able to get a room at the Holiday Inn in Middletown, not too far from the festival site.

August 15, 1969, the first day of Woodstock, finally arrived. It was muggy and still, and the four of us—me, my friend Neal Cohen (who had just returned from serving in a combat unit in Vietnam), Wendy (the wife of our friend Ken Kaltman, who'd had the misfortune of pulling National Guard duty that weekend), and a friend of Wendy's— piled into my '68 GTO and headed northward. Over fifteen miles away from the venue we hit a four-lane traffic jam. Everyone was headed for the same rural destination.

The traffic jam was a cultural event in itself. Miles of four-lane highway had become inbound lanes, but we still weren't moving. At all. For hours on end. Many people simply gave up, abandoned their cars, and walked the rest of the way to the festival site. Yet, in those hours of cramped gridlock, as we fumed both literally and figuratively in the overheating GTO, a sense of the Woodstock event began to assert itself. If a car grazed another by mistake, there was no road rage, nobody got angry. Frustration at being stalled for hours in the oppressive wet heat never boiled over. Instead, there was a sense of shared experience, a quickly gathering feeling of community; joints were passed from one car to another, strangers became instant friends, smiles all around. This was something special, a signpost for the summer and the generation, and you couldn't escape it.

Unfortunately, cars don't grasp the concept of landmark cultural events, and eventually my '68 GTO began to seriously overheat. (Lesson for the day: never bring a muscle car to a traffic jam.) I veered off the freeway onto the grass and headed for the nearest exit. The concert would have to wait: we had to get the car to the hotel as soon as possible.

The traffic and our unfamiliarity with the Sullivan County roads made for a longer trek to the hotel than I would have liked, but after some driving around, we found the Holiday Inn, parked the car (just in time), and went inside to register. As we entered the hotel, we saw the reception desk to our right and a small waiting area with couch and chairs to our left. Next to the desk was a large picture window overlooking the parking lot. We soon discovered that we'd accidentally booked ourselves into the event's headquarters. I stood, slack-jawed, watching Richie Havens check in and Arlo Guthrie relaxing in the corner. Part of the lobby had been turned into the communications center for the festival, and there were walkie-talkies and assorted pieces of shortwave and telephone equipment strewn about. There was no way we were going to be allowed to stay here, but miraculously, our reservations were honored and the desk clerk checked us in.

Neal and I walked down the corridor to our rooms, eyes bugged out and unblinking, thinking, if not saying, "Holy shit!" at every step. We passed Ravi Shankar's shoes, neatly placed outside his door. We saw folk legend Tim Hardin sitting on his bed, shooting up. Every door we passed, to the left and to the right, another star. We dropped off our stuff and headed back downstairs to eat lunch and see who else was in the hotel.

The corridor had been just a warm-up for the restaurant—a modest affair furnished with Formica-topped tables and a handful of booths. The people sitting in the restaurant—Roger Daltrey and Pete Townshend, Janis Joplin, Stephen Stills, David Crosby, Neil Young, Richie Havens, and Arlo Guthrie, all eating lunch, just as casual as you please—made Neal and me feel like interlopers, as if we had "uninvited guest" branded on our foreheads. As we choked down our sandwiches, we tried our best to look cool. We probably failed.

After a while, Wendy and her friend came down, and the four of us decided to make our way to the concert. My GTO had cooled in the parking lot, so we loaded up. We were leaving the hotel grounds when a security guard

- **May 23, 1969: The Who releases the rock opera *Tommy*.**
- **July 20, 1969: Astronauts Neil Armstrong and Edwin "Buzz" Aldrin, as members of Apollo 11, become the first men to land on the moon.**
- **August 9, 1969: Actress Sharon Tate (the pregnant wife of director Roman Polanski) and four others are found brutally murdered in Beverly Hills. Charles Manson and members of his "Family" would later be convicted of the crime.**

waved us over. Never a good sign. To our surprise, Wendy jumped out of the car and gave the guy a big hug; turned out he was not only an old friend of her parents, but head of artist entry for the festival as well. He gave us a pass, which I placed on the GTO's dashboard, and then he told us to join the end of the artist caravan now heading out to the festival site. The motorcade began to make its way through the huge crowds, lights flashing and sirens wailing. We were surrounded by performers, many of them already legendary, receiving a full police escort into the venue. Amazing.

The pass also allowed us into the backstage areas, so we watched the spectacle unfold from the wings. I want to say that standing mere feet from a list of performers too lengthy to mention, too important to describe, was amazing—and it was—but a violent and unrelenting rainstorm had blown in, and after a few hours we were ready to go back to the hotel. We trekked to the GTO, only to discover it was mired in a slurry of mud. While we were trying to find a way out of this dilemma, Arlo Guthrie happened by and asked us if he could hitch a ride back to the hotel. Great—now Arlo Guthrie is helping push my GTO out of the mud. This couldn't get any more bizarre.

Back at the hotel, we headed straight for the bar, where many of the performers were freely sharing all sorts of intoxicants. The place was small and dark, with only about ten tables, but I will never forget the image of Janis Joplin, bottle of Johnnie Walker in hand, dancing around the bar.

We didn't sleep at all for three days. We watched the never-ending concert unspool before us in the hot mire, the haze of humidity, exhaustion, and drugs blurring afternoon into evening and evening into epic night. The Who; Crosby, Stills, Nash and Young; and on and on—we didn't want to miss a minute of the adventure. Of the hundreds of thousands camped out on Yasgur's farmland, I'm not sure that any could claim to have gotten more out of Woodstock than I did. I still wonder whether this experience was the fates foreshadowing the events about to unfold.

3

A Converted Buddahist

Get a job—The interview—Fucked on the couch—Family and
the Mob—Learning the ropes—Payola—Ron and Buck—
Selling records in the bathroom—Cecil Holmes—Cornered at
the Apollo—Held at gunpoint—"Whatever it takes"—
The Bitter End—Reprimanded—DJs—Barnstorming—
The three-foot joint—WBCN—Signing bands

September 1971
The Buddah Group offices
1650 Broadway
Manhattan, New York

After I met Neil Bogart for the first time, more than nine years passed before I heard anything more about him. In September 1971, my parents came home from a wedding and told me they had seen Cousin Ruthie there. She'd said that I should call her son Neil about a job. Good thing, too—I needed one.

I phoned Neil the following evening, and he asked me to come down to Buddah's offices at 1650 Broadway in Manhattan. The office suite belonged to the Buddah Group (comprised of Buddah, Kama Sutra, Hot Wax, Curtom, T-Neck, and Sussex Records, among others, which collectively were home to a stunning list of big-league players that included The Isley Brothers, Sha Na Na, and The Lovin' Spoonful). Scepter Records, run by the legendary Florence Greenberg (who had helped steer The Shirelles to stardom), called 1650 home as well, as did many music publishers and artists. After the Brill Building, it was probably the most famous address in the music industry. Hell, even I'd heard of it, and I knew virtually nothing about the business.

The next day, I arrived at Neil's office and entered the waiting room. Gold records adorned the walls, but the room was decorated in the most awful purple you could imagine, like some sort of toxic grape soda. Even in an era of lime-green leisure suits, the designer responsible should have been cited for second-degree eye-slaughter. I sat in that violet-colored nightmare for over three hours, waiting for Neil. He had completely forgotten our conversation of the night before, and he called his mother to find out who the kid in his waiting room was. I was a little embarrassed to have to repeatedly explain to the receptionist and Neil's secretary who I was, but since I was only twenty-three, my ego hadn't developed much, so I wasn't too offended.

Three hours is a long time to wait, but the names on the walls provided ample distraction. I was impressed by all the posters and gold records, with names like Brewer and Shipley ("One Toke over the Line"), Melanie ("Candles in the Rain"), Curtis Mayfield (Neil called him the "black Dylan" whenever possible), The Isley Brothers, and my favorites, Sha Na Na. With another glance I saw The Lovin' Spoonful ("Summer in the City"); the Brooklyn Bridge featuring Johnny Maestro ("Sixteen Candles," "The Worst That Could Happen," and many other hits); and from Buddah's just-ended bubblegum days, artists such as the 1910 Fruitgum Company ("Yummy, Yummy, Yummy"), The Lemon Pipers ("Green Tambourine"), and Ohio Express.

Finally I was summoned into Neil's office, which was not purple but was larger than I expected it to be. It had been quite a while since our first meeting, and his appearance surprised me. I'd remembered him as taller and thinner, but he looked like a pudgy Richard Simmons, curly hair and all. Aside from his dark-brown Afro, his most prominent feature was his penetrating, almost bulging eyes. Despite his Brooklyn upbringing, he had only a trace of a New York accent (I more than made up for him in that department) and spoke in an engaging mid-tenor voice. Neil was almost endlessly enthusiastic, but he wasn't one of those exhausting people who are perpetually "on." He has often been described as an amazing salesman, and he certainly was, but this stemmed from his ability to make you believe in an artist or song and think it was all your own idea, not something he'd browbeaten you into believing.

We said the obligatory hellos and talked about WNEW-FM, the city's premiere progressive rock station. Neil was in awe of WNEW, as he had never had a bona fide rock-and-roll hit. He knew he didn't understand rock the way he understood Top 40 and R&B, and due to the tremendous amount of flack he had received from the critics over the many bubblegum hits he had overseen for Buddah, his aim was to be a player in the rock arena.

I bluffed my way through the meeting by talking about the DJs at WNEW. I had brushed up on their names—which was not too difficult, as there were only a handful of them. But, despite the fact that I had majored in communications in college and had a stronger handle on what was happening in radio than your average twenty-three-year-old, my inexperience was on full display. After our meeting, Neil sent me to chat with Jerry Sharell, Buddah's head of national promotions, and Buck Reingold, who ran promotions on the East Coast.

I got the job because they needed someone immediately to do local promotion for the New York market. The last person to hold the position had recently been fired for an interesting lapse in judgment. Neil and the president of Viewlex (the conservative educational company that had bought Buddah in 1969), returning to the office after a dinner meeting, had walked in on the promo man having sex on the waiting room couch with the music director of one of the top East Coast radio stations.

If Neil had been alone, he would have walked over and given the guy a raise and a promotion. I mean, what better way to ensure that your music gets played than to bang a prominent music director? But because he was with the president of Viewlex, Neil felt forced to feign indignation and fired the guy on the spot.

The other reason I was hired was nepotism, a policy in which Neil firmly believed. ("All things are relatives," was a favorite saying of his.) Plus, at $125 per week, I was the cheapest option that had walked through the door. And, just like that, I became Larry Harris, local New York promotion man for Buddah/Kama Sutra Records.

Buddah had been culled from the older Kama Sutra Records, which was secretly owned and controlled by John "Sonny" Franzese, a powerful member of the Colombo crime family. This was not an uncommon arrangement; before the music business became attractive to corporate America, organized crime had established a strong foothold in the industry. By the time I joined the label, all of the original Kama Sutra owners were long gone, their stock purchased by the Viewlex Corporation three years prior. Artie Ripp had left in a huff in late 1969, when Viewlex refused to release the Woodstock soundtrack for which he had acquired the rights, and Sonny Franzese was in jail for armed robbery and conspiracy—although he wasn't completely out of the loop, despite his cellblock D mailing address.

Buddah, as you may have noticed, is spelled incorrectly. There are a few theories about this. Artie Ripp said he thought it was irreverent to spell Buddha like the Buddhists do; he also claimed he could never say "ha" at the end of the name, only "aah." Since Buddha was a mystical figure, they thought the reference would give the label a cool, hip aura, and it went with the whole Kama Sutra vibe. But when I first joined the company, I was told it was a printing mistake discovered after it was too late (or too expensive) to change. I suspect it was spelled wrong because nobody knew the proper way to spell it. As for which theory is the correct one, take your pick.

The next day, I reported to my new office, which I had to share with Buck Reingold and Ron Weisner, head of artist relations. I was not in the office that much as my job entailed going to all of the reporting retail record outlets in town and building relationships with them so they would send positive sales reports about us to the trades (*Billboard*, *Cashbox*, *Record World*, and *The Hamilton Report*) and the radio stations (WWRL, WABC, WPIX-FM, WNEW-AM, WNEW-FM, and WOR-FM, among others).

After I'd had some tutoring from Buck and Ron, I knew that the way to succeed was to give the record stores free product in exchange for the reports. Usually, I gave them singles, but as time went on and things became more competitive, I started giving them whatever albums they wanted. Keep in mind that even when giving away commercial product for free, we still needed to account for those units when it came to calculating artists' royalties. Any records not used for promotional purposes usually carried a royalty fee to the artist. In some cases, the artist's contract called for X amount of free goods for use in making sales deals, but in many cases, labels buried the giveaways and never accounted for them. If artists' business managers or accountants came in to check the books and were thorough enough in their endeavors, they would find a discrepancy and the label would be held accountable for the royalties.

Part of my job was to visit radio stations in New York on their "music days," which were the days they agreed to see promotion people. When it came to WNEW, WPLJ, and WLIR, the three FM rock stations in the market, I could go whenever I wanted and deal with each DJ individually.

I also had to play diplomat with the program directors to keep feathers from getting ruffled.

WPIX-FM, the lone Top 40 FM station in town, had a gem of a program/music director named Barney Pip. Barney was very nice—the type of radio guy who would take a shot on a record he liked. Because of that, WPIX was the first station in the market to play songs like Bill Withers's "Lean on Me," or "Scorpio," the hit instrumental by Dennis Coffey, both of which I shopped. You could visit Barney anytime, even when he was on the air. I also visited the FM rock DJs while they were on the air, but if they were on after normal business hours I called ahead. Back then, the vibe of the industry was open to chance and the moment-to-moment whims of the DJs, who held positions of far greater power

- **March 5, 1971: Led Zeppelin performs "Stairway to Heaven" for the first time, at Ulster Hall in Belfast, Northern Ireland.**
- **July 3, 1971: Jim Morrison is found dead in his Paris apartment, possibly of a heroin overdose.**
- **August 1, 1971: The *Sonny & Cher Comedy Hour* debuts.**

than their modern-day counterparts. Every day I had the opportunity to deal with people willing to take a chance on music that hadn't been tested and retested before it was exposed to the public. In the case of progressive rock radio, you had a good six or more opportunities to have your music played. If the morning guy didn't like the record, there was still a chance that the afternoon or night person would.

Up until the late 1990s, to have a record played on a station in a decent-sized market you needed to prove that it had all kinds of credentials and, in many cases, you needed to hire an independent station-approved promotions person (called an "indie") to bring the record in. Just to have your record added was big bucks to the indie promo guy, who in turn paid the station a fee to be its music consultant. The owner of a radio station could make in excess of fifty thousand dollars per year working with an indie.

Is this payola? Yes, more or less. Instead of the record companies giving money (or drugs, women, and various other favors) directly to the radio stations, an independent promotions middleman is paid to do it for them. One key difference is that with the independent promoter in the picture, the money goes to the station owners rather than to the often-underpaid program director or DJ. This keeps the record companies at arm's length when it comes to actual money changing hands between them and the stations. In my mind, the arrangement creates an ethical gray area. I'm not sure what the substantive difference is in the end: the record companies are still paying to have their music played. Nobody in the music biz or the radio biz wants a repeat of the highly publicized Alan Freed payola trials of the 1950s or other, less-well-known investigations that were conducted throughout the 1970s and 1980s. The current method somehow nullifies that legal risk.

This does create an unbalanced playing field in that the smaller labels cannot compete for airplay; they simply don't have the money to pay the indies. When all is said and done, it could cost a label hundreds of thousands of dollars just to cover this new form of payola for one record.

As always, the large corporations are most invested in keeping the status quo, and they know that this independent system of promotion protects their turf from any young innovators. This suppression of the entrepreneurial spirit is one of the reasons the music business of today is facing such hard times. Evolving musical forms are what keep music exciting and keep people buying new artists and product. Rap, disco, and even rock and roll were not spearheaded by the majors but rather the little independent guy. Look at the careers of Elvis, Donna Summer, and LL Cool J. It was the small labels that took a chance on them.

Although the indies were not as crucial in the 1970s, even then there were people who had the ability and contacts to control what music was played on key radio stations in major cities. Paying these promotion people with cash, drugs, or records was not uncommon, and it could mean the failure or success of a record.

Ron Weisner, vice president of artist relations, was a great teacher and mentor. He was of average height and build; he had a head of thick hair, a big mustache, and a weird and distinctive gait. Ron had *the push*—the ability to get our artists on local and national TV shows. That's what he spent most of his time doing, when he wasn't busy acting as in-house psychiatrist for many of the artists and a few of the employees. He also helped book tours and gigs for the artists.

Ron had major clout with WWRL-AM, the leading R&B station in New York, due to his close relationship with Norma Penella, the station's music director. It always seemed a little ironic to me that Norma, a middle-aged Italian woman, chose the music for the station that so heavily influenced the city's black population, but in this she was hardly unique. A big—and here I'm being kind—Italian gentleman named Joe "Butterball" Tamburro was the music and program director for Philadelphia's WDAS-FM, the leading R&B station in the market. But most stations were owned by white folks in those days, and I suppose they felt more secure having white executives in charge.

While Ron was a gregarious and gentle soul, Buck Reingold was a totally different story. This former short-order cook was a very forceful guy. Buck was built short, square, and hard with red hair and a lot of freckles. He had very little understanding of music, which didn't bother him in the least. When Buck (or Bucky, as some called him) needed a record played, it would get played, and if something or someone got broken in the process, oh well. He was hired after he married Neil's sister-in-law, Nancy—who was the twin of Neil's wife, Beth—and he therefore became yet another beneficiary of Neil's steadfast nepotism. He did his job well, and if getting those records played meant parading down Broadway naked with a record hanging from each ear, then he would do it.

Buck had a set of brass balls. Rick Sklar, the program director of WABC-AM (the most powerful station on the East Coast) was arguably the most influential person in the world of music radio. Not surprisingly, it was very difficult to get a meeting with Rick, and if you were lucky enough to see him, you would have very little time to play your music; more often, you'd just drop it off and he would listen to it when he was ready. Just after I joined the company, our Kama Sutra label released "Put Your Hand in the Hand," by Ocean. It was receiving substantial airplay around the country, and Neil, who was not one to let go of a record that was beginning to show promise, was walking around the office repeating to anyone who would listen, "Keep pushing it, guys. Keep pushing it. We're this close to breaking this thing big. I can feel it." Buck decided that he was going to impress Neil by getting Rick Sklar to play the record before it had risen high enough on the charts to be automatically added to WABC's playlist. Buck went to WABC's offices and camped out for hours in a men's room stall, knowing that eventually Rick would have to use the facilities. Rick finally came in, and as soon as he was comfortable in his stall, Buck began to play the record at full volume on a portable record player. Rick was so taken by this (and the fact that it was a great song) that he started to play it on air immediately.

Buck once followed a program director to a baseball game, sat behind him, and played him a song while he watched the action; another time, he paid someone to let him hang a banner hyping one of our artists out of a twentieth-story window directly across from a radio station's offices. As obnoxious as he was, he fit right into the promotion-man mold Neil loved.

But Buck's aggressive, abrupt style didn't always work. While he had close relationships with a number of Top 40 programmers, when it came time to deal with many of the more laid-back artists and the rock radio people, Neil tended to steer Buck out of the office. Buck was a loaded weapon, and Neil had an innate sense of when to deploy him.

Buck was also Neil's gofer. If Neil was having a party at his home in New Jersey, Buck would be there to carry in the tables and chairs, and he would also take care of much of the food prep. Although he could probably rip Neil in two without much effort, he would dutifully take Neil's public berating when he screwed up. This was a bit out of character for Neil, whose typical reaction to a mistake was to shoot you a look, his expression grim and eyes bulging more than usual, or to have a terse but civil discussion with you in private. Not so with Buck. Neil would fly off the handle and scream in front of everyone. This seemed to happen very frequently. Buck never said a word in response; he knew Neil was his meal ticket.

The other promotion man I worked with at Buddah was Cecil Holmes. Cecil was a tall, good-looking, well-dressed black man with a large Afro. He was very well respected in the industry, and of all the people I ever worked with, Cecil is the only one who never cursed or had anything bad to say about anyone. He also never did drugs—ever. Cecil was a gentleman, and he knew how to take care of business.

One evening, Cecil and I went to the Apollo Theater in Harlem to see a show by Honey Cone, an all-girl vocal trio coming off a string of hits for Hot Wax Records, which we distributed through Buddah. Cecil drove us there in his big Cadillac through Central Park. Just when we were about to leave the park, he locked all the doors. I was taken aback, and I immediately thought, "These are his people. Why is he locking the doors?" When I mentioned this, he replied, "These definitely are *not* my people!" In 1971, Harlem was not the safest place to be; even the cops walked three or four abreast for protection. But Cecil's action surprised me, as I frequently went to Harlem to visit record shops and WLIB-AM radio. I had never felt threatened, and I couldn't possibly have been more Jewish or more white.

My sense of security vanished that evening. In the Apollo, we both had a growing sense that we were being sized up. For what reason, we didn't know, but we were both New York kids, and that sixth sense comes with the territory. We left the show fearing a confrontation outside the backstage entrance, which is where Cecil had parked. By a stroke of luck, the boyfriend of one of the Honey Cone girls was at the theater that night, and he came outside with us. His name was Thad Spencer, and he was a professional boxer who had come very close to fighting Muhammad Ali for the heavyweight title in late 1967, before the government stripped Ali of his mantle for dodging the draft for the Vietnam War. The unsavory types who had seemed intent on confronting us behind the theater clearly recognized Thad, and they parted like the Red Sea. No one came close to touching us.

Around this time, we had another close call. One day, two big black guys with equally huge Afros walked into our offices. They waltzed by Neil's secretary, Barbara, went into Neil's office, and shut the door. Taking out their guns, they laid them on the desk in front of them and told Neil he was on trial. They claimed we had purchased a certain record and the deal included distribution rights; they were concerned that the original distributor, who happened to be a popular gospel disc jockey named Joe Bostwick whose contract we were not aware of, was being pushed out into the streets by "the Man." In this era, there was a movement in the black community against "the Man" who was making money on the backs of black performers.

Barbara called Cecil Holmes, maybe figuring that because he was black, he could help calm the situation. Cecil walked into Neil's office and addressed the two thugs as "brothers," but he was quickly told to sit down and shut up. He had no stroke with these guys. They told Neil that he had twenty-four hours to get the situation taken care of and that they would return the following day—if Neil didn't make it right, there would be trouble. In the meantime, Barbara, cool as she was, sat at her desk trying to scheme a way out of this mess. She called a guy named

Nate, who was our "cleaner," so to speak, and who was likely involved with the Mob in ways I never knew. The next day, when the thugs returned, they found Nate standing in Neil's office. They turned on their heels and walked quietly out of the building. In an attempt to reach a middle ground, we gave Bostwick mail-order rights to the record.

Of course, this event shook Neil, but the fact that he had the protection of some major crime figures probably made him a little more comfortable about the situation. Mafia protection was a dual-edged sword, however, and he always told me that he had never wanted to ask a favor of "those people," as he would be paying it back for the rest of his life. The Mafia would have connections in the music industry for many years to come.

One day, Neil received a call from a disc jockey friend of his in San Francisco, who told him about a record that was burning up the local airwaves. The song, called "Oh Happy Day," had been recorded by a religious group, The Edwin Hawkins Singers. Neil had the DJ play the song over the phone and then decided that he wanted to put it out on Buddah immediately. Neil called Edwin Hawkins right away, but he could not close the deal over the phone—he would have to go to San Francisco and work the deal in person.

When an unsigned band has a hit on its hands, the competition among the labels to sign the act develops at a lightning pace, and Neil was fearful that while he was in transit from New York to San Francisco someone else would call Hawkins and close the deal on the phone. Hawkins had implied to Neil during their conversation that he was fielding offers from other labels and was waiting to hear back from them.

Reasoning that Hawkins wouldn't be able to field other calls if he were on the phone (luckily, call waiting had yet to be invented), Neil had Artie Ripp call Hawkins and keep him talking. While Neil traveled half a day to get to San Francisco to lock up the record, Artie kept Hawkins on the phone, determined to prevent someone else from beating us to the punch. When Hawkins was done talking and hung up, Artie would immediately call back with something else to discuss. This lasted for hours, until Neil finally arrived. Buddah got the record, and it was a monster hit.

One of the more colorful characters I met during this time was Paul Colby. Paul was a strange little man, and he owned The Bitter End in Greenwich Village. He had a reputation for being difficult, but due to the amount of money we spent at his club, we got along wonderfully with him. I would go to the club at least once a week to see various artists (Bette Midler with Barry Manilow on piano stands out), and I was always given a great reception and the best seat in the house, no matter how packed it was. Although the cramped venue was maybe seventy-five seats jammed together to the point where you couldn't even walk around, it was famous. It was our first choice when we wanted to impress out-of-towners. My first meeting with Brewer and Shipley, for instance, was at The Bitter End. It was also my first meeting with cocaine. The duo may have been famous for songs about weed ("One Toke over the Line" and "Tarkio Road"), but they seemed equally at home with blow. The backstage area at The Bitter End was nothing more than two rooms containing a beat-up old couch, a table, and a few chairs. Between shows that night, we were smoking some weed when Brewer and Shipley began to do some lines of coke, scooping up the dust with long pinkie fingernails that they kept manicured in a spoon shape for just that purpose. Initially, it did nothing for me, but after a few minutes the coke overrode the pot and I began to feel a different kind of buzz. It wasn't a big revelatory experience, but I didn't hate it, and I continued to do the stuff for years.

The early days at Buddah were filled with that anything-can-happen sense you have when you're young and your life is spread out before you. Each day was a learning experience. After the work day was over, between 6:00 and 7:00 p.m., a few of us would gather in Neil's office to smoke pot and drink Blue Nun. These hangout sessions were not structured meetings; but, looking back, I'm sure Neil knew that sometimes things would happen during them. The West Coast was still open for business, so a call or two might come in during the sessions. No one wanted to rush home, especially if they did not live in the city, and many of us had regular dining engagements with industry people, so we used the time to cool our heels (and avoid the traffic) while we waited for the dinner hour to roll around. We would sit and bullshit or listen to some product by bands on the label or new artists Neil was considering signing. I began to see a little more of Neil's identity during these times.

He was maybe a little less insistently enthusiastic, more reflective about what he doubted or didn't like. We'd discuss other labels, or artists and their managers, occasionally drifting into the realm of politics. (Neil was a fan of Richard Nixon; he believed that Nixon's economic policies helped put money in his pocket.)

The gatherings would go on for an hour or more and were often attended by people from various departments, including Nancy Lewis (who avoided the drugs but usually supplied the Blue Nun) and Sherrie Levy from publicity, Jerry Sharell from promotions, Joe Fields from sales, Jude Lyons from creative services, as well as me, Neil, Cecil, and, on occasion, Buck. No business environment I've been in before or since has created a more intimate bond among coworkers than those hangout sessions in Neil's office did. It was us against the world. It was family, and that's exactly the way Neil wanted it.

Neil hadn't always been so expansive or casual. When he started at Buddah, he had been far more conservative, insisting, for instance, that all the women—with no exceptions—wear skirts. He was so militant about it that during one of his trips to the West Coast, all the women in the office wore pants as a form of rebellion, but his secretary ratted them out—she called Neil and told him about the fashion coup. Drugs and that whole scene were completely verboten as well. Anyone caught doing drugs in the office was fired. In those early days, despite the fact that he was married to Beth (his first wife), Neil had lots of girlfriends on the side, one of whom, Mitzi, worked for Buddah. Neil was more serious about Mitzi than the others, and they would often stay late at the office and have sex on his desk. At some point in 1970, Mitzi convinced Neil to start smoking pot. Not long after that, Buddah released a debut LP by a singer/songwriter named Biff Rose. A press party was held in a small recording studio, and it was the first time Neil endorsed open drug use at a company function. He wanted tons of joints to be on hand, and Soozin Kazick, Buddah's publicist, had to roll them all herself at home during the evenings leading up to the party.

～ ～ ～

One evening, a few months after I had joined the company, Neil walked into my office and informed me that I wasn't doing my job well. He wasn't screaming, and he didn't appear to be mad; his voice completely matter-of-fact, he told me I wasn't living up to his expectations. I'd been blindsided. I turned green as my stomach rolled over. How could he say this? Here I was, putting in fifteen-hour days (and loving it), visiting record stores and radio stations that had never seen a representative of the company before. I was establishing myself and Buddah at all three of the area's major rock stations. WLIR in Long Island had been particularly easy for me, as I was good friends with both the program director, Mike Harrison, who coined the term AOR (album-oriented radio) and his eventual replacement, Ken Kohl, with whom I'd gone to college.

I couldn't believe that Neil was disappointed with my work. When I asked him what he meant, he pointed to my expense account. I cringed. And then I began to get mad, because I knew that I was always very frugal with my expenditures. How could he possibly think I was being wasteful? Then Neil said, "You're not spending enough." I blinked. Huh? "Larry, you can't do your job well unless you're spending money, and you're not spending enough of it." I thought that by being money conscious I was helping the company. But, what the hell, if he wanted me to spend money, I would accommodate him.

I began to spend more freely. I found that it was pretty easy to have breakfast with a DJ, lunch with a music director, dinner with a program director and drinks with a writer, all on Buddah's dime. Sending chocolates to the secretaries, buying gifts for the elevator operators—it all became second nature to me. I would visit WPLJ or WNEW in the small hours of the morning and bring the on-air DJ food and drinks, and often marijuana or blow. The drugs were never a gift, but rather something we did together to build the bond of friendship. Mike Klenfner of WNEW and I would go out for some massive, expensive dinners. We were both well over six feet tall, and although I was thin at that point, Michael was a big guy and could eat the kitchens bare.

My favorite Mike Klenfner story involves a folk artist named Steve Goodman, who had been brought to us by Paul Anka. Goodman recorded a self-titled album for us that featured a song called "The City of New Orleans," and I got him a considerable amount of airplay throughout the country. However, I could not get as much play as I wanted on WNEW. One day, when we were in the elevator, Steve told me he had leukemia and did not know how long he was going to live, but he wanted to leave his wife and baby daughter something when he passed. I just about broke down in tears, and the next day I went to see Mike at WNEW. I told him that he had to play the album more frequently because the guy was going to die. Klenfner was convinced I was bullshitting him, and for years (fortunately, Steve lived until 1984) he kept asking me when the guy was going to die. He really thought I made the whole thing up just to get airplay. I did resort to some ridiculous maneuvers to get a record played, but even I would not stoop that low.

The list of contacts I had made was impressive. Or at least I thought it was. John Zacherle at WPLJ was a particular favorite item on my expense reports. I would visit him at 2:00 a.m. and give him a ride home when he went off the air. I loved Zach—still do. As host of a very popular local TV show, *Chiller Theater*, he was an influence on me when I was growing up, and he is one of the kindest people you will ever meet. Alex Bennett was the overnight man at WPLJ from 2:00 a.m. to 6:00 a.m., and I was the only promotion man—or one of very few—to bring artists to visit him when his interview/music show was running. I brought Charlie Daniels when "Uneasy Rider" came out, and comedian Robert Klein joined us numerous times. Dick Neer, the overnight person at WNEW, and I were never very close, but Mike Klenfner often filled in for him.

Alison "the Night Bird" Steele was on from 10:00 p.m. to 2:00 a.m. Alison was great; she played all our artists, and we didn't even have to ask her to do it. She and her boyfriend, who was an assistant district attorney of New York, spent enough time with Neil and Buck on a regular basis that I never really needed to drop in and see her on my promotion rounds. When Alison was on the air, I spent time with John Zacherle, as his show was on at the same time as hers and he had no relationship with either Neil or Buck. I also devoted a great deal of time to all the WNEW talent during their Summer in the Park events—a series of live performances at area parks. It seemed like we had an artist doing an event almost every week—

- **October 1, 1971: Walt Disney World opens outside of Orlando, Florida.**
- **February 14, 1972: "Steppenwolf Day" is declared in Los Angeles, California.**
- **August 22, 1972: Actress Jane Fonda broadcasts an anti–Vietnam War polemic from a hotel room in Hanoi.**

everyone from Jim Dawson and Buzzy Linhart to Sha Na Na. Buddah probably supplied more artists for Summer in the Park than any other label.

When my overnight visits were done, I went home, slept for a few hours, woke up, showered, and headed to WNEW to be with Pete Fornatale and later, in the day, Mike Harrison or Dave Herman.

Middays I spent with Scott Muni (even in the early 1970s, he was a living legend in the radio and music industries), and I would watch him drink his lunch. I also became friends with Dennis Elsas, who succeeded Klenfner as music director when he left to become the first album promotion person at Columbia Records, which at that time was the largest label in the world.

I was able to get almost anything played on WNEW, WLIR, and WPLJ (though I could never corner the impenetrable Jonathan Schwartz, who would run and hide when he saw a promo person). I was, at least by my own reckoning, off to a very good start.

A year or so after I joined the company, we moved to 810 7th Avenue. Brand new offices in a classy building. This was nice. I still had to share an office—this time with the new head of album promotion, Jay Schick—but I didn't mind in the least. Jay came from Florida, where he had been a court reporter. After a few too many "trips," he decided to venture into the music business. I watched Jay closely to see how he worked; I saw that although he worked hard, he had trouble concentrating. He introduced me to what would become not only my new favorite drug but also the preferred drug of the early-to-mid 1970s: Quaaludes. We were at a concert together, and he casually offered me a couple of pills. I shrugged and thought, "What the hell?" I swallowed two of them. It was a very nice kind of high. It made my fingertips tingle and slurred my speech a bit, but rather than feeling mellowed out, I felt like getting up and doing something, anything—sex, cleaning, cooking. It just felt good to be active. The drug would prove to be Jay's undoing, as it would cause him to pass out at very inopportune times, like when we were all in a meeting. He left the company shortly thereafter to return to Miami and his more lucrative court reporting gig. But he taught me one important lesson: never take 'ludes before dusk.

The biggest advantage of my new office was that I was right next to Joe Fields, the head of sales. Joe, who was short in stature, had more energy than any ten people I have ever known. I absorbed a host of great sales skills just listening to Joe on the phone. He was a master, given that much of our product was very difficult to sell, especially in the inflated quantities Neil asked him to move. Joe could also hold his own with any radio person; the format did not matter. I can honestly say that he sold the Brooklyn Bridge to a few people and mean it literally and figuratively (the band The Brooklyn Bridge, that is).

One story illustrates just how crazy Joe was. Joe and Neil went to a convention for Heilicher Brothers, a very influential distributor in the Midwest. To make an impression, they hired an old-fashioned prop plane and dressed as 1920 aviators; then they had the plane buzz the convention hotel a few times and land on the hotel grounds. After that stunt, who do you think was the talk of the convention?

One of our major artists was Curtis Mayfield, who, before going solo, was the lead singer of The Impressions. Curtis, along with his manager and partner, Marv Stuart, had his own label: Curtom Records. Buddah manufactured, sold, and promoted the product, but Curtis had total control over the content. Neil usually wouldn't hesitate to correct an artist if he thought his or her music needed a little something, but when it came to Curtis Mayfield, he would never assume he knew better. Curtis was a true superstar in those days. His albums always went Gold (half a million units sold), and he became a household name in the summer of 1972, when he created the music for the smash movie *Super Fly*, the soundtrack for which sold over three million units. But, as exciting as his albums were, he was incredibly dull in concert, anchoring himself in front of the microphone and barely twitching a muscle.

In September 1972, I was sent to Hofstra University in Hempstead, New York, to act as liaison between Curtis and the ABC people during the taping of the infamous pilot episode of ABC's *In Concert* TV series. Also on the bill was Alice Cooper, the original shock rocker, whom Curtis was to follow onstage. The taping was a mess. ABC's people did not have it together, and everything was way off schedule. We had been slated for a 12:00 a.m. start time, and at 2:00 a.m. we were still waiting to go on. To make matters worse, none of the thirty people in Curtis's entourage had any rolling papers left. There was smoke, plenty of smoke, but nothing to roll joints with, and certainly no pipe—pipes were not part of the hardcore pot repertoire at that point. This was a major catastrophe. It was intolerable to have to while away the time without being stoned. Not to worry. In amazement, I watched as a member of Curtis's posse ripped open a paper grocery bag, filled it with marijuana and menthol tobacco from numerous Newport cigarettes, rolled it, fitted one end with a rolled-up piece of cardboard (a perfect filter) and—viola! The biggest joint I had ever seen. It was at least three feet long and four to six inches wide. After two passes to each person, it was gone, but it had served its intended purpose. We were now all in a better mood.

Eventually, Curtis went onstage before a less-than-enthusiastic audience. The *In Concert* people had not allowed audience members to go to the bathroom for hours because they were afraid they would leave the hall, and that would make for terrible audience shots. They were also afraid that, once out of their seats, people would not return at all, leaving the production staff to find replacements in the middle of the night. But some audience members decided that they were leaving, and locked doors were not going to stop them. The fact that it was illegal to lock these people into a theater did not seem to bother the show's producers; they had a show to shoot, and there had to be an audience, no matter what.

In Concert was, in fact, an excellent opportunity for Curtis, as the target demographic for the show was young white males into rock and roll, and he needed exposure to that audience. I am sure Ron Weisner was responsible for setting it up.

Neil was a visionary, and he was one of the first people (if not the very first) to use a TV spot to promote an album release. In most cases, the thirty- and sixty-second commercials were cut-down versions of pro-motional films (essentially music videos), which were mainly created if you needed to promote your product in foreign territories, or if you needed a moving image on a local dance show or news broadcast. Some of those spots, including one for Stories's ("Brother Louie") 1973 album, *About Us*, are even available on YouTube.

Neil had a wonderful working relationship with two of the principals in the New York production company Direction Plus, which we occa-sionally hired to produce promo films and TV spots for Buddah. While certainly no one knew it at the time, both of those principals, Bill Aucoin and Joyce Biawitz, would go on to change our lives forever, as we would change theirs.

The Curtis Mayfield three-foot joint scenario may have been an amusing eye-opener for me, but it was nothing compared to some of the situations I found myself in on Curtis's behalf. He called me at the office one day (I'm sure one of my Buddah colleagues put him up to it, as I can't imagine he thought I was cool), and he asked me to meet him at his hotel suite. When I arrived, I found him in bed with several women. He called me over, handed me two thousand dollars, and gave me an address where I was to pick up a package for him. I went to this seedy part of town knowing full well that I had two grand on me and that the package was not going to contain a pastrami sandwich. Carrying around so much cocaine made me very paranoid. I returned to Curtis's suite, but this time I was not invited in. He opened the door a crack, took the blow from me, and slammed the door shut. No thank-you—nothing. Probably shouldn't have expected a gratuity, either.

That one occasion aside, Curtis was always very nice to me. In fact, I don't think I ever saw him be anything but congenial to anyone. Yet I was totally struck by the irony. This guy had written the music to *Super Fly* and was hailed by everyone as a genius for delivering the antidrug message through songs like "Freddie's Dead" and "Super Fly," and now he was doing an entire ounce of blow.

As Christmas 1972 approached, we all anticipated a great present from Marv Stuart and Curtis for the effort we had put into helping the *Super Fly* soundtrack become a hit. When Marv showed up with little jars of jam for the staff, Joe Fields went ballistic and ran down the hall yelling at Marv for being such a cheapskate. Considering the rest of us didn't have the balls to say anything to Marv, we all loved Joe for doing it for us.

I spent many evenings with Joe going to see artists perform—those on our labels and others. Joe would always take the train from his home in Long Island, and since I had a car and was heading back in the same direction, I would take him home late at night when the trains were not running so frequently. Just hanging out with Joe during these outings, I received the best education I could have had in music business history and theory. Joe would later start his own jazz label (jazz was his true love). From what I understand, he then sold it and bought it back several times, making a great deal of money in the process.

One of the many lessons he taught me was that what people want you to perceive is not necessarily the way things are. Before my first trip to Boston to visit the very influential radio station WBCN-FM, Joe gave me a primer on what to expect. He told me that the people I would meet there would like me to believe that the sales guy, Kenny Greenblatt, was the music director. This was to prevent the DJs from being pressured by record people. The station would also use this as a tactic to get advertising from the labels: you would drop off a dozen albums (one for each DJ), and if they decided to play the record, Greenblatt would call to say he could get it played but would need some advertising to show the label supported it. This was all a ruse. Joe explained that the real deal was the program director, Norm Winer, who (in my opinion) ran the station in too democratic a fashion. All of the on-air people, including the newspeople, had a vote in what music was played. Knowing this on my first visit to WBCN, with the new *Super Fly* album in hand, I made it a point to deal only with Norm.

I became very close to WBCN's staff, and Boston grew to be one of my favorite destinations. I rarely stayed in a hotel there, opting instead to stay in the house that Norm shared with three DJs: John Brody, Tommy Hadges, and Joe Rogers, who went by the appellation Mississippi Joe. I usually slept on an uncomfortable couch in the living room, but it was more fun hanging with them than being in a hotel by myself. It's not like I was able to get a lot of sleep when visiting Boston anyway. We would stay up into the wee hours getting high and talking about life. I was to view many a Boston sunrise.

WBCN was the station that helped introduce Monty Python to American audiences. A few of the WBCN people were already Python fans because they'd read about the comedy troupe in *Melody Maker*, the popular English music and culture magazine, and the person most into Python was Mississippi Joe. So we set up a showing of the Python movie *And Now for Something Completely Different* for the WBCN audience in a local movie theater. The film was not much more than a series of highlights from the troupe's BBC show *Monty Python's Flying Circus*, but the event was a big success. Everyone in attendance was thrilled at the reception the movie received, and the screening helped make the Boston PBS television station aware of the potential of broadcasting *Monty Python's Flying Circus* to American audiences.

On one occasion, I invited a few of the on-air people out to lunch. One of them asked me if some of the staff could join us. I agreed, and, to my surprise, there were about twenty people waiting for us when we got to the restaurant. The entire staff was there, including the elevator operator and the janitor, not to mention the accountant's nephew. Of course, I was stuck with the bill and had to look like a good sport, but I felt used and abused. Neil was pleased with my expense report that month.

When a group of WBCN staff made a special trip to New York to spend a few days, I arranged for us all to see *National Lampoon's Lemmings* show (with Chevy Chase and John Belushi in their pre-*Saturday Night Live* days) at the Village Gate, a famous jazz club in Greenwich Village that often hosted small off-Broadway acts. Buddah had nothing to do with this show, but I thought everyone would enjoy it. *Lemmings* was a Woodstock parody (the festival in it was called "Woodchuck") that mocked the hippie generation, and the Village Gate was so jammed that a number of us had to sit on the floor in front of the stage. Taking the staff to the show helped solidify my relationship with the station, but, to be truthful, it didn't really seem to matter how close I was to them; they never played many of my records.

One of Neil's more lucrative ventures was a prestigious deal to distribute Charisma Records through Buddah. Charisma was founded by a former journalist named Tony Stratton-Smith, and it was home to several noteworthy artists, particularly Genesis, then fronted by Peter Gabriel, and the Monty Python comedy troupe. Neil had come to know Tony via our association with Nancy Lewis, who ran publicity for us and had been publicist for The Who. Python had yet to experience their big American breakthrough (that would come in 1974, with the theatrical release of *Monty Python and the Holy Grail*), but their BBC show was a huge success in Britain. Similarly, Genesis had made a lot of noise in Europe but hadn't yet found their footing in the states. The band is best known for their later pop stylings when Phil Collins was their front man, but back in the early 1970s, Genesis was a high-concept art-rock outfit whose epic and complex songs (frequently clocking in at over ten minutes) could not find a place on US radio. They had received a great reception in their native England, and *Melody Maker*, in particular, had been raving about their extravagant stage shows for years, so this was something of a pressure project for Buddah. Their first album for us was *Nursery Cryme*, and although some people, like Scott Muni at WNEW, played them in his English hour each week, we were having a hard time getting airplay as Peter Gabriel's vocals were very hard to understand. I had to come up with a way to make everyone pay attention and realize this band had a great live show, and that their music, esoteric as it was, was still accessible and relevant.

I met with Muni and discussed what could be done to get Genesis more exposure on the station. He had no real ideas, as he did not often push his on-air staff to play specific groups unless their music directly related to the station in some fashion. I came up with an idea: we would throw a Genesis concert for the WNEW audience and the small admission fee would go to charity. Buddah and Charisma would pick up the tab. I ran the idea past Neil and Tony Stratton-Smith, and they both agreed. The caveat was that I had to make the concert as high-profile as I could. The show was scheduled for December 13, 1972 at the Lincoln Center's Philharmonic Hall in Manhattan. I sent out invitations to every noteworthy progressive FM program director in the country I could think of: Bernie Kimball from WCMF-FM in Rochester; Tom Starr from WOUR-FM in Utica; Mark Parenteau from WABX in Detroit; Jerry Stevens from WMMR-FM in Philly; even West Coasters like Mary Turner and Richard Kimball from KMET in LA. We put everyone up at the Americana Hotel.

WNEW plugged the show like crazy, and on the night of the concert almost every DJ played Genesis constantly to increase excitement over the event, which, at three dollars a pop, had sold out easily. Genesis blew everyone away, with Gabriel in his bizarre garb flying over the audience. It was a major success. The number of ads (the industry term for a radio station adding a song or artist to its playlist) were too numerous to count. Only Mark Parenteau, as I recall, left the building unimpressed.

A few days after the event, I was smugly sitting in my office feeling oh so impressed with myself—I'd pretty much made Genesis in the US, by my own reckoning—when in walks Buddah comptroller Eric Steinmetz, who was angrily pointing to a bill from the Americana showing a case of champagne charged to Parenteau's room. Mark had taken the entire case home and charged it to Buddah. I called and bitched him out for a good fifteen minutes, but we wound up laughing about it, and I didn't press the issue; I knew I would have an IOU with his name on it in my pocket for the foreseeable future. Neil could not possibly have cared less, as he knew it was money well spent. Eric, with his bean-counter mentality, was a pain in the ass about it for weeks, until Neil finally told him to back off and leave me alone.

As 1972 gave way to 1973, Neil, Cecil, and I, along with the Buddah Group, were plowing ahead. We had big hits with Barbara Mason's "Give Me Your Love" and Stories's "Brother Louie." I was getting to spend quite a bit of time with Sha Na Na and their manager, Ed Goodgold. He was a very funny and likeable guy (his quick wit had earned him the nickname "the Rabbi"), and he had one of the most difficult managing gigs in the business. Sha Na Na was comprised of twelve guys, all of whom had equal say in the direction of the band. I always enjoyed seeing them in concert. They put on a great show, and the crowd was always part of the pageantry, dressing in 1950s garb. Before one show, in Detroit, I arrived at the hotel early, so I took a few 'ludes and headed out to the pool. Trying to impress some sweet young thing in a bikini, I dove nonchalantly into the water, not realizing I was at the shallow end. I surfaced with a gash on my forehead and a slight concussion as reward for the stunt. Leaving the tour, I flew home and spent a few days in the hospital in traction.

When I returned to the office, Neil had big news for me. He'd had his eye on acquiring Gladys Knight & the Pips, whose contract with Motown Records was about to expire. Gladys wanted to branch out into gospel, blues, and country, but Berry Gordy, Motown's founder and driving force, wasn't keen on that career path. Neil had called a meeting and announced that he had secretly signed Gladys to a deal. She was currently working with songwriter Jim Weatherly on her next album, *Imagination*, her first for Buddah. As if the clandestine signing wasn't interesting enough, Neil also told me that he wanted us to work Gladys's final Motown single, "Neither One of Us (Wants to Be the First to Say Goodbye)." Pushing another label's song is tricky work, but we managed to promote the single very quietly, and it eventually sold over a million copies, peaking at No. 2 on the charts. Once the song had peaked, Neil released *Imagination*, which spawned the biggest single of the group's career: "Midnight Train to Georgia." The song would top the charts and go on to win a Grammy.

Business was also going well for Bill Aucoin and Joyce Biawitz's production company, Direction Plus, which by the summer of 1973 was producing a thirteen-episode rock-music-based TV series for national syndication called *Flip Side*. Each half-hour episode would focus on one or two acts performing in a recording studio, and it was usually hosted by either the president of their record label or their A & R rep. For the Curtis Mayfield/Sha Na Na episode, Neil was the MC, dressed in black leather (in keeping with Sha Na Na's outfits). I was in the recording studio with him as he videotaped his segments. The program was broadcast in New York on December 22, and I couldn't help but think it was odd to see the president of a label on television taking up time that rightfully belonged to the artists. However, the feeling left me quickly after the taping, and it wasn't until years later that I realized it had been a portent.

I felt lucky and fulfilled, and I frankly couldn't imagine a better place to be than right where I was. Fortunately, Neil never thought like this. He had already quietly begun conspiring to make a move that would officially certify his legend and make Cecil, Buck, and I co-owners of a lucrative piece of the American Dream.

4

Leaving the Nest

Doing it alone—Approaching Warner—Supernova on 54th Street—Signed—The Who—Going shopping— Resurrecting the Fillmore—LA bound—House guest in Bel-Air—Alison Steele and *The Fugitive*— Setting up the Casbah—A house on a cliff

First week of August, 1973
Buddah Group Offices
810 Seventh Avenue
Manhattan, New York

"Do you want to own a record company?"

What actually came out of Neil Bogart's mouth was more like, "Larry, I'm starting my own record company with backing from Warner Brothers. I think you've got a good ear for rock, and I want you to help run that part of the company. You'd own a piece of the business, but you'd have to move to LA. You want the gig?" He'd walked straight into my office while I was working my way through the daily glut of calls, and he broke the news in a completely oh-by-the-way fashion. No fanfare, no lead-up. Nothing. Just like that.

The offer left me dizzy. I was game, of course, but I felt baffled by Neil's overture—I had no idea what he thought I could bring to the table. There were many other players he could have approached, most with years more experience. Yet here was Neil, standing in front of me, insisting that I had a great understanding of the rock side of the industry and that's where my attention should be focused. I was young, still felt invincible, and wasn't quite experienced enough to know what I was getting myself into. What the hell—I was up for it.

Neil explained, "Larry, you know I'm not unhappy here. We've had a lot of success for Buddah, but we can do more, and I think having to answer to Viewlex for everything we do is hindering us." He was right.

We'd had quite a bit of success—scoring six Gold albums in 1973 alone—but Neil always had the Viewlex Corporation looking over his shoulder, he held a sizeable amount of stock (reportedly valued at over a million dollars) that he couldn't sell for reasons I don't recall, and he felt that he never received enough credit, so his decision to start his own company made sense.

I was surprised to learn that Neil had started to lay the groundwork a year earlier, in the fall of 1972, when he hired Jeff Franklin of ATI (a major booking agency) to secure funding and distribution for this new label. Jeff was Neil's close friend, and he acted as his business manager when needed. Their friendship dated back to 1968, when Jeff had brought an artist named Jack Wild to Neil's attention. He negotiated the hell out of the deal and got Wild signed to Buddah with a very favorable contract. Neil had been thoroughly outclassed by Jeff, and he did not soon forget it. Once his embarrassment had subsided, he took the if-you-can't-beat-them-join-them approach and convinced Jeff to represent him. Jeff took the offer and did a lap of the industry, pitching Neil's plan to anyone who would take a meeting. Many companies passed on the opportunity—including Warner, which turned Franklin down on three separate occasions—but he was finally able to set up a meeting with Warner's three top men: cochairmen Mo Ostin and Joe Smith, as well as vice president Ed West. After his initial failures, Franklin had changed his pitch, realizing (correctly) that if he could get the three Warner execs in a room with Neil, then he was halfway home. Once he adopted the ploy of selling them Neil instead of his company, things started to happen. Within seventy-two hours, a seven-figure deal was in place wherein Warner would provide financial backing and distribution for the new company. Before the ink was even dry, Franklin was brokering a deal for Neil to buy out the last three years of his contract with Buddah.

Neil already had a logo and artwork, designed by renowned artist David Byrd, for his new label, which he called Casablanca Records. Not only did *Casablanca* have the cachet of being arguably the best film ever made, but Neil also liked the surname connection he had with the film's star, Humphrey Bogart. Plus, the film was owned by Warner Brothers, which would serve as the new parent company, and this eliminated any risk of legal action against us for the choice of name.

We had ourselves a new label. Now we needed a big signing. On Friday, August 17, one of the *Flip Side* producers, Bill Aucoin, called in a favor and asked Neil to listen to a demo tape from a band he was managing, a four-man glitter-rock outfit from New York called KISS. Neil passed the five-song tape to Stories coproducer Kenny Kerner and asked for his opinion. Kenny agreed to check out the tape over the weekend and get back to Neil on Monday. The demo not only sounded great, but it was also produced by the legendary Eddie Kramer (Led Zeppelin, Jimi Hendrix), which surely made KISS seem even more of a desirable commodity. When Kenny reported back on Monday, his enthusiasm about this upstart band aroused Neil's interest, and a showcase was hastily arranged.

A few days later, on a warm weekday evening, Neil asked me to accompany him to a small studio at the Henry LeTang School of Dance on 54th Street in Manhattan. Neil had been warned that the performance we were about to see was on the outer fringes of the absurd. He told me to have an open mind, but he also insisted that I be very critical, because this group could play an important role in the survival of our new record company.

On the way to the performance, we stopped for a quick dinner at Tad's Steak House, a serve-yourself, tough-steak-for-about-a-buck type of joint. Neil loved food, but he would inhale his meals, not wanting to waste time eating when there were more important things to do. Dining with him was usually a race to finish before he left the restaurant.

We were running late, so we jogged the few blocks from Tad's to the dance studio. Arriving quite out of breath, we were surprised to see only a few people in the room—a dozen, at most—among them record producers Kenny Kerner and Richie Wise; KISS's managers, Bill Aucoin and Joyce Biawitz; the KISS drummer's wife, Lydia; KISS's soundman, Eddie Solan; and Sean Delaney, an associate of Bill's who was helping develop the band's material and stage show.

The room was fairly small, maybe twenty feet wide by thirty feet deep; several rows of battered folding chairs were set up in front of the stage. The space was typically used for the kind of dance rehearsals and recitals attended by the moms and pops of the performers—kids decked out in tutus and toe shoes who would stumble through something vaguely resembling ballet or tap. The stage was elevated about a foot above the worn hardwood floor. Behind a small set of drums were at least six stacks of amplifiers and speaker cabinets, and huge PA fills flanked the stage. Had it been a twenty-five-hundred-seat theater, this would have been a modest equipment arsenal. In that small room, it was ridiculous.

I quickly took a seat near the back of the room. Four seven-foot monsters in eight-inch platform boots took the stage. The makeup they wore that night was close to what would become the trademark KISS visage: whiteface, with a different design around the eyes for each band member. Paul Stanley's black star was in place, as were Ace Frehley's silver explosions, and Gene Simmons and Peter Criss had their respective batwings and cat whiskers under development. But the makeup looked cheap. The whiteface was more like powder than greasepaint. It was pale and transparent rather than stark; it lacked a bright-whiteness that would have provided a contrast to the blacks and silvers, and it ran off their cheeks as they began to sweat. There were no costumes to speak of, either. Gene, who was by far the most comfortable in his alter ego, wore a tight black skull-and-crossbones T-shirt. Paul had on a heavy leather jacket with suede or velvet pants and bright-red platform shoes; Ace wore head-to-toe black with white platform shoes, while Peter had donned a black tank top and red leather pants. I don't recall the exact set list, but the band stormed through five or six songs, including "Deuce," "Strutter," "Nothin' to Lose," and an unrecorded song, "Life in the Woods." They had been performing in New York–area dives for several months, and, for them, it had all come down to impressing Neil and me.

There was no production at all. None of the trappings of the show that KISS would later make famous were evident—no blood, no fire, no explosions or drum risers, just pure energy and sound. And more sound. The volume level in that small room was indescribable. I'd attended more concerts than I could possibly catalog, and loud music was hardly new to me, but KISS's decibel level was so high that standing in the jet intake of the Concorde would have been more restful. I couldn't hear for two days afterward, and during that time I was afflicted with earaches. But, despite the onslaught, I couldn't help but be impressed as I watched the performance. As green as its members were, KISS was an incredibly compelling band. These guys demanded your attention, and there was no way you could walk away from them feeling apathetic. Love them or hate them, you were going to have a strong reaction, and Neil and I both knew that anyone capable of provoking this type of visceral response was the stuff of future superstardom. I did not spend any time with the band before or after the performance; they did their thing, and then the rest of us went our separate ways—except Neil, Joyce, and Bill, who stayed on to hang awhile. I hopped into my car and went home to suffer the pain.

A few days later, at Neil's insistence, I arranged to meet with the band at offices belonging to Howard Marks, who ran an advertising agency that Bill and Joyce were involved with and that would later become instrumental in KISS's financial success. I gave the band a quick critique of their performance, though I don't think they paid attention to a thing I said. That didn't matter—my sole objective for the meeting was to make them feel that Casablanca was the only label for them. Not that anyone else was breaking down doors to sign them, but I dramati-

- January 30, 1973: G. Gordon Liddy begins serving a twenty-year prison term for his involvement in the Watergate burglaries.
- March 17, 1973: Pink Floyd releases *The Dark Side of the Moon*; the album would spend a record-breaking 741 weeks on the *Billboard* 200.
- July 20, 1973: Bruce Lee dies mysteriously at age 32.

cally underscored the fact that Casablanca would stop at nothing to promote them. If the relationship was going to work, I needed them to cooperate totally with whatever we asked them to do. I also suggested that they put their logo on the drumhead and figure out a way to use more speakers and amplifiers in their production so it would look more massive. We later accomplished this on the cheap by using fake speaker cabinets; the band didn't need any extra volume, and empty cabinets were far less expensive. I also wanted them to find a point in the show to destroy some guitars, as The Who, my favorite group, so often did.

The band spent much of September and October refining their performance and song arrangements with the help of Bill, Joyce, and Sean Delaney. Meanwhile, Neil and Bill had been working on a contract to make KISS Casablanca's first artists, and on November 1, 1973, a fifteen-thousand-dollar deal was struck. Technically, it was a production agreement between Casablanca and Rock Steady (Bill Aucoin's company); KISS hadn't signed anything.

Before the ink was even dry, the band was recording their debut album at Bell Sound Studios in Manhattan, with Kerner and his partner, Richie Wise, coproducing the sixteen-track sessions. We had chosen Bell over other, more famous studios, such as Electric Lady or the Record Plant, because we'd had a working relationship with Bell at Buddah; Bell was owned by Viewlex, the company that had bought out Buddah in 1969. The album was recorded in less than a month, and without much hype or drama.

In early December 1973, I invited KISS to join me on a trip to Philadelphia to see The Who perform at The Spectrum, a big sports arena. Gene Simmons, Paul Stanley, Ace Frehley, Peter Criss, and I piled into a Mercedes leased by Jerry Sharell, who had just left Buddah to work as VP of promotion at Elektra Records in LA. Jerry had given me the use of his car when he took the job, and it was quite a step up from my two-seat Opel. The band and I started to get to know each other during the ride from Manhattan to Philly, and it soon became apparent that Gene was the KISS spokesman. I also felt that the other members of the group had been told beforehand to be on their best behavior and say as little as possible. We spent most of the ride without talking much; I could usually carry on long, rambling conversations with anyone, but these guys were so tight-lipped that at times I felt like I was in the car by myself. We arrived at the sold-out twenty-thousand-seat arena and were met by the promoter of the gig, my soon-to-be good friend Larry Magid, who was, and still is, the major promoter of live concerts in the market. We were ushered upstairs to a VIP area to watch the show.

The members of KISS were knocked out by The Who's performance, as was everyone else in the arena, and on the ride back to New York they did not stop talking about it. Finally, some conversation! I had been dreading the ride home, figuring it would be a repeat of the awkward two hours of silence on the way down, but I was happily surprised.

KISS agreed to break guitars onstage (mimicking The Who's Pete Townshend) if I could find a way for them to afford it. I arranged a deal with the Gibson Guitar Corporation, which would supply the instruments if we would feature the company's name and logo on KISS's album covers as well as in the band's trade and consumer print advertising. We also discussed how we could make Peter Criss's drum set a centerpiece of the show without actually destroying it, the way The Who did. Though he was no Keith Moon, I always thought Peter was a very solid drummer, and everyone agreed that more attention needed to be paid to him. Shortly thereafter, KISS's live production began to include a levitating drum riser: Peter would rise up behind the band in a massive bombardment of smoke and explosions.

A week or so later, Neil and I took the band to several magic shops around New York City to get ideas for KISS's stage show. None of us really had any idea of what we were looking for. Neil was fascinated by the stuff on display, and he kept pointing to things or picking them up and saying, "Larry, come over here and look at this!" One thing that particularly caught his eye was flash paper. Magicians use it all the time to create little fireballs from the palms of their hands. Neil fell in love with the stuff, and for the next year he used it at any meetings involving KISS. We'd be meeting with the Warner people, DJs, promo men, or rack jobbers—any audience, really—and he would suddenly say, "KISS is magic!" and unleash a burst of flash-paper flame. It never failed to impress. He did it so often that I started to predict it—"Oh no, here we go again." Once you'd seen the man behind the curtain a dozen times, the trick lost a lot of its gee-whiz factor. KISS incorporated a couple of flash-paper effects into their shows for the next year, then they moved on to bigger, more impressive displays.

At the end of December, KISS played a few last small gigs in the New York area and, in a crafty move, a private performance was set up at the Fillmore East, the legendary if short-lived New York concert hall. The invitation list was restricted to members of the local and regional press as well as some New York–based Warner Brothers employees. Prior to this January 8, 1974 show, someone from Warner—which, as a company, was skeptical about KISS's makeup gimmick—called Neil and asked him to tell the band to drop the makeup. Neil "got" KISS, and he knew that their look would be vital to their, and our, eventual success, but he wasn't in a position to flat out tell Warner no. So he dutifully obliged, making a halfhearted attempt to convince Bill Aucoin to go along with Warner's wishes. It was obvious Neil didn't believe in the pitch he was feeding Bill. When Neil wanted to convince you of something, he convinced you of it. His smile would never waver as he told you in a bright, enthusiastic voice how fantastic this new artist or song was. He wasn't obnoxious about it; he was steadfast and incredibly effective at removing all doubt. But he was convincing no one here—not me, not himself, and certainly not Bill, who responded with an emphatic no. Neil quickly and, if I had to guess, gladly told Warner of the band's decision.

The KISS members were working with Bill and Joyce to craft their appearance and show in front of video cameras. We knew that to become successful KISS would have to use television effectively, and the only way to make sure they would come off as an exciting performance band on a real television show was to get them to feel comfortable in front of the camera. Bill and Joyce's experience in television was therefore the perfect complement to the band's already over-the-top presence.

As for the rest of us, just prior to Christmas, Neil and his family, our partners Buck Reingold and Cecil Holmes and their families, and I hopped on a 747, settled into coach class, and headed off to California to begin what was to become the journey of our lives.

∼ ∼ ∼

Our arrival in LA was littered with good omens: the weather was fair and warm, and we were greeted at the airport by three limousines, one for each family. Being odd man out without a family of my own, I rode with Neil, Beth, and their kids. I spent my first month or so in LA living with them at the property they had bought in Bel-Air, a very exclusive section of Beverly Hills. Cecil and Buck bought houses in the San Fernando Valley—an area less exclusive than Bel-Air, but still far too expensive for me. I felt both excited and dislocated; I hadn't had time to look around LA beforehand for a place to rent, and I was in no position to buy a home.

Arriving at Neil's new house—a spacious, two-story domicile set against a hillside across from the Bel-Air Country Club—we were met by Milt Friedman, the owner of a local rental car company. He presented us with seven Mercedeses courtesy of Warner Brothers. One for each of us, plus the wives. The vehicles would become a familiar sight in the Casablanca parking lot, so much so that Joe Smith, the co-chairman of Warner Brothers Records, would often joke about the irony of "all these Jewish New Yorkers driving German-made cars." He was certain that wasn't kosher.

Living with Neil, Beth, and the kids was fun for me, and it made LA feel much more like home; it was like I had a family, even though I was just borrowing Neil's. It was during this time that I saw firsthand how family-oriented Neil was. He adored his children and doted on them every chance he got. He even brought the New York winters of his childhood to LA for them one Christmas by renting some of the large snow-making machines used on movie sets to create a winter wonderland in his front yard.

He and I were both early risers, and helping him to get the kids fed and off to school each morning helped ease my transition from New York to LA. Beth was a joy to be around, too. She was the complete package. She was beautiful by any standard—a prepossessing woman with an olive complexion, a stunning face, and large, intelligent eyes. Beth would also not hesitate to give her opinion on a vast array of subjects. With her combination of beauty, confidence, and wit, I thought she was just about perfect.

A few days after we arrived, Alison Steele, our good friend and renowned radio personality from WNEW in New York, called to say she was in town and asked if she and a couple of friends could come over to say hello. Neil said yes without hesitation, despite the fact that the furniture was still in transit and the house was almost empty. Alison arrived not long thereafter with her two friends in tow: David Janssen and his fiancée, Dani Crayne. The New Yorker in me couldn't help but note how very LA the whole scene was. Here I was hanging with the star of *The Fugitive*, the wildly popular TV show; its final, climactic episode in August 1967 had garnered the highest ratings in television history to that point. David and I quickly segued from making polite conversation to sitting on the bare wood floor of an unfurnished Bel-Air living room smoking a joint. I was getting high with Dr. Richard Kimble—amazing! Despite the bizarre situation, I found David and Dani to be very friendly, and we were to see them again at various events we staged through the years.

The fact that our arrival in LA occurred in December was a bit of a blessing. Not only did it allow us a delightful change of weather, but it was also good timing in terms of business. In December, the music industry generally shuts down for two to three weeks for the holidays, and this industry-wide vacation gave us time to get things together at the offices we had rented. Neil had filed the paperwork with the State of California to incorporate Casablanca Records a few weeks earlier, on November 27, 1973, but there was tons of work for us to do before we could officially open our doors for business.

We set ourselves up in a twentieth-floor apartment at 1155 North La Cienega Boulevard—a stopgap measure until we could find a more permanent home. Toward that end, we hired a woman named Briana, whose working knowledge of Warner, LA, and the music business in general was advantageous for us New Yorkers. She helped us find some ideal office space, and she furnished the place and installed the telephone system in short order. We hired two or three people to answer the phones and deal with some administrative duties, but it was a bare-bones operation to start, with most of the substantive support being provided by Warner Brothers.

Our first permanent offices were located at 1112 North Sherbourne Drive, just off the Sunset Strip, in a converted two-story house with a three-room guesthouse in the rear. The two houses were connected by a kitchen and a shared, gated yard. Neil, Cecil, and I had our offices in the main house, while Buck took the guesthouse, happily making full use of the relative isolation to do what he wanted without being bothered. Buck could carry on with women at all hours without his wife, Nancy, finding out. He was the only one of us to have an assistant—coincidentally, also named Nancy (Sain)—and although she worked in the guesthouse, her presence apparently did not hinder Buck's impressive womanizing at all. Despite the fact that Buck's wife was Neil's sister-in-law, Neil didn't seem to mind. Hell, he practically encouraged it. Maybe this was because of the times we were living in, or because Neil was no saint himself, although he was nowhere near as unfaithful to Beth as Buck was to Nancy.

The front entryway served as our reception and waiting area. It could accommodate about four people, including our receptionist, Lisa Sepe, who was one of the most naturally beautiful and sweet women I have ever met. She was only about eighteen years old, tall, well built, with long, thick, naturally blonde hair. She had a music industry lineage; her father had been Barry White's longtime road manager. (We'd soon use Barry to produce the second album Casablanca released, Gloria Scott's *What Am I Going to Do?*) The kitchen and dining room were used as office space, as was a sunroom on the other side of Neil's office. The sunroom was initially used by Neil's secretary, but it would later become the hub of the production and international departments. The basement of the main house was our mail room, which was run by a kid named Kenny Ryback, who also served as our all-purpose gofer. We had no parking lot, so after the driveway filled with cars, people found ample parking on nearby streets.

The offices were decorated to look like Rick's Café in the Bogart film, with high-back cane chairs, rattan sofas, and palm trees. Neil even had a near-life-sized stuffed camel named Bogie installed in his office. After a while, the nails began to come out of the finely crafted cane chairs, and you'd rip your clothing if you weren't careful. Middle Eastern rugs were laid out generously throughout the house, and anyone who wasn't paying attention to where they were walking was likely to trip over them. An inordinate amount of greenery adorned the space; while certainly impractical, the plants did give the office an oasis feel and reinforced the whole *Casablanca* vibe.

Having our offices so close to Sunset Boulevard afforded us proximity to many of the local radio stations and music retailers without the added hassle of being on such a busy thoroughfare. It didn't hurt that clubs like the Whisky and the Roxy were just down the block. Another of our frequent gathering places was a popular LA club called Pips. It was a nice dance club, but its real drawing card was the backgammon room in the back. Backgammon was extremely popular at the time, and high-stakes games were played at Pips almost every night. In order to get into Pips, at least one person in your party had to be a member of the club. I don't recall what the membership dues were, but they weren't cheap—maybe a few thousand dollars. Buck was the first to join, and Neil and I were ready to get our checkbooks out, but then we found out that Pips was refusing to allow Cecil to join because he was black. The checkbooks immediately went back into our pockets. Cecil was our brother, and we wanted no part of any club that wouldn't accept a member of our team. It was a sickening reminder that abject racism still percolated close to the surface in an allegedly enlightened time. Buck stayed on at Pips as a member, mostly for the women, but Neil and I never returned.

Once we were settled into our offices, I began to look for a house, and I eventually found a place to call my own. It was a small, two-story, two-bedroom house that was hanging—and I do mean hanging—over the side of a cliff near the famous Hollywood sign. Its proximity to such a drop-off caused me some trepidation: I was afraid I would fall off the deck into the abyss below while I was stoned one night. Despite being surrounded by the metropolis, the house was very peaceful and quiet. I found its sense of relative isolation very relaxing. I hired a painter to redo the interior of my new place, and while I waited for him to finish I stayed on with Neil and Beth. I had little money for anything else, so the house had virtually no furniture except a waterbed, which Beth Bogart and Nancy Reingold had helped me select from a nearby Wonderful World of Waterbeds superstore.

During our trip to the waterbed store, Beth mentioned to me that I should not feel hesitant about having a girl visit me in their home. Nancy jumped on her, insisting that it would be totally inappropriate for me to have sex in Beth and Neil's house. As the two women argued about this, I realized that although they were twins (as were my older sisters), their opinions and values varied wildly. I felt much closer to Beth.

My house also contained a leopard-print sofa bed, which I had brought with me from New York, and the dresser and rolltop desk I'd had when I was a kid. So my little home was decorated in a very eclectic, no-taste bachelor style. The entryway was upstairs, and it opened into a kitchen that was separated from the living room by a long countertop. There was no furniture whatsoever on this floor of the house. Absolutely none. And I liked it that way, because when I was home—which was not often—all I wanted to do was to go to bed and mellow out. If I did have a female visitor, I did not want to be able to offer her anywhere to sit but my bed, because I hoped that this would make it easier for me to get laid. The entire back of the house was glass, providing a breathtaking view of the valley below. The final perk of this cliffside isolation: I could grow my own weed in large flower pots hanging on the deck.

It sounds completely ridiculous these days, but owning a microwave and a twenty-seven-inch TV made me something of a cutting-edge gadget collector. The microwave and a refrigerator were sent to me by the Zamoski Company in Baltimore in exchange for some albums. The television, which was a very large model in 1974, was Neil's suggestion. At Zamoski's, they were so cool that they were open to trading anything from carpeting to electronics for vinyl records: this was barter at its best. We would often order prizes for our contests or gifts for artists and DJs from Zamoski's.

Soon after I moved in to the house, one of our former Buddah Group artists, comedian Robert Klein, came to stay while he was performing at the Troubadour on Santa Monica Boulevard. I had gotten to know Robert very well back East, and once I'd moved out to LA, he'd frequently stay with me when he was in town doing shows. Because most of us think of comedians as relative no-names doing five nights a week at the local improv, we tend to forget that the top guys and gals in the field are like rock stars. Robert is solidly old-school now, but at the time he was as hot as any comedian on the planet.

During this particular visit, I drove him around the city and showed him LA's hot night spots—like the Whisky and the Roxy—and listened to him rant about his managers, Buddy Morra and Larry Brezner. Robert, who had done *The Tonight Show* more times than any other comedian, had just signed a lucrative contract with HBO, and his live shows generated good money as well. He felt (justifiably so, according to the half-hour sales pitch I was hearing) that his managers should be treating him as their top guy, but instead they couldn't stop raving about this new comedian—some guy named Robin Williams.

After that, I attended a gig of Robert's at the Troubadour; I knew his routine so well that I could have jumped onstage and done it myself. I found it helpful to drop his name when trying to pick up pretty young things at nightclubs, and his name could equally impress the older set. Robert was nice enough to have dinner one evening with me and my parents, spending most of the meal raving about me. This not only made me proud, but it wowed my parents that a guy who'd done Johnny's show so many times would say such nice things about their son.

5

Our First Kiss and a Ride on the Mothership

Bill Amesbury—Introduction in Acapulco—Ostin, Smith, Saul, Regehr, and Rosenblatt—The biggest launch party ever—KISS premieres—Progam directors (in the biblical sense)—No one wants to KISS—KSHE and the big storm—Crash at the Agora—The WABX fiasco—Way ahead of our time—George Clinton and the Purple Gang

Mid-January 1974
Casablanca Records Offices
1112 North Sherbourne Drive
Los Angeles, California

In early 1974, KISS's debut album was still not quite ready to be released, as we needed time to prepare Warner Brothers for what was about to befall them. Additionally, January was not typically a good month to release albums, especially those of new artists, since so much product had just hit the market for the holiday shopping season. Instead, a record by an artist named Bill Amesbury, who was referred to us by a Canadian producer whom Neil knew, became Casablanca's first release. Amesbury's single, "Virginia," was not a great record, and I had nothing to do with its promotion as it was tailor-made for Top 40. The record allowed Buck the chance to become familiar with some of the Warner people he would be working with, and it also bought us some time to set up the KISS marketing blitz, which would include several different full-page ads in *Billboard*, *Cashbox*, and *Record World*, as well as a sixty-second radio spot featuring a Humphrey Bogart sound-alike doing *Casablanca*-themed voice-overs.

I spent much of this time getting to know the Warner Brothers staff and trying to understand how their company functioned. Most of the people at Warner were less than thrilled about our label. They were used to labels that had (in their opinion) relevant artists—such as Chrysalis, with Robin Trower and Jethro Tull; or Capricorn, with the Allman Brothers. It was beneath a company with such a classy image to be associated with a group that wore makeup—though they did have Alice Cooper. Somehow, Alice's makeup was upscale in their eyes.

We weren't exactly acting like shy, unassuming neophytes. When you have no experience (and we didn't, compared to Warner), you're expected to be deferential, to quietly and respectfully pay your dues. We didn't. We were loudmouthed New York guys who drove nice Mercedeses and drew bigger paychecks than our Warner counterparts. We bragged publicly and loudly in the trades about ourselves—we Casablanca people, not just the company itself or our artists. More often than not, we acted like we were inventing the business, not like the kids who'd just arrived at the party. I can't imagine that sat well with most of the Warner folks.

This created two huge challenges for us: one was marketing KISS, and the other was getting Warner Brothers to work with us. To anyone with a pair of functioning eyes, KISS was a supernova waiting to explode, but igniting the fuse was proving far more difficult than we expected. KISS was an uphill battle for us as far as Warner Brothers was concerned, and at the crux of that was the black-and-white contrast between the Casablanca and the Warner ways of doing business. We were a small group of kids out on a new adventure, and Casablanca was as shoot-from-the-hip as you could get. From the start, Neil boasted about us to anyone who would listen. He especially played us up in the January 1974 edition of an in-house Warner newsletter called *Circular*, saying that I had walked into Buddah right off the streets and now knew more about the world of FM radio than guys who had been doing promotions for ten or twelve years. A great compliment, but Neil was being an overzealous braggart and had wildly overstated my experience. In the same article, he also explained the infrastructure that made Casablanca not only successful but also unique among record companies: we were a team of promotion men. It was unusual for a record company president to do promotions himself—to call radio stations, to go out on the road and visit them— but Neil did it, and he loved doing it too. Promotion was the name of the game for us, and that's what we were: a promotion company.

In sharp contrast, Warner Brothers was a cumbersome bureaucratic maze in which every department clung desperately to its own turf. Buck or Neil or I couldn't have cared less who got the credit, we just wanted to succeed. Warner's staff seemed intent on their proprietary success. It was a classic study in contrast: entrepreneurial creativity versus the old-style corporate mentality. Working for Warner was a dream come true for most Warner employees because it made them part of the WEA (Warner Elektra Atlantic) Corporation, and while the prestigious labels Elektra and Atlantic had great acts, the Warner roster was cooler and hipper.

By the middle of January 1974, we were ready to begin work, but then we were sidetracked when Warner invited us to its convention in Acapulco. This was a major event within Warner culture. The company would fly in its entire promotional and sales staff from around the country and present them with all kinds of awards, but the event's primary function was to bolster morale. Dinners were massive events, and the convention hotel, the Acapulco Princess, was the height of tropical opulence.

The convention was my indoctrination into Warner Brothers, and it was there that I first met many of the staff members who would play a large role in our day-to-day operations. I was particularly impressed with Warner's cochairman, Joe Smith, a gregarious and likable man who had a remarkable ability to remember the names of everyone he had met in the industry, and even the names of those he hadn't met. In the conference's initial reception line, through which everyone was funneled into the room, Joe greeted his guests, and although I was not with Neil or anyone else from Casablanca, he knew my name. Joe was the kind of person who immediately put you at ease, and since he, and not Warner's president, Mo Ostin, was actually responsible for us being there, I felt a certain warmth toward him.

Three key members of the Warner staff were Ron Saul, the promotions director; Bob Regehr, who ran marketing, publicity, and artist relations; and Eddie Rosenblatt, who was the head of sales. We immediately developed a good rapport with Regehr, but our relations were considerably cooler with Saul and Rosenblatt. Rosenblatt, who later left to become president of Geffen Records, thought that we weren't good enough for Warner. But Saul was far worse, and he seemed to be doing everything he could to ensure that his promotion staff gave us as little

help as possible, a tactic that would later backfire on him. Saul was
replaced shortly thereafter by Gary Davis, though our relationship with
Davis wasn't much better.

Fortunately, Bob Regehr and his staff were very nice, and usually
helpful. While they didn't seem to understand why Warner had made
this deal with us, they were willing to give us a shot. It was important to
have them in our corner, as they had a separate budget that we could tap
into and a great deal of clout with concert promoters throughout the
country, all of which would prove highly valuable to us when it came to
booking KISS. Regehr and his right-hand man, Carl Scott, knew the concert business. Regehr's department was also responsible for publicity, and
we had a nice relationship with them until our need for publicity outpaced their ability or desire to provide it. I always got along well with
Carl Scott; he was accessible and fair, and I did believe he was honest
with me in terms of what he could and would do. I also had dealings
with another member of the artist relations group, a very small and
dynamic young lady named Paulette Rapp, who was Regehr's lieutenant.

The Warner sales department was made up of some fine industry
veterans, and we worked well with all of the field people. Our problem,
which did not become apparent until months later, was the head of the
department, Eddie Rosenblatt. If it were not for the efforts of Russ
Thyret, Rosenblatt's second in command, we would have been at logger-
heads immediately. Russ, who would later become company chairman,
was in charge of single sales, and he was a particularly skilled politician,
always attempting to smooth over disagreements we were having with
Eddie, which usually involved how many records to ship and what sales
promotions we should use. Russ had our interests in mind, and he was
one of the very few inside Warner who recognized that we were not
being treated fairly. Then again, given the politicking that goes on in the
industry, Eddie and Russ may simply have been running a good cop/bad
cop routine.

KISS's debut album was finally ready. Our labor pains began as we
prepared to deliver it. There was no shortage of enthusiasm for the
album on the part of Neil and me and the rest of the Casablanca staff. It
had all the energy we'd hoped for. It was filled with the songs that
would be the cornerstones of the band's sound and stage show for
decades: "Deuce," "Strutter, "Cold Gin," "Firehouse," all crashing to a

thunderous conflagration at the album's end in "Black Diamond." The finished product made Neil feel vindicated for stonewalling Warner's attempts to dilute these garish misfits and make them more palatable. To celebrate the record's release on February 8, 1974, Warner decided to throw a party welcoming us to the label. This would give us the opportunity to showcase KISS live for the Warner staff, West Coast radio, television, retail clients, and critics. The event grew in size and scope until it became the most expensive music industry party in history to that point. Factoring for inflation, it may still hold that distinction.

The party, held on February 18 in the Los Angeles Room of the Century Plaza Hotel, was simply amazing. The caterers had turned the ballroom into the *Casablanca* set. There were palm trees, camels (both live and stuffed), rattan furniture, and actors dressed in period costume playing the parts of Rick, Ilsa, and other characters. Warner had even gone so far as to dig up original set decorations and props from the movie. In attendance were rock stars like Alice Cooper and Iggy Pop, and famous television personalities, including David Janssen, and Ted Knight from the *Mary Tyler Moore Show*. Casablanca

- **February 2, 1974: Barbra Streisand scores her first No. 1 single with "The Way We Were."**
- **February 4, 1974: The Symbionese Liberation Army kidnaps millionaire heiress Patty Hearst.**
- **April 4, 1974: Van Halen performs its first gig at Gazzarri's on the Sunset Strip in Los Angeles.**

added to the guest list, flying in numerous radio friends and retail contacts from around the country. I particularly remember Mark Parenteau (from WABX in Detroit) at the event—he'd go anywhere for a free party.

At the evening's midpoint, KISS took the stage. The retail people, who tended to skew older, walked out en masse and congregated in the lobby, taking cover from the painfully loud performance in the ballroom. The younger attendees remained, but the room's poor acoustics and the band's sheer volume gave some of the Warner staff more reason not to like KISS or Casablanca, and they weren't lacking for reasons to begin with. Nonetheless, the extravagantly staged party marked our coming out: Casablanca was open for business.

Neil was an eternal opportunist, and since KISS was already out on the West Coast for the Casablanca launch party, he arranged for them to perform on ABC Television's *In Concert* three days later. They also did a great deal of publicity with West Coast publications and radio. This initial glut of exposure was crucial in establishing KISS as outrageous. The party was equally crucial in that regard, as the members of its captive audience were the exact movers and shakers we needed to leak word of KISS's overpowering and explosive flamboyance. The music trade papers and many of the big-city media outlets ran stories about the band, and people called us for weeks after to rave about what a great time they'd had at the event. Many who called were genuinely happy for us, but a number of the West Coast elite clearly wanted to see us fail; we were the brash New Yorkers who had come to show the laid-back West Coast country clubbers how it was done.

To no one's surprise, our first release, the Bill Amesbury record, went nowhere (it peaked at a mild No. 86 on the *Billboard* Top 100), and this meant that I had to do the KISS album promotion and marketing almost all by myself. The Warner Brothers field staff were no help at all, providing little more than delivery service, except for a select few of their regional guys, like George Gerrity out of Boston. They did not push anyone to play the record, which wasn't atypical: Warner had a no-pressure reputation to uphold. However, due to the AOR airplay we were beginning to receive, the group was becoming hard to ignore. By early March, we'd made "most added" in *Record World* and had succeeded in getting KISS added at WRKR-FM (Kalamazoo), WMMR-FM (Philly), WPLR-FM (Connecticut), WVVS-FM (Valdosta, Georgia), and KSHE-FM (St. Louis). Others—like KMET (LA), WOUR (Utica, New York), WCMF (Rochester, New York), and WNEW-FM, WPLJ, and WLIR (all in New York City)— quickly followed suit. Buck was working possible singles, but even with all our efforts, Top 40 radio was not yet buying the fact that this was a viable group.

Although I finally convinced KMET to play the KISS album, I still had to figure a way to get KLOS, the big ABC-owned station, to jump on the record. I normally worked with just one progressive station per market, except in New York City. I always believed that if a station worked with me, then I should work with it in an informally exclusive agreement, which meant that I would be working *against* the competing stations in the format. I would often set up promotions that had nothing to do with my product, just to help a station. I'd also help a station out by asking the promoters I knew to work with it before another. This had worked very well for me at Buddah, back in New York. Now that I was with Casablanca and based in LA, I had to get KLOS on board.

I went to visit the station for the first time right after the KISS album came out. I walked into the programming office to see the station's program director, Tom Yates, but in order to meet with him I first had to go through the attractive young woman who served as music director. As soon as she and I made eye contact, it was all over—we fell passionately for one another. We went out to have a picnic in a park, and then we went back to my house. She stayed for hours. In the coming weeks, she would come over to my house often, and it would just be sex, sex, sex. No drugs, just sex. She was stunning, and I'd fallen so hard for her that I even called my friend Norm Winer, the program director at WBCN-FM in Boston, to tell him I was in love. She was about five foot four and beautiful, with the cutest face, a remarkably hard body, great legs, and a very sexy, husky voice. Problem was that she had a live-in boyfriend, so it didn't become a long-term relationship. No matter, I got KISS added to KLOS, and I got laid many times in the process. What great leverage. I'm sure Neil was very proud.

Despite our best efforts, we were not able to sell KISS singles. KISS turned out to be very unusual in that regard; many of their most popular songs were not hit singles by any stretch of the imagination, although we did everything we could think of to make people believe they were. Our failure to sell singles on KISS was something completely different for Neil. Prior to this, he'd been renowned for his ability to sell and promote singles. The fact that we couldn't move them for KISS was a source of surprise and consternation for us, until we realized that the landscape of the industry was changing. It was a new world, and album sales were king.

It took no experience or industry acumen whatsoever to see that the key to KISS was their live performance. Even at this neonatal phase in their development, their concerts were a cauterizing experience for the uninitiated. Their look and vibe today is pure comic book—wry and admittedly (even gloriously) over the top. But in 1974, nothing like KISS had ever been seen. The field was then populated by the likes of John Denver, the Grateful Dead, and Elton John, so the KISS guys felt dangerous. Their costumes were more developed than they'd been at the Manhattan dance studio performance nine months earlier. There were no more T-shirts or velvet or red pants. They all wore leather, and everything except Paul Stanley's lips —clothes, platform boots, backline speaker cabinets, drums—was black, white, or chrome. Their shows would start off with one of the crew, usually their tour manager, barking out a P.T. Barnum greatest-show-on-Earth introduction: "Put your two lips together and welcome KISS!" It was a call to worship, which was immediately followed by a few crashing guitar chords. Then the stage seemed to vaporize in a fusillade of smoke and deafening explosions. The three guitarists—front man Paul Stanley, lead Ace Frehley, and bassist Gene Simmons—would run around the stage with an energy and abandon matched only by The Who, windmilling power chords and galloping through dry-ice fog banks with an electric fury. But at those early shows, the stunt that drew the most gasps through its sheer originality and shock value was Gene Simmons vomiting blood. Most audiences had seen bass solos (many of them interminable, thanks to the burgeoning art-rock scene, with its unchecked musical interludes), but to see Simmons writhe as he played made no sense to them. *What is he doing?* His lips would then begin to spasm away from his teeth into an altogether malevolent grin. Then the first trickle of blood would appear—a thin, crimson thread from the corner of his mouth. When I watched the audiences at these shows, I saw the wheels spinning in their heads. *This isn't right. Something's wrong with him!* And then Simmons would convulse in a violent seizure and blood would spew in all directions.

The stunt was deeply unsettling to those first crowds who saw it. Other bands had explosions (though not quite so many), other bands had smoke, or lights and lasers, but the blood spitting hit people in their blind spot. They never saw it coming. I distinctly remember seeing their genuine looks of concern turn to horror, disgust, and fascination. One poor girl at an early show seemed convinced that Gene's intestines were spilling out onto the stage.

And this wasn't even the show's climax. "Black Diamond," the most epic-sounding of the band's tracks, usually capped the evening. During the song, Peter Criss's drum riser would be elevated ten or more feet and another blast of smoke and concussion bombs would provide an added flourish.

KISS's show was truly jaw dropping, and what the band needed was a really good booking agent. Enter Jeff Franklin, again—the same man who had helped Neil set up distribution through Warner. Though he was the top man at ATI, the industry's leading concert-booking agency, Jeff tended to stay out of daily operations, preferring to focus on brokering bigger deals. His two direct reports, Ira Blacker and Wally Meyrowitz, were outstanding at their jobs and kept the day-to-day bookings off Jeff's desk.

We quickly came to realize that KISS was going to represent a huge challenge to ATI. The problem was, in brief, KISS was too good. No one wanted to follow the band, and fewer and fewer acts were willing to share the bill with them. Those who did would often sandbag KISS by limiting the band's use of the PA system or refusing to allow their pyrotechnical displays because they were afraid of being upstaged. Audiences expected headliners to be as entertaining as KISS, and they never were.

We had to work KISS differently. The standard method for booking new acts was to put them on a bill with big-name headliners in order to expose them to as many people as possible. We couldn't do this with KISS. As nice as it was to have such an obvious skyrocket on our hands, KISS's potential was so volatile that it scared off would-be promoters. This put us in the disadvantageous position of having to treat KISS, a new and mostly unknown act, as a headliner, and that meant committing to spending amounts of money commensurate with headliner status. We would have welcomed better-known bands taking KISS on as an opening or middle act, but with the show they had and all the equipment it required, it was very difficult to find bands willing to go on after them. This led to canceled bookings with some pretty big bands—among them, Genesis, Queen, and Aerosmith.

I decided to take a different approach. I went to various cities and arranged for KISS to perform for free for the AOR stations in the market, a tactic I had used to great success with Genesis a few years earlier at Buddah. As long as we were paying for them to headline and losing money on every show, why not get the most out of the band's performances?

KSHE-FM in St. Louis was (and still is) the oldest rock station in America, having been the first in the country to switch to an all-rock format, back in 1967. It was run by Shelly Grafman, a really nice guy from the old

school of radio. If you showed Shelly how playing a band would put
money into his station's coffers, he would cooperate. I'd had a good
relationship with him when I was at Buddah, and when I took on the
job of getting KISS airtime, he was one of my first calls.

Casablanca bought time on the station and booked KISS for what was
termed a "live performance promotion," which turned out to be a headlining spot at KSHE's Kite-Fly on March 31.The kite fest, the station's big
annual outdoor event, was held in Forest Park, St. Louis's version of Central Park. To help promote it, we scheduled an on-air appearance at KSHE
a week or so before the concert. The day of the band's radio appearance,
one of the worst storms in decades hit St. Louis. When the band and I
showed up at KSHE, it was closed. No one was there. The station, the size
of a shoebox, was located about ten feet away from a drive-in theater on
old Route 66 in Crestwood, a St. Louis suburb. Both the theater's enormous screen and the station had been damaged by the storm. So, there
we were, the band members (sporting their costumes) and I, standing on
top of a hill at the side of Route 66, the wind blasting us with dust and
debris, wondering what the hell we were going to do. Afterwards, Shelly
felt so sorry for us and was so impressed that we'd even shown up in
that weather that he began to play KISS like they were the biggest thing
ever to hit the city. It paid off: the kite fest drew over forty thousand
people, and KISS was a smashing success. Given that KISS was still
almost completely unknown and had released their first album just a
few weeks prior, getting to play in front forty thousand people was an
astounding opportunity. St. Louis and KSHE would become strongholds
for KISS. Shelly, his wife, Emily, and I remained good friends for years.

With the KSHE success in mind, I tried to set up as many radio-oriented
concerts for KISS as I possibly could. Booking them proved to be a difficult
task for ATI, as the timing of the radio gigs did not always make geographic
sense. ATI might normally book Chicago one night and Indianapolis the
next, but my reliance on radio-sponsored gigs could have KISS going
from Memphis to Chicago and back south to Charlotte all within a few
days. I'm sure KISS's road crew adored us for this, and I did have one
major argument with Wally Meyrowitz and Jeff Franklin during which I
insisted that they couldn't book KISS in several cities because I needed
the band hundreds of miles away at some Midwest station to do a radio-
sponsored gig. I empathized with ATI's plight; I knew the schedule made

absolutely no sense in terms of normal tour routing, but I was not trying to make sense. We were desperate to break out the band, and if a powerful radio station was willing to help us out, then we would take advantage of it. Touring at this point had to be focused on cities or stations where we could maximize radio exposure. If a market didn't have a radio station that would back us up and play the band, then we would have to ignore that market until we could find a foothold in it.

Cleveland was an ideal target. The market was dominated by two radio stations: WIXY-AM, the powerful Top 40 station; and WMMS-FM, which had a progressive rock format. WIXY was directly handled by our independent representative in the Midwest, Bruce Bird, who was one of the first independent record promoters, and a very good one, at that. Bruce had some pull with the program director (PD), Marge Bush, and he helped us to get almost all our product on the station.

WMMS was more difficult. Their PD, John Gorman, had little to do with the music—he left that up to his star DJ, Kid Leo. Leo was not thrilled about KISS. His main love was David Bowie, so we knew we would have to bring the band into the market and show WMMS how a live KISS show worked.

In terms of concert promotion, the market was repped by Mike Belkin of Belkin Productions, and he was not warm to the idea of booking KISS. To reduce his risk, we booked the band as an opening act for Rory Gallagher at the Agora Ballroom, a small, old-fashioned, low-ceilinged venue that was furnished with tables and chairs. It was far from the best place to showcase the band, but we had no other choice. The night of the show, April 1, I had Bruce and his younger brother, Gary (who eventually took over Bruce's business and grew it into one of the most powerful independent promotion firms in the country), arrange for Kid Leo to join us at the venue. As soon as Leo showed up, I handcuffed him to a chair so he couldn't leave.

The show was going great until Peter Criss's drum riser began to go up. The ceiling was too low to accommodate this, and before anyone realized it, Peter had crashed into the ceiling and fallen off his drum riser. I rushed over to him and saw that he was unconscious. With the help of road manager J.R. Smalling, I managed to revive him. Meanwhile, the rest of the band, used as they were to mishaps—Gene had set his hair on fire and Ace was constantly falling down because he couldn't walk in his space boots—didn't miss a beat. Despite this, or maybe because of it, Leo was impressed enough to begin playing the band, and Cleveland would eventually become one of their strongest markets.

KISS's April 7 gig was another example of how this marketing angle worked. Mark Parenteau was at WABX, the local rock station in Detroit. He was not initially impressed by KISS; he preferred another new act, Aerosmith. Mark was openly gay—why he was married, I never understood—and he had a crush on Steven Tyler, probably because Tyler reminded him so much of Mick Jagger. I arranged a special trip to Detroit to present KISS's album to WABX. When I arrived at the station, Mark was on the air, so as we talked we were frequently interrupted; we also took breaks to toke a bit of weed or snort a line or two of blow off the KISS album jacket. At first, Mark was totally against playing KISS; the makeup really put him off, though he was a big fan of Alice Cooper (the same contradictory reaction I'd seen among some Warner staffers earlier that year). I eventually cut a deal with Mark whereby Casablanca would pay all the production costs for a KISS concert in Detroit. He could arrange to have any other bands he wanted on the bill, but if KISS blew away the audience within the first five minutes of taking the stage, then he would have to play them like it was the Second Coming. He agreed, and the show was on. The only problem was that Aerosmith insisted on closing the show to make the audience believe they were the bigger act. But, knowing what KISS was capable of, I was fine with this. Besides, the deal stipulated that on-air mentions would be the same for both bands.

WABX hired a local man named Steve Glantz to promote the show. Glantz was an entrepreneur in his early twenties whose father was bankrolling his promotion company. He had little experience beyond promoting several area college events, though he grew to be a very important contact for KISS. The station arranged for the show to be held at the Michigan Palace, an old five-thousand-seat theater in downtown Detroit. It sold out immediately—I think the ticket price was only ninety-seven cents, since ninety-seven was WABX's frequency on the radio dial—and the WABX staff showed up in force: David Perry, Dave Dixon, Dan Carlisle, general manager John Detz, and Ken Calvert. Mark and I walked through the audience as KISS began to play. The minute Gene Simmons spit fire, everyone froze. You could hear the proverbial pin drop for about two seconds. Then there was a deafening roar. Mark yelled in my ear, "You win!"

The gig was plagued with production problems, likely stemming from Glantz's inexperience with larger gigs. The amount of time between acts (Bob Seger and Ted Nugent were also on the bill) was an issue. At multi-act shows, the first bands on the bill do not typically use their full production, which helps shorten the gaps between acts, but I was paying for the gig, and the last thing I was going to do was let KISS take the stage with anything less than their full production. Following KISS's set, the venue's representatives threatened to close the building at midnight in compliance with their contracts with the stagehand and security unions. By the time I resolved the matter, it was approaching 2:00 a.m. To compound the problem, the audience was leaving the hall, exhausted after rocking through six hours of music. Steven Tyler threw a screaming hissy fit. Mike Klenfner was there representing Aerosmith's label, Columbia Records, and he wound up on the receiving end of Tyler's rant. The image of Tyler, about five foot two and about one hundred pounds wringing wet, yelling up at Klenfner, at least six foot four and three hundred and fifty pounds with hands the size of catcher's mitts, was by turns hilarious and surreal. I was expecting Klenfner to lift Tyler off the ground and throw him from one end of the backstage area to the other, but he kept his cool, and Tyler lived to sing another day.

KISS clearly needed to headline. This would be tricky in markets where they had little or no airplay. ATI had to skip over whole areas of the country until we could establish the band on radio there. In the case of San Francisco, we never got airplay from the legendary KSAN-FM; station PD Tom Donahue was not crazy about the band, even though he was friends with Neil.

KISS did play small gigs in the market, and they began to establish a following, but this still did not translate into KSAN airplay. We waited until the demand for a live show in the market became overwhelming due to airplay and exposure from KFRC (the Top 40 station), outlying AOR stations, and the print media. Then the band went back to San Francisco and did a headlining arena show for Bill Graham. Graham had avoided presenting KISS in other markets. I think he just did not like the band and the kind of rock they represented. I found his reluctance interesting, because he shared a Hungarian Jewish heritage with Gene Simmons.

With KISS finally off and running, we turned our attention to other ventures. One of the more interesting plans was for Neil to do a series of musical greeting cards with Bob Crewe of BC Generations. (Bob was famous for writing songs with and producing The Four Seasons.) The first card was to feature the song "My Happy Birthday Baby." The idea was decades ahead of its time, and unfortunately it went nowhere; musical greeting cards are, of course, sold widely today.

We also concentrated on expanding our roster of artists, and one of the first we signed was Parliament, fronted by creator George Clinton. To call George unique would be a vast understatement, and there was nothing understated about George Clinton. He was a creative genius whose music was new and fresh and totally of his own devising. Never mind that this music—an almost indescribable mix of doo-wop and gospel-tinged jazz with heavy grooves and the volume of Black Sabbath—was almost completely unmarketable. Clinton had taken his music, his flair for the dramatic, and his indomitable personality and carved out an exclusive market niche. He called his music P-funk, and everything associated with it was funkified. He didn't invent the term or the music (it had grown out of jazz and R&B circles decades before, and James Brown had pioneered it in the 1960s), but he took it in an extreme direction, blending over-the-top ideas and quirks to create his own brand. George was especially adept at role-playing. He was fond of claiming that he had thirteen distinct personalities—including Dimwit, Sneaky, Speedy, Doped, and Sexy—whose names he'd recite like the names of the dwarves in some spaced-out reading of *Snow White*.

Clinton had created a following that was far more intense than those of groups like the Ohio Players or Average White Band. Parliament's fans, which he lovingly dubbed "maggot brains" (making George the "maggot overlord"), would be there for every album and every concert. But, given the way that George wrote and recorded his music, the band would not produce a hit single, at least not one that would cross over from R&B to pop radio.

The origins of Parliament are confusing, at best. George grew up in Plainfield, New Jersey, where he formed a doo-wop ensemble called The Parliaments in the late 1950s. That group eventually expanded, and, owing to a dispute with the record company that owned the rights to the band's name, George renamed the outfit Funkadelic. He released several successful albums for Westbound Records under the name Funkadelic, but by 1974 he'd decided to revive the Parliament moniker and was looking for a record label, even though the player rosters of Funkadelic and Parliament were almost exactly the same. This was an unusual scenario, because we were entering into an agreement whereby we would forgo any proprietary ownership of Parliament; plus, it could be argued that the coexistence of Funkadelic and Parliament would water down the impact of both bands. But Neil didn't care; he was convinced that George was a moneymaker, no matter what name he used.

Everyone at Casablanca thought Clinton's management team of Ron Strassner and Cholly Bassoline were hoods. They looked just like Damon Runyon characters, with their fedoras and long black coats, and their attitude was reminiscent of the Mob. But I liked them and their realistic way of looking at the business and the people they were representing. They were certainly not Mob-oriented. Rather like their client, George Clinton, they had their own Detroit Purple Gang kind of flair.

George and Archie Ivy—who was, more or less, George's personal assistant—would visit me at Casablanca, and over copious piles of weed and blow (George once brought in some uncut and very potent coke, declaring that anyone who tried it would speak Spanish, as the stuff "hadn't cleared customs yet"), they would pontificate for hours about how they were going to develop Parliament's stage show into an other-worldly display of pageantry and pomp and how they needed half a zillion dollars to do it. Many times, I had no idea what they were talking about. My eyes would glaze over, and George would ramble on, giving voice to every thought that came into his head, stream-of-consciousness-style, like William Faulkner gone jive. I would stare at him and wonder, "Man, do you come with subtitles?" I often had to ask Archie or one of the two Purple Gang look-alikes, Cholly and Ron, to translate George for me, but sometimes even they didn't have a clue. But so what if we didn't understand what they were trying to explain to us? We gave them the money anyway. These advances were always against future royalties, and Parliament sold enough product to make us comfortable with the arrangement. This eventually became a point of contention, as George would claim that he was owed royalties—he seemed to have forgotten about the tour advances.

To look at Parliament and their absurd stage show—which eventually came to include an enormous UFO called the Mothership (which would land onstage in a billowing cloud of dry-ice fog), and a giant skull with a glowing four-foot doobie dangling from its mouth—you would think there would be a never-ending series of strange Parliament tales to tell. But, to be truthful, the band was really fun to work with, and aside from a few battles of the kind that typically occur between artists and their record companies, everything went well between us. In fact, I believe that we were the only people who were able to understand and put up with some of their shenanigans—and they with ours.

6

Kiss-Off, America!

Eddie's idea—Scott's bigger idea—The biggest mall in the world—Two sloppy seconds—Roy's—Getting fucked by Warner—The Hudson Brothers—Ira's offer—A huge strikeout—Three's a crowd—A divorce—Neil's new place— Guns and the panic button

April 22, 1974
2836 Lambert Drive
Hollywood, California

Late one night in April 1974, I received a call from Eddie Pugh. Eddie was Warner's Florida promotion man, and for him to ring me at home at such a late hour was a real surprise. I was half asleep when he called, and he was talking so fast that he was ten seconds into his story before I could figure out what he was talking about. I pieced together something about a progressive rock station in Fort Lauderdale (WSHE) that on April 20 had held a kissing contest in which the couple who kissed the longest won some prizes, including a few KISS albums. The response to the contest had been great, and Eddie wanted to bring it to our attention. I was elated to hear the news, seeing the potential for a national marketing blitz.

I cannot overemphasize how vital it was to our early success to have relationships with people like Eddie—people who not only had the acumen to recognize a good thing when they saw it but also the generosity to bring it to our attention. Eddie Pugh was different from most promotion people, even within Warner Brothers. Warner had very little black product in the mid-1970s, and Eddie, who was black, was the kind of promotion man who was always looking for a challenge, so rather than stay within the narrow confines of Warner's small R&B catalog, he would promote whatever he had, regardless of its genre. Here was a guy who covered all the bases. Neil and I were so impressed by Eddie that we eventually hired him.

As soon I said goodbye to Eddie, I called Neil. By the next morning, he had a plan. We would arrange for radio stations throughout the country to compete in a huge national Kiss-Off. Eddie had not been the only one to notice the success of the WSHE contest. Scott Shannon, a DJ at WMAK in Nashville, had the inspired idea for KISS to record a cover of Bobby Rydell's "Kissin' Time" as part of the promotion. Neil loved it. KISS hated the thought, however. They and their producers, Kenny Kerner and Richie Wise, were dead set against it; they didn't want to record a cover song when they were perfectly capable of writing their own material. Neil always tried to be positive—positive people were successful people, as far as he was concerned—but if he couldn't get his way through ebullient enthusiasm, he had no problem rolling up his sleeves and wrestling you to the ground. After his cajoling had failed (and, I'll admit, KISS doing Bobby Rydell struck me as pretty odd, but I wasn't about to tell Neil that), he told them, "Look, either you record the song or we'll pull our support for you."

It was pure bluff. KISS was our first signing, and, frankly, they were the only thing we had going for us. Neil would never have purposefully killed their career. I knew this, but the one bit of leverage Neil had was that the KISS team was even greener than we were. And with the band's outlandish appearance and their refusal to tone down their gimmick, they had to recognize that their chances of finding another record company that believed in them were limited. They caved. Neil won, but he didn't want to fracture the relationship, so he softened his stance. "C'mon guys, the promotion will work great, and it's just one song. As a concession, I promise that the song will only be a single, and not part of any future KISS album." By April 26, KISS was back at Bell Sound Studios in Manhattan, cutting the track in one twelve-hour session. We rush released "Kissin' Time" as a single and, in direct violation of Neil's promise, we included it on all new pressings of KISS's first album starting in June.

The series of kissing contests, which were collectively dubbed "The Great Kiss-Off," began on May 10. The single's lyrics contained the names of many cities around the country, and we used this to our advantage, matching those cities to radio markets: WAYS (Charlotte), WOKY (Milwaukee), WIXY (Cleveland), WSAJ (Cincinnati), WCFL (Chicago), KLIF (Dallas), WFIL (Philly), WQXI (Atlanta), WMAK (Nashville), KJR (Seattle),

CKLW (Detroit), KILT (Houston), and WPIX (New York). The names of all these stations/markets, except for Houston and New York, were included in the reworked lyrics for the single. We ran a prominent ad in the May 18, 1974 issue of *Billboard* (which would have hit newsstands around May 7) to bring national industry attention to the events. The lyrics made radio airplay easier to come by, because radio stations loved to play songs that mentioned their city.

Here is how the event worked. First, the stations would have a kissing contest in their own markets. Then the local winners would compete for the national title. The publicity would be enormous, and it would go on for many weeks, because it spanned both the local contests and the final national event.

On June 8, the day of the National Kiss-Off, Neil, Buck, Joyce, and I went to Woodfield Mall (then the largest in the world) in Schaumburg, Illinois, just outside of Chicago. KISS came too, and they walked around the mall in full regalia. There was heavy local media coverage for the event, and many Chicago-area celebrities were on hand. Radio personality Larry Lujack was master of ceremonies. A stage had been erected in a large open area in the middle of the mall. Neil got up on the stage and started asking the crowd for donations to a local hospital charity. He was failing miserably—I don't think he raised a single dollar. After an hour or so, he had Buck go up to the next level of the mall, stand at the railing where he could see the stage below, and wait for a cue. Again Neil addressed the respectably large crowd that had gathered on both levels, but this time he made it about the children: "C'mon folks, the children really need your money." At that moment, Buck released a big stack of one-dollar bills into the air, and suddenly it was raining money. People on all parts of the upper level started throwing down ones and fives, and a few tens and twenties—hundreds of them. People on the lower level were picking up the bills, crumpling them, and throwing them toward the stage. It's a miracle Neil didn't incite a riot. Aside from performing these onstage fiduciary duties, Neil or I, using a bank of phones, reported every half hour to the participating radio stations on how their contestants were faring. The stations, in turn, aired the results, building excitement in each city. These were mostly Top 40 stations, as Neil wanted to use the outlets that had the highest ratings. Besides, few rock stations would participate in such an obviously commercial event. The national media, television and print, picked up the story, and the Kiss-Off became one of the most successful KISS promotions ever, though the contestants seemed to garner more attention than the band.

While our relationship with Warner Brothers had been touch and go to this point, near the end of April 1974, Warner asked (and paid) us to put two of their bands on our label. The company had finally come to realize that certain bands—for reasons related to their type of music, their band members, and/or their management—just did not fit within their organization. But Warner had contracts to fulfill. Placing these bands with us killed two birds with one stone: contractual obligations were met and the artists were gotten rid of with no hard feelings. One of these artists was Marc Bolan of T.Rex ("Bang a Gong [Get It On]") fame. Neil and I had both followed Bolan's career to some degree (it was impossible not to), but we didn't become huge fans of his until we met him. Marc had lived a fast, hard life. He'd enjoyed (probably a bit too much) the spoils of stardom, but he impressed us no end with his renewed vigor

- April 5, 1974: Stephen King's first novel, *Carrie*, is published.
- April 6, 1974: Two hundred thousand attend the California Jam. Performers include Black Sabbath, Deep Purple, the Eagles, and Black Oak Arkansas.
- April 8, 1974: Hank Aaron breaks Babe Ruth's long-standing home run record.

and earnest commitment to living a clean life and recapturing the status he'd enjoyed in years past. In retrospect—knowing that Marc would die just a few years later—it's easy to view this as an example of signing someone on the way down (even though we'd been persuaded to do so), but neither of us had seen it that way at the time. Casablanca was nothing yet, and Bolan gave us credibility in the rock arena, as he was considered by many to be a member of the English rock elite. Marc was an extremely nice guy. He only visited the offices a handful of times, usually with his girlfriend, a pretty woman with refined features and a café-au-lait complexion. Despite his stature in the biz, he was easy to work with and not the least bit elitist. To this day, I can't imagine what caused Warner to want to get rid of him.

The other artist was Fanny, one of the first all-female rock bands. Despite their pioneer status, Fanny is never mentioned in any of the latter-day "women in rock" documentaries. Roy Silver, Fanny's manager, was a major character in the business (he also managed Jackson Browne). He had a flair that was definitely different. We became involved in various ventures with him, including a new restaurant concept. Roy's restaurant, aptly called Roy's, fused Asian and American cuisines. It became popular with industry types, and it featured a private room—not much more than a large booth with three walls and a curtain—where sex or drugs were almost guaranteed upon entry. Since Neil (or maybe it was the company; I can't recall) was a big investor in the restaurant, we were asked to have our expense account meals there whenever possible.

Roy had many close friends in the music business, including Bob Gibson, Gary Stromberg, and Stewart Levine, all of whom worked with us in various capacities. Neil hired Gibson and Stromberg's firm to do our publicity, which caused a rift with Warner—its PR department took the hiring as a slap in the face. But Neil hadn't done it because he thought Warner was incompetent; rather, he'd wanted to make sure we had the attention necessary to generate as much press for our artists (especially KISS) and our company as possible. With Warner being so large, we had some concern that a new subsidiary label like ours would be a low priority. Shortly after hiring Gibson and Stromberg, we began to hear rumors that we would no longer be getting any help from the Warner PR department. I'm sure it did not sit well with Warner that we were paying Gibson-Stromberg with Warner money. Bob Regehr, the head of Warner's PR, was not pleased with us, and things got sticky between us and his department. Make no mistake, this was his department: Mo Ostin and Joe Smith did not make Regehr do anything he did not want to do.

The one cool thing that his PR people came up with was a black T-shirt that had the name "KISS" spelled out on it with hundreds of rhinestones. The band's road crew had made their own shirts using this design. Someone from Warner must have seen them at the Casablanca launch party and made the shrewd observation that a mass-produced version might be good promotional merchandise. Unfortunately, they only produced a few hundred of the shirts, which almost immediately became collector's items. I was able to send some out to contacts in the radio biz, but because of the limited supply, not everyone got one. The shirts were snug, so they definitely looked best on women. Even though I was fairly trim at the time, I could never wear one. When we told the Warner people that we would need more shirts, they explained that they cost almost $20 apiece to manufacture (a fortune in those days); all the rhinestones had to be hand applied, and there was no way they were going to spend more money on them.

With the excitement surrounding KISS and all the publicity, airplay, and concerts, we thought the album would sell like hotcakes. But for some reason, we were stuck at about one hundred thousand units. Looking into the problem brought us more conflict with the Warner promotions department. Buck Reingold was given a tape from an unknown source of a conference call in which the head of promotion, Gary Davis, told his field staff to ignore the product of the custom labels and only work the Warner-owned artists. This really pissed us off, because part of our deal with Warner was that they would help us promote our product. We knew that alone we had very little pull at Warner, so we distributed copies of the tape to Warner's other subsidiary labels. After enough complaints from the likes of Chrysalis and Capricorn (who meant a lot more to the bottom line at Warner than we did), Davis was looking for another gig. We also ferreted out the real reason the KISS product was stuck in sales limbo: it was back ordered to the tune of over one hundred thousand units. Warner Brothers claimed that they were having some manufacturing problems, so they were only pressing their albums and not the custom-label product like ours.

Although our tenuous relationship with Warner was weighing on us, there was plenty of exciting news at the office. In June we'd signed the Hudson Brothers, a musical trio out of Portland. Mark Hudson would go on to become a very successful songwriter, Brett Hudson became a movie and TV producer, and Bill Hudson married Goldie Hawn, with whom he fathered actress Kate Hudson. The Hudson Brothers came with the added bonus of a deal with CBS Television to produce an hour-long summer replacement series featuring the band. *The Hudson Brothers Show* was already in production, with a premiere date of July 31. Neil became friendly with the show's producer, Chris Bearde, who had helmed the incredibly popular *Sonny & Cher Comedy Hour* for the previous four years. We also got to know the Hudson Brothers' manager, David Joseph. These were good people to know, as they would provide us with several key artists for our roster in the years to come.

But one opportunity that we were presented with turned into a low-light of my career—I struck out in spectacular fashion. During this time, former ATI booking-agent-turned-manager Ira Blacker pitched me a band he was representing. Ira had been KISS's booking agent, but he had left ATI to form his own management outfit, I Mouse Limited. We'd enjoyed a good relationship during his short time with KISS, and he wanted to give us first dibs on an act he was representing: a Canadian trio hailing from Toronto who had developed a strong following that far outpaced their bar band status. They weren't much of anything yet, and Ira even admitted that outright, but he was making a strong case for them nonetheless. At Ira's behest, I traveled to Canada to see them perform live.

The trip was doomed from the beginning. The flight from LA to Toronto should have taken five hours, but it took closer to ten. The plane had mechanical difficulties at the gate at LAX, the weather during the flight was terrible, and I was developing a nasty case of the flu. To compound matters, the club where the performance was happening was a dark, dingy place called the Colonial Tavern, which had a threadbare sound system that couldn't come close to keeping up with the band.

Despite the venue and the flu I was fighting, I could appreciate the fact that the trio gave the high-energy type of performance that Ira had promised. Their downfall in my eyes was their look. They were ugly. I say this with a great sense of amusement, because the members of KISS (behind the makeup) were some of the worst-looking guys I'd ever seen. Nonetheless, Ira's group just didn't cut it visually. They were all gangly looking, and their front man, the bassist, had a huge hook nose that Barbra Streisand could only aspire to. On a visual level, these three Canadians simply couldn't compete.

I flew back to LA and gave Neil my impressions. Neil was always so positive about everything that I almost felt compelled to sell him on this band, but something held me back. I told him, "I thought they were decent. They have energy, but their songs are only OK. I just don't think they're the band for us, at least not right now." Had we been a little less cash poor, I would have taken a flier on them, but there wasn't enough money in the Casablanca coffers to afford a ham sandwich, to say nothing of another recording artist. After hearing my spiel, Neil said, "Look, you've seen them and I haven't. I have faith in your judgment, Larry, so whatever you decide, we'll do it." I was deeply grateful that Neil held my opinions and abilities in such respect, but my practical side couldn't ignore the incredibly tenuous position Casablanca was in. We couldn't afford to fail. I decided not to make an offer.

I called Ira to let him know that we were passing on his band. He took the news well, and, like the pro he was, he had them signed to Mercury Records in an instant. He did a masterful job of pulling the wool over Mercury's eyes, too, calling in favors with a distributor in New Jersey, who told Mercury that the trio's first album was the most-requested import he handled. A nice bit of fabrication on Ira's part, but it worked.

This was my first big decision on which act to sign, and as the years went on, the wrongness of my choice just grew and grew. Even now I cringe just looking at these words: The band I chose not to sign was Rush.

And to highlight the quality of Neil's character, never once, ever, did he tell me I blew the deal. That's exactly why so many of us were willing to run through walls for him.

As our problem with Warner was becoming apparent, a really messy situation was coming to the fore between Neil and Beth due to Neil's infidelity with Joyce Biawitz, KISS's comanager. I had first noticed there was something more than business between them at KISS's showcase the previous year in New York. It probably didn't help matters that the weekly magazine for the touring industry, *Performance*, ran a blurb saying that Neil and Joyce were seen "looking very cozy together" at an LA concert by one of our former Buddah artists, Melanie.

During the summer of 1974, Neil rented a beach house in Malibu to take full advantage of being in LA. Everyone would go out there on the weekends to hang out, get high, and have fun. On one particular week-end, near the end of the summer, Gail and Dominic Sicilia came out from New York to visit. Gail was the music director of WOR-FM, a Top 40 hybrid station that leaned more toward a younger demographic and came off as more hip than other Top 40 stations. Dominic was a brilliant promoter and entrepreneur who had worked for us at Buddah as a creative director and also managed the band Stories.

Gail was very good friends with Beth Bogart and Nancy Reingold. However, she knew things that the two sisters did not, as she was present at all sorts of music events. Dominic would also tell her what was going on, so she knew about Neil's various trysts, though she'd always kept mum on the subject. That weekend, Joyce was also at the beach house. Gail couldn't hold her tongue any longer. She told Beth about this and the many other affairs Neil had had with people Beth knew—his former secretary, and on and on. Beth blew up. She felt betrayed and embarrassed, and rightly so.

Beth and Neil argued about it for weeks, and Neil promised to be good, but Beth finally kicked him out of the house. He stayed at my Hollywood Hills hacienda for a few days while he looked for a place to rent. Neil took the breakup very hard. Each night, he cried himself to sleep. He knew he would see the kids less, and I believe he still really loved Beth—I think he always did. After Beth kicked him out, he was always trying to be around her twin sister, Nancy, so he could maintain the family connection. Neil never admitted publicly that Beth had thrown him out. He would always tell people that he, not she, had chosen to end the relationship.

Neil eventually found a furnished house to rent in Beverly Hills. It was a stern and imposing home, much bigger than he required, but he needed the prestige of a Beverly Hills address. The company was paying the rent, anyway—so what the hell.

I felt bad for both of them. It was hard for me to hear negative things about Beth, as I'd always really liked her, but Neil needed a sounding board, and I was it. I don't think Neil ever got over the divorce, but he did start dating a few months later. He met and began going out with Lucie Arnaz, daughter of renowned TV stars Lucille Ball and Desi Arnaz, and a talented actress and singer in her own right. Lucie was married, but she was separated from her husband. Soon after they started dating, Lucie invited Neil to her mother's house for dinner. Neil came to the office the next day acting like he had gone to the Mount and seen God. All he could talk about was meeting the redheaded legend and how wonderful she was. He was also perplexed. He couldn't decide whether he should continue going out with Lucie (he was very taken with her), because if he did he would risk losing Joyce. He went back and forth, mentally listing the positives and negatives of the situation. I don't remember why he stopped seeing Lucie. I guess he just decided that Joyce would be better for him, especially since she would do anything for him—*anything*—while Lucie probably would not.

Then one day, as Neil and I were returning to Casablanca after a meeting at Warner Brothers, Neil said to me in a very emphatic manner, "Whatever you do, and whatever anyone says, do not leave my side, no matter what." I had no idea what he was talking about. Then we walked into Neil's office, and I saw tall, gangly, tough-talking Hy Mizrahi and his girlfriend. Along with Artie Ripp and Phil Steinberg, Hy had been one of the original partners in Buddah. Hy began to scream at Neil that he owed him money, and he ordered me to leave. I said no and stood my ground, at which point Hy pulled open his jacket and revealed the handle of a .38 revolver. Neil made a move toward the panic button discreetly located in the fireplace behind his desk, but Hy told him if he pushed it he would shove him up the chimney. Someone from the outer office yelled that they had called the police. Hy and his girlfriend (I think having her there made him more macho) took this as their cue to leave, though Hy continued to threaten us as they departed.

Neil was shaking, and with good reason. He told me Hy allegedly had Artie Ripp beaten up in a parking lot because Artie would not give in to his demand for a kickback. As soon as Hy left the office, Neil called Arnold Feldman, who had been our accountant for years and was rumored to have connections to the New York Mafia. Neil related to Arnold what had happened, and by that evening two really tough-looking Italian fellows had flown in from New York to act as Neil's bodyguards. I, on the other hand, had no one to protect me, so I went out and purchased a handgun, which I kept at my house. A little while after Hy had left our offices, Buck Reingold, who was not lacking in confidence himself, returned from an errand. When Neil and I explained to him what had happened, Buck became livid and asserted again and again that if he had been there he would have kicked Hy's ass. And he probably would have.

A few days later, we discovered that Hy had also threatened Art Kass, prompting Art to contact Hy's old partner, Phil Steinberg. I had never met Phil, but from what I was told, you did not mess with the man. While working at Buddah, I once asked about an empty office that no one ever used. I was told that it was being saved for Phil, who would be coming back from Mexico after the heat over some alleged crime had died down. In any case, Phil loved both Art Kass and Neil, and I guess he was none too happy with Hy. Phil called Hy, but he couldn't get him on the phone, so he left a message with his girlfriend, saying that if Hy ever bothered Neil or Art again, he would find Hy and break him into little pieces. I guess Hy believed this, or maybe Arnold Feldman's acquaintances got to him. He called Neil a few days later to apologize profusely.

7

Steppin' Out
and Comin' Home

**Meeting with Mo—Farewell to Warner—All alone—
Gribbit!—Building the Casbah—Mauri—Meeting Candy—
Lemon Pledge and cocaine—Brian and A.J.—
Fanny and "Butter Boy"**

August 1974
Warner Brothers Records
3300 Warner Boulevard
Burbank, California

As the summer of 1974 wore on, our battle with Warner came to a head. It was time for a face-to-face with someone at Warner who could make big decisions. In August, Neil and I arranged for a meeting with Mo Ostin, cochairman of Warner Brothers. Despite the "co" designation, Mo was the top man in the company. No one questioned that.

Mo was a short, balding fellow who was a good fifteen to twenty years older than us. He had become head of Warner many years before as a colleague of Frank Sinatra's. As the story goes, Warner had offered Sinatra his own label, Reprise. He'd placed all of his buddies with the label, including Dean Martin and Sammy Davis Jr. Frank had needed someone to watch out for his interests, and that person was his accountant, Mo Ostin. During this period, Reprise became very powerful, driven by the popularity of Frank, Dean, and company, and it proved to be the mainstay of the entire Warner family. Mo artfully worked his way into the position of boss. He did very well for himself, especially when the Warner/Elektra/Atlantic merger came together.

Warner's offices were located in Burbank, in the San Fernando Valley, and they were jammed to the rafters with people. Desks were set up in the hallways. The company had clearly outgrown its surroundings. Even

Mo's office was small—certainly smaller than Neil's—and it was not at all in keeping with his towering status in the industry.

Our meeting with Mo started out very cordially, with Mo expressing his happiness with the label arrangement. Then we started to complain. We told Mo that we felt something was drastically wrong with the sales picture. Our retail contacts were telling us that when they ordered a KISS record, it was not shipped to them. Mo claimed to know nothing about a back-order problem, so he called his head of production into the office and asked him if there were any issues that he knew of with the Casablanca product. He explained that over one hundred thousand of our units were back ordered due to pressing-plant issues. Mo then called in Eddie Rosenblatt, head of sales, and asked him to explain why steps had not been taken to rectify the situation, and why he had not been notified. Eddie apologized, offering some ridiculous explanation, which even Mo did not seem to believe. Finally, he and the head of production admitted that since the plants they were using could not keep up with all the orders, they were pressing Warner-owned product before they pressed the product from the subsidiary labels. This was becoming a tired routine. First, we'd been ignored by promotion, and now we were getting screwed by production and sales.

Mo knew that not having the sales we deserved would hurt our account balance with Warner. Because Warner had thus far paid almost all of our expenses—five Mercedes sedans, office rent and build-out, money to sign and produce artists, tour support for KISS, and so on—we had already racked up a debt to the company of about seven hundred and fifty thousand dollars (which would be worth in excess of $3.1 million today). Neil had originally been told that Warner's investment would be somewhere in the area of a million dollars and that if we did not show signs of scoring a major success, Warner would take us over. The current situation was hurting the development of KISS by negatively affecting chart positions and sales momentum. Mo seemed very embarrassed, and he offered Neil a deal that stipulated that we could leave the label and owe them nothing. Neil took the out, but he refused to allow Mo to whitewash the debt. We paid back every penny of it.

While Mo appeared mostly sympathetic to our plight, it had not been his idea to bring Neil into the Warner family in the first place. It was Joe Smith's idea. Joe came from the radio and promotion end of the business, and he had become cochairman of Warner when Mo decided he needed someone to cover for him in areas where he didn't excel. Smith was one of the best speakers in the music industry—or any other industry, for that matter. He had a way about him that was endearing to everyone. He was able to joke about Morris Levy breaking kneecaps in front of industry bigwigs, including Morris himself, and get away with it (Morris was president of Roulette Records and allegedly the Mafia's music connection). In fact, Morris would laugh louder than anyone else at these jibes. Joe was our main and probably only supporter at Warner. He'd had to lobby Mo hard to make the Casablanca deal become a reality. Because of this, I will always wonder if Mo engineered the exit strategy for Casablanca when we became too much of a pain in the ass.

On the ride back to the office, Neil and I were mostly silent. I glanced over at Neil as he drove. His face had that thousand-yard stare of someone utterly lost in thought. He was trying to convince himself of something. Then his face brightened and he said, "Larry, this isn't bad. This isn't a bad thing at all. In fact, this is the best thing that could have happened to us. We were coming to the end of our financial rope with Warner anyway, and they would have pulled the plug on us any minute now. Warner's not a bottomless money pit. But now we're free to do whatever we want without answering to anyone but ourselves."

This was Neil in his element. The circumstances for a neophyte label (just months old, really) that had its corporate umbrella suddenly yanked away were dire. Most companies, most men, would have done the sensible thing and folded their tents. But not Neil. I knew he was very nervous about these new developments—we were now orphans—but by the time we'd reached the office, he had prepared what he was going to say to Cecil and Buck, then Joyce, Bill, KISS, the other groups and managers, and, of course, the press. He immediately began to lay out a strategy for exiting Warner Brothers and shifting distribution over to independents.

Leaving Warner, I felt like we were in this old *National Geographic* special that everyone's seen. A gazelle is born and falls to the ground in a wet heap. The camera pans over to a pack of hyenas approaching in the distance, looking for dinner. The newborn gazelle has to figure out how to run, to learn something in three minutes that it takes humans two years to do. Either that or be eaten. How daunting was the task of establishing Casablanca as fully independent? Put it this way, I was jealous of the gazelle.

As we found our footing, we took account of what we needed to do to move forward as a self-sustaining company. We quickly realized that we would have to double or triple our staff just to stay afloat. Warner had handled all production, sales, some publicity, all international relations and deals, as well as most of the local and regional promotion. That was all up to us now. But being alone and exposed didn't mean we had to stop bragging about Casablanca—quite the contrary. We placed full-page ads in several industry publications featuring a drawing of Neil, Buck,

- **July 1, 1974: Isabel Peron of Argentina becomes the Western Hemisphere's first non-royal female head of state.**
- **July 29, 1974: Cass Elliot of the Mamas and the Papas dies at age 32.**
- **August 7, 1974: Frenchman Philippe Petit astonishes New Yorkers by performing a high-wire act between the top levels of the World Trade Center's Twin Towers—more than 1,300 feet above the city streets.**

Cecil, Nancy Sain (Buck's assistant), and me walking past Rick's Café on a Moroccan street and proclaiming, "We're steppin' out and comin' home! Casablanca, we're now independent!"

In order to expand Casablanca, we had to do some restructuring. Though Neil had some unique philosophies when it came to running the business (mostly related to choosing artists and his wildly extravagant promotion efforts), when it came to setting up our new departmental infrastructure, we followed the general blueprint that most record companies employ.

The legal department plays a key early role, as it's responsible for the language of the contracts that new artists sign, as well as any agreements the record company has (and there are dozens) with various outside companies, such as manufacturing plants, printers, and ad agencies. This department also handles the inevitable influx of legal issues that arise in the course of business (someone is always suing someone).

The production department is responsible for coordinating the manufacturing process. It gets the master tapes for an album from the recording studio to the mastering lab, and from there to the production facility, where the vinyl is grooved and mass produced; and it gets album artwork to the printer that will produce the cover and/or liner. All of this requires a tremendous amount of coordination and patience, and an eye for detail. It also helps to have someone around with a degree in psychology to talk management off the ledge when the inevitable delays crop up.

From there, the publicity and promotions department takes over, designing marketing campaigns, placing print ads, scheduling TV spots, and shipping out press kits by the crate. This department often works very closely with the distribution and sales people, who are responsible for selling and positioning the product (albums, singles, and so on) with retailers, working their list of radio, TV, and industry contacts to get the product on playlists.

Casablanca was still small enough for Neil and me to cover functions that at a larger company would have been handled by an entire staff. Neil ran all the production, working with the manufacturing plants, as well as all the international deals. I worked with the distributors on a daily basis to make sure they were paying attention to our product and knew what airplay and marketing plans we had in the works. I had never done this before, but I had carefully watched Joe Fields perform his magic at Buddah, so I had some idea of what to do. On occasion, Neil would jump in to help me, especially when my lack of experience caused me to be too aggressive and a distributor would call him to complain. But, inexperience aside, I did feel that the distributors could, if they really wanted to, push out more product than they did.

Art and production were just two of our new responsibilities, and in this a company named Gribbit! gave us a huge hand. A Gribbit! rep named Chris Whorf helped Neil develop the artwork for our albums; he also helped us to design our new stationery and implement the changes that needed to be made to our old Warner-distributed product. Early in the relationship, Neil would go over every LP, inner sleeve, and label design with Chris and do several passes if necessary to get the artwork just right. Gribbit! did most of the Casablanca albums, except those of KISS, which is why there's somewhat of a theme linking the various Casablanca covers.

All of the Casablanca albums distributed through Warner bore the catalog designation "NB," followed by a four-digit number. "NB" was simply Neil's initials. The first Casablanca album (KISS's debut) was labeled NB 9001; the second (Gloria Scott's *What Am I Going to Do?*), was NB 9002, and so on. With Warner now out of the picture, all future Casablanca albums (excluding special releases, like picture discs) would have the designation "NBLP" and a four-digit number. For reasons I do not recall, we started with NBLP 7001 (again beginning with KISS's first release) and went on from there.

Our assuming of multiple responsibilities was a prime illustration of the fact that Neil understood all aspects of the record industry. He was a creative genius when it came to knowing what was needed, and he was acutely aware of every step necessary to make something happen. This applied not only to developing artwork; he also knew his way around the recording studio, the mastering lab, the manufacturing plant, and even the mailroom. His broad knowledge of the business made us bullet-proof from scams and schemes: no company involved in the production process could cut corners or take advantage of him.

With the influx of new employees, it was vital that we set an example, so Neil and I always came to work early. Furthermore, most LA record companies would begin the business day at maybe nine or ten in the morning, but Neil and I were New Yorkers at heart—we liked to begin early so we could catch up with the East Coast. We'd typically put in a good twelve hours, usually leaving the office at 6:00 or 7:00 p.m., and then we'd go home or out to dinner and drinks at Roy's, where we would network with other industry types. Roy's was the only place in LA run by industry people, and the music crowd, and occasionally the film crowd, would fill the bar, hanging out and carrying on. The bar was narrow and small, which made for more intimacy and camaraderie. A night at Roy's was a rite of passage for newbies at record companies such as A&M, Warner, and Capitol.

Having so much new responsibility on my plate, I required some edu-cation (you can only fake so many things at once). I attended as many meetings as I could with Neil and Chris Whorf. I paid close attention to their decision-making methodology. The experience I gained in those few months when we created what Casablanca was to become was ten times more worthwhile than anything I could have learned at business school. Simply attending meetings, hanging out at recording studios, and watching from the sidelines at mastering labs and manufacturing plants was the single greatest learning experience of my life. I absorbed years of book learning inside of a few months.

We were doing everything we could to distinguish our artists from those of other labels. When it came to album artwork, for instance, we insisted that the album title be in the top third of the cover so a customer flipping through a record store bin could read it easily. Also, Neil had the mastering lab cut our records much hotter (louder) than normal. This mastering ploy would help make our records sound more sharp and alive on radio. For my part, I insisted that the titles and artist names on the spines of our albums be maximized so that when one of our records was sitting on a radio station shelf with only its spine visible, it would be easier to read than the competition's.

Neil and I could only do so many things at once, and we needed help. Our first hire, made sometime in mid-September, was Mauri Lathower, a man with a sterling reputation developed during a seventeen-year career with Capitol Records. Mauri would handle international deals for us, and he had witnessed it all, from Sinatra to The Beatles. He was a small, charming guy with a white Van Dyke beard, and he was a jazz musician in his own right. He began with us at a lower salary than he'd had at Capitol, and he was refreshingly willing to tackle all the new-record-label challenges that he knew lay ahead. We trumpeted the hiring to the industry press and also announced that I had become vice president, even though I had been VP for well over six months at that point. It didn't matter. Any excuse to get our name out there was an opportunity we never passed up.

A few weeks later, we hired Dick Sherman as our national director of marketing and sales. He knew everyone in the distribution arena and always had a joke at the ready. Dick had played professional basketball with the New York Knicks for about three seconds when he was a lot younger and a lot thinner. He was a very funny guy who rarely had a good word to say about anyone, but he was a true character, so he fit the Casablanca mold.

Both Dick and Mauri were a generation older than the rest of us, but we all worked and played together without age becoming an issue. If it bothered them when we told clients that they'd been around since before radio was invented, they did a good job of hiding it. When it came to some of our more questionable activities (like smoking grass or other drug-related pursuits), Dick was an old-line conservative; but owing, I assume, to his experiences as a jazz musician, Mauri was much more open to such things.

Neil always tried to make everyone feel that they were part of the company. In all the years I was at Casablanca, and over the ensuing decades, very, very few people who worked for the company ever said to me that they didn't love working there. Neil wanted Casablanca to have a family atmosphere, and, accordingly, we would have birthday celebrations with crates of Dom Pérignon and lavish cakes for everyone, from the top-level employee to the lowliest mail-room worker. We always tried to make tickets available for our artists' shows to everyone who wanted to go, until the company became so large that holding back several hundred tickets to each show became unwieldy and expensive. We also gave out lots of T-shirts and other promotional stuff—Neil had satin Casablanca jackets and very nice leather briefcases made for everyone in promotion, PR, sales, and legal.

One Monday morning, after returning from a weeklong trip, I walked into the office to find it populated by new people: bookkeepers, secretaries, and other staffers, including Randee Goldman, who would become Neil's personal assistant. Neil, beaming, shot me a glance as if to say, "Look at all the new stuff I bought for us!" I could envision him hiring people as if he were on a shopping spree: "I'll take three accountants, two of those secretaries over there, one of those, a dozen of these." Neil had hired so many new people that we had no office space for them. The dining room between Neil's office and the kitchen was filled with people, desks, and phones.

As I entered the room, I encountered the most beautiful woman I have ever seen. I took a deep breath, and, with as much cool as I could muster, I walked over and introduced myself to Mary Candice Hill, whom Neil had hired to handle production for us. To this day, I've no idea why she didn't burst out laughing at me. Here was this tall, lanky guy standing in front of her—sans shoes, for some reason, but wearing ridiculous socks with individual slots for all ten toes, each slot a different color. What possessed us to think that any 1970s attire was cool I have no idea. A grown man wearing toe socks? Really, I have no explanation.

In retrospect, I realized that I was largely responsible for hiring Candy (she preferred that name to her given one). A few days before my trip, I had walked into Neil's office, sat down, and started to make small talk. Part of the joy of working in a completely independent company without adult supervision was that we could kill time like this whenever the hell we wanted. Despite the fact that each of us was handling several jobs, there wasn't all that much to do because we had such a small roster, so whenever we got sick of what we were doing, we'd while away the hours bullshitting, or smoking grass, or dreaming out loud. As we sat there talking about nothing in particular, I was leafing through a copy of *Billboard*. I ran across a story about Blue Thumb Records going out of business. One of the people they referred to in the article had production experience, so I mentioned it to Neil. Never one to hesitate over a good opportunity, Neil picked up the phone and called Bob Krasnow, president of Blue Thumb and an old nemesis of his from the Buddah days. Bob had left Buddah shortly after Neil arrived as they just did not see eye to eye, but they eventually buried the hatchet. Neil asked Bob about this production person, and Bob gave her a glowing recommendation. Neil hired her a few days later.

I eventually summoned the chutzpah to ask Candy out to dinner, and she accepted. As we drove to the restaurant she had chosen, Candy explained to me that she did not like Neil. I was dumbfounded. She was comparing him to her former boss, Bob Krasnow, and she apparently felt Neil didn't measure up. In her eyes, Neil was a glib snake-oil salesman—nothing more, nothing less.

Candy's relationship with Krasnow was interesting, to understate things a bit. When she had begun working at Blue Thumb, one of her responsibilities had been to make sure that Krasnow's office was clean in the mornings. He would frequently hold meetings with artists and managers that ran late into the evening, and he'd leave the place in a state of disarray. One morning, Candy had entered Krasnow's office and noticed that his desk was covered with dust. She dutifully cleaned the desk with Lemon Pledge and straightened up the office. Of course, it hadn't been dust on the desk, and when Krasnow came in he went crazy. Bob Emmer, another music industry vet, walked into the office to find Bob on his hands and knees, desperately trying to inhale the coke that had been brushed onto the floor and screaming at Candy that she was fired. He hired her back a few minutes later. This kind of thing was typical of the music business in the 1970s. Krasnow went on to create a viable black music department at Warner Brothers (signing Funkadelic, Parliament's alter ego) and later played a major role in resurrecting Elektra Records. He was an excellent records man—the Pointer Sisters were also among his signings.

I told Candy that she had Neil completely wrong, and that, oh by the way, I was his cousin. To my surprise, she didn't care at all that we were related. After dinner, we went back to my place, dropped a few 'ludes, and stayed together all night. The next day, I took her back to her apartment, and she introduced me to her cat, Sally, a beautiful white feline. I fell in love with Sally. In fact, I fell in love with them both. Candy was not only beautiful but also smart and funny and, most importantly (as I would find out later), she was in love with me, too. We were together almost every night after that, and working with her during the day and being with her at night, I found myself in the kind of relationship I never thought I could have.

Candy initially split her time between working with Mauri Lathower on international deals and handling production. Both the international and production departments began to grow so quickly that she soon began to focus on production alone. She and Mauri shared their office area with our TWX machine—a bizarre contraption that looked like a typewriter glued to a stock ticker. The TWX was AT&T's answer to the Teletype. If you're wondering what a Teletype is, remember the amusing scene in *Almost Famous* where Ben Fong-Torres from *Rolling Stone* magazine excitedly tells the Cameron Crowe character to submit a story via Teletype, as "it only takes eighteen minutes to send one page." That gives you an idea of where our communications systems were at during the Casablanca era. Neil conducted all of his overseas correspondence via TWX.

Candy was phenomenal in many regards. She could type very quickly, knew the TWX, and had a strong grasp of grammar and writing; she helped out with our overseas correspondence. Her overseas production responsibilities consisted of making sure that all audio and art were sent and received by our licensees and distributors—if one piece went missing, all hell would break loose. When she transitioned out of the international department, she recommended her sister, Christy, for the

job. Neil replied, "Great. Hire her now." Casablanca was family, literally
and figuratively. Christy was outstanding at the international stuff, especially in her dealings with the new overseas artists and producers we
began to sign, and she became close friends with many of our overseas
distributors.

Sales, both domestic and international, and production coordination
were taken care of, but promotions remained. Neil and I knew it was
vital to the company to have the very best promotions people available.
Problem was, we couldn't afford them. But we didn't care, and we hired
them anyway. Neil's ever-positive, full-speed-ahead mantra was exciting
and addictive, and I eagerly adopted it. We all did. But somewhere in the
sensible region of my mind, red flags were rising.

Neil and I came up with a short list of the most talented promotions
people we could think of and began offering them more money than
they were currently making. The results were mixed. We hired Brian
Interland, from the Northeast, and we loved him; he had a fantastic rep
and seemed to enjoy the challenge of the new company environment. He
fit right in. On the other end of the scale was A.J. Cervantes, from the
Midwest. Buck was taken with him for some reason, though I was never
particularly impressed by his work. A.J.'s father, Al, was mayor of St. Louis
from 1965 to 1973, which had provided A.J. with opportunities that he
might not have had otherwise. A year later, when I took one of our
artists, Angel, to St. Louis to perform for the first time, A.J. arranged for
limos to take the group to interviews. Trying to show the band how
much clout we had in the market, I mentioned to the chauffeur that our
employee's father was the previous mayor. He remarked that Al Cervantes
had left office in disgrace. Lesson: be careful when you drop names.

We did not hire representatives in Chicago, opting instead to use
Bedno-Wright, an indie promo firm that had very strong influence with
some of the Top 40s in the market. For the Southeast, we got a great
promo guy named Wynn Jackson, a smooth-talking, good-looking
southerner, and we periodically used Wade Conklin, a Buddah alumnus
and close friend of Charlie Daniels, who knew the Nashville scene well.
Our team was augmented by staffers at several of our distributors, and as
a group we managed to canvas the country effectively.

In the midst of all the human resources chaos, we were still trying
to conduct business. Fanny's debut, *Rock and Roll Survivors*, was released,

followed quickly by KISS's sophomore effort, *Hotter Than Hell*. We also solidified an arrangement with Quality Records for them to become our distributor in Canada, and in short order we had somewhat of a hit with the Hudson Brothers' "So You Are a Star" from their album *Hollywood Situation*, the last album we'd issued under the original Warner distribution system.

We had to resell the KISS and Parliament catalog titles and begin to work the Fanny and T.Rex product. While I understood Warner's trepidation when it came to KISS, I never could fathom why they had a problem with Marc Bolan. He had both the T.Rex connection and the all-important English pedigree so favored by the big conservative companies. Even though we only had Marc for one album (until his contract with Warner expired), we were deeply saddened a few years later when he heard that he had been killed in a car crash.

Fanny was on the verge of a monster hit. Their single, "Butter Boy," exploded onto the Top 40 and pulled album sales along with it. It was one of those songs that seemed to be an automatic hit; once it got played, radio station phones started ringing off the hook, and then the sales began. It had Top Five written all over it. But, just as we were preparing to ride the wave of its success, the song came under heavy attack for having inappropriate sexual references (today no one would bat an eye). Its fast climb was stalled, and it was dead in a matter of days. I found a deep irony in the situation, considering that the band's name, Fanny, which had been suggested to them by George Harrison, was slang for "pussy" in most of the English-speaking world. Only in North America did it have a more innocent connotation.

Patti Quatro, the lead singer of the group (and sister of musician/actress Suzi Quatro), provided me with a great distraction from all of this. I was quite taken with her; in plain terms, I thought she was hot, and I developed a crush on her. Soon after, I overheard Neil talking with the band's manager, Roy Silver, about Fanny. He mentioned not having the money to "pay her royalties for 'Butter Boy,'" and I assumed that "her" was Patti. Roy told Neil not to worry—she was a sweet girl and would not press the matter. That killed any hopes I had for the two of us. I felt far too guilty about her not getting paid for the song to ask her out.

8

Here's Johnny!

**On empty—*The Tonight Show*—A conflict of interest—
Joyce divorces KISS—Distribution network—Dead on
arrival—Lost in the desert**

November 15, 1974
Rainbow Records Pressing Plant
Santa Monica, California

We were out of money.

The divorce from Warner Brothers and the collateral damage it had caused—it had forced us to hire an army of people to replace those Warner had provided for us—had drained our accounts. We had drastically expanded our overhead, advertising, and payroll, in particular, and our cash flow was still just dripping along. Every dollar that came through the door went toward hiring, or placing a full-page blowout in *Billboard*, or fluffing a prospective artist with a party, or buying some new gadget or first-class airfare somewhere. If Neil saw a dollar sitting on your desk unspent, he knew you weren't doing the job the way he wanted you to do it.

But the equation still left us nowhere: no money + spend + spend + spend = a bad moon rising. This wasn't difficult math to fathom. We justified what we were doing by believing that we were following the old adage "It takes money to make money." And yet we spent money as if the second half of the equation didn't exist.

As part of the exit agreement we'd made with Warner Brothers a few months earlier, Neil had arranged with Mo Ostin to take a promising and lucrative Johnny Carson album with us. The Carson project was a two-disc set of "magic moments" from *The Tonight Show*. Both Joyce Biawitz and Neil had invested a great deal of time and energy in it over the previous year.

The album had been set up through Richard Trugman, an attorney recommended to us for his experience with these types of negotiations.

Neil had come to know him when an associate of Trugman's accidentally sliced a golf ball through a window of Neil's house, which was located across the street from the Bel-Air Country Club. Trugman had the added advantage of being a cousin of Henry Bushkin, Carson's attorney and deal maker, whom Johnny often called "The Bombastic Bushkin."

At first, Neil was not crazy about Trugman—no one at the office was. This was not an uncommon reaction, as Trugman was somewhere south of cordial. But once Neil realized that Trugman had a lot of Hollywood contacts, he quickly began to warm to him. This was typical of Neil: he would leverage any situation or evaluate any potential relationship in terms of how many players, Hollywood or otherwise, it would give him access to. When we'd first arrived in LA, Neil had joined one of the larger LA temples because he knew that so many of the Hollywood movers and shakers were members. While Neil was a man of faith, he wasn't all that interested in organized religion; the temple was a net-working opportunity, and so was Trugman.

Richard was a very tough cookie who knew how to scam and scheme with the best of them, and Neil liked that type of shifty bravado. When it came to music, Richard tried to fit in with the rest of us and create a cool and hip image for himself. He was anything but. One day, I borrowed his car, and while I was driving down Sunset Boulevard, I noticed that he had an 8-track Beatles tape in the car. I took it from its cardboard slip-case and saw that it was not a Beatles album but a Beethoven symphony. I looked at Richard's other tapes—they were all classical recordings in contemporary slipcases.

Finding material to include on the Carson album placed an incredible load on Joyce, as she had to sift though untold hours of kinescope reels from *The Tonight Show*'s Steve Allen days, in the 1950s, and then work her way through the thousands of shows from the Carson era. Much of the footage she was seeking, such as Johnny's early broadcasts from New York, no longer existed. Even when she found a funny sketch or highlight, age and poor archiving techniques would often render it unusable—I clearly recall her complaining to me about the condition of some of the old footage. In many cases, the sound on the old kinescopes was almost completely eroded.

Locating clips was only half the battle. There was also the problem of getting the rights to use them, as NBC and *The Tonight Show* had not always retained (or had subsequently lost) the artist-signed clearances for this kind of use. There were also budget constraints: Carson wanted one hundred thousand dollars up front, and Ed McMahon, who would be the spokesperson for the album, was to receive fifty thousand just for doing the TV and radio spots. In fact, we'd set aside four hundred thousand dollars in TV ad buys to run before Christmas in eighteen different markets. The entire album, advertising included, would cost more than $1.2 million to produce.

When the project had started at Warner, they had some question as to whether Joyce was up to the task. There were singularly few people who were qualified, but Joyce was unquestionably one of them, and in 1974, being one of only a handful of women in the field, she was something of a pioneer.

The project (and Neil certainly understood this well) also gave Joyce a good excuse to spend more time out on the West Coast with him. However, while their relationship continued to grow, Joyce's relationship with Bill Aucoin and KISS came into serious question. Like many bands then and now, KISS never fully trusted their record company. Sure, they put up a good front for the outside world, and I always believed they sincerely liked and appreciated us, but they kept us at arm's length. I understood why: no matter how honest or pleasant someone appears to be, there is no altruism in this business; the only person you can, or should, trust at all times in all circumstances is yourself. This mistrust between band and label turned Neil and Joyce's relationship into a major conflict of interest, at least from KISS and Bill's vantage point. If the tables had been turned, Neil's mindset would have been 180 degrees different, as he loved it when our reps were nailing program directors or anyone else in a position of power over us. He saw the value of that leverage. KISS and Aucoin didn't; they saw half their management team in bed with the president of their record company, which meant that Joyce was susceptible to listening to and fighting for Neil's point of view instead of KISS's. The problem festered, and ultimately Joyce parted ways with Aucoin and KISS. It was an amicable divorce. Her interest in Rock Steady (the management company she had founded with Aucoin) was bought out for the reported sum of fifty thousand dollars, and she continued to pull a percentage of the profits for a while.

With the Carson album drawing closer to completion, Neil began to crank up the promotion machine, making sure that there was a great deal of industry prepublicity to create an aura around the release. *The Tonight Show* was doing great. It had a nightly audience of over fourteen million, and it was the largest profit center for NBC Television. Who in their right mind would think that a record featuring major guest stars from the show's history would be anything but a huge seller? Before anyone had heard one second of the album, Neil had us all believing we had a historic, record-break-ing release on our hands. Neil had had great success with a similar project at Buddah, called *Dick Clark: 20 Years of Rock n' Roll*, which had sold in excess of one million copies. Dick claims to this day that he was able to buy a house in Malibu because of it. If Clark had worked, why not Carson? Neil's confidence level was

- **August 9, 1974: Richard Nixon becomes the first US president to resign from office.**
- **September 8, 1974: Daredevil Evel Knievel attempts to jump his "Sky Cycle" over the Snake River Canyon in Idaho, and fails.**
- **October 1, 1974: Horror classic *The Texas Chain Saw Massacre* makes its debut in Austin, Texas.**

so high that he anticipated as many as three more *Tonight Show* high-light albums, which would cover even the earlier Steve Allen and Jack Paar eras of the show. The initial print run of the album was seven hundred and fifty thousand. And it wasn't just inside the walls of Casablanca that the album's promise shone brightly—the rest of the industry saw the dollar signs as well. The Carson album greatly eased our transition from the shelter of the Warner umbrella to full independence.

A major logistical hurdle that we faced when we left Warner Brothers was that we now needed to find distributors for our product. The Carson album was very appealing to many wholesalers, and it was a nice carrot to dangle in front of the major independent distributors. Thanks to the album, Neil had great leverage in his negotiations. He was firm: if you could not come up with some advance money, you did not get to be our distributor. Such a move took tremendous balls on Neil's part, since we had almost nothing to offer as a label. Most of the distributors bought into the pitch, and those who didn't would soon rue their decision, as

Neil refused to work with any who turned him down. He eventually cobbled together a roster of twenty-six independent distributors, many of whom he knew from our days at Buddah. Among them were Record Merchandising (LA/San Francisco), Heilicher (Dallas/Houston/Miami/Minneapolis), Southland (Atlanta), Music Merchants (Boston), MS Distribution (Chicago), Universal (Philadelphia), London Records (New York/New Jersey), Action Music (Cleveland), and my old reliable apartment furnisher, Zamoski's (Baltimore/Washington, DC).

The amount of each advance the distributors paid to us directly was related to the markets in which they were prominent. Problems arose in several regions where the distribution lines were blurred; for example, Cleveland may have been shipping to certain Chicago accounts, and Chicago may have been selling to accounts as far away as Los Angeles, so things could get a bit complex at times. Most of the disputes were settled without getting too heated, but our involvement in independent distribution required us to referee the occasional turf war. Additional monies came in from distributors in England and Germany as advances against royalties. We did not have much of a track record of meaningful overseas sales, so these advances were rather small.

Neil personally presold *The Tonight Show* album to everyone he could think of. Not only did he presell the album to the distributors, but he also called many of the major rack jobbers (glorified suppliers who decided upon the product assortment for major retailers and stocked it for them), such as the Handleman Company, and talked them into carrying the album. Normally, Handleman (like Walmart) did not take product for their accounts until it was on the charts or already a proven seller, but Neil had a strong relationship with them, and he was able to persuade them to bend their rules.

Neil not only worked the phones for the Carson release, but he also went out to meet each distributor personally. He would stop at nothing to get them excited about our two-LP magnum opus. He'd hype the album and play the TV commercial for them. He even went so far as to award cash prizes to salespeople who correctly answered certain *Tonight Show* questions. He'd gather a distributor's salespeople together and ask, "OK, who knows who Aunt Blabby was?" Those who knew got a hundred dollars. Or he would ask if they knew the Magnificent Carnac; those who did won a hundred dollars. These salespeople later told me that they were completely blown away and became big believers in the Carson album. Even thirty years later, most of these guys still fondly remember Neil coming to spend time with them. Many of them have told me that they were great friends of Neil. But they weren't—Neil just made them feel that way. Spending an hour with someone doesn't make you a lifelong friend, but Neil's talent for instant bonding left an indelible impression upon countless people. Many of these distribution companies were located in old warehouses in less-than-upscale neighborhoods. The sales guys were almost never in the office, and even when they were, they probably had to share a phone or a desk, so a visit from someone whom they had read about in the trade papers was a major event. It was probably more important to them than a visit from an artist.

In order to generate the cash flow we needed to pay the bills and secure the advances from the distributors, Neil presold over seven hundred and fifty thousand units. This was an impressive amount for a major label, but for a one-month-old independent like Casablanca, with no artist roster to speak of, it was nothing short of staggering.

On November 15, 1974, the Carson album, *Here's Johnny: Magic Moments from The Tonight Show*, was released.

The album bombed.

More accurately, it BOMBED. It hit the floor with a lifeless, echoing thud. An enormous (and very dead) elephant in the room that was the music industry.

The only time we would get a sales bump is when Johnny held the album up during *Tonight Show* broadcasts, and even then it was just a small spike. Johnny did this maybe two or three times during the entire promo campaign, and he had to be begged to do it. I was able to get a handful of my album-oriented stations to play a few cuts, but no one in radio gave it much exposure. In the throes of our love affair with the promise of Johnny Carson, it never dawned on us that audio highlights of a TV show were simply not radio friendly. The show did not translate well without Johnny's facial expressions and those of his guests. The album quickly became the laughingstock of the industry, the joke being that we'd shipped the LP Gold and it was returned Platinum. A funny line, to be sure. Sad thing was, it wasn't far from the truth.

This begs the question: How can you have more returns than sales? As illogical as it seems, it is possible; it has largely to do with accounting practices and your definition of "sold." Back then, record companies would give albums—"free goods"—to their accounts instead of offering them a straight discount. When the company sold an account ten albums, for instance, it might include two free albums in the order, so about 20 percent of the records sold went out as free goods. By way of illustration, in the production agreement we'd signed with Bill Aucoin's company, Rock Steady, it was specifically stated that we would give 20 percent of KISS's albums and 30 percent of their singles away as free promo product. We didn't do this with every transaction, only when we were trying to move quantity or position a product to make it more appealing for the retailers and distributors to purchase larger quantities. This practice allowed record companies to promote their albums through free product without having to pay artist royalties (which also generated no money for the labels). Almost all artist contracts stipulated that no royalties would be paid on free goods. If a label had simply given a big discount on an album, the sale would still count, and royalties would have to be paid.

One major problem with this system was that the 100 percent return policy offered in the business at the time made it impossible track the free goods given to any one distributor over the course of a product's life. If an account paid us for ten albums and received two more for free, it could technically return all twelve for a full refund because the two free ones hadn't been tracked. That's why when we "sold" seven hundred and fifty thousand albums, we were opening ourselves up to nearly a million returns.

Before the returns began flooding in, *The Tonight Show* album did receive Gold status from the Recording Industry Association of America (RIAA), which in lieu of actual financial success provided us with the opportunity to blow our own horn. But this was a hollow victory. We made hundreds of framed Gold records and sent them to the distributors and retail buyers in the hope that this would keep the product out there a little longer. Gold status was a bit of a sham. At the time, the primary requirement to achieve this status was shipping (not selling) half a million copies. The actual number of albums sold to consumers was not taken into consideration, as there was no one to track that. Eventually, Sound-Scan (the method *Billboard* currently uses to monitor sales to the end consumer) was created, and it gave subscribers access to everyone's exact running sales totals. If we'd had to take back the entire lot of unsold Carson product immediately, it would have been even more of a disaster than it already was.

All of us knew it was a bomb, but we could not let anyone know that we felt that way. Neil, Dick Sherman, and I all fought with the distributors and accounts to keep the Carson albums on the shelves. We refused to take them back until a distributor was threatening to walk. We had to keep the album out of the return cycle as long as possible. We would get no money from the distributors for new product as long as all of this old product—namely, the Carson album—was coming back, so it was imperative that we support the perception that the album still had some life left in it. We knew that it didn't, but that was no reason not to extend the product as long as we could. Failing to do so would have spelled the end of Casablanca, as we would have been forced to file for bankruptcy if we'd had to credit all our distributors at once.

It's funny what you'll tell people when the very existence of your company hangs in the balance. We made up all sorts of stories about new and grandiose advertising campaigns that were coming down the pike. "Oh, we've got this whole series of radio promotions," I'd shout, "where the winners are going to be flown to LA to be in *The Tonight Show* audience. And be sure to watch the show tonight, because Johnny is going to be talking about the album a lot." If that didn't work, I'd offer them in-store advertising credit—I'd give them a discount on the album if they placed it in a high-profile spot in their record stores. I didn't believe a single word that was coming out of my mouth, but I had to say these things anyway. If I had to tell a distributor that God himself was going to come to his house and wash his Buick for him once a week if he moved twenty-five hundred copies, then that's what I told him. Casablanca's existence depended upon us telling these distributors literally anything to get them to believe the album still had legs.

The end of Casablanca seemed so close at hand that I was already considering what I would do when I moved back to New York. But as time passed, the Carson album took on an interesting role in Casablanca's history: it nearly killed us, but it also saved us. Due to oddities in the way the RIAA awarded it Gold status and the fact that we kept it on the shelves for as long as we did, the album gradually generated enough money and prestige to keep us afloat.

Our first major release after leaving Warner Brothers, and we'd fallen flat on our faces. The name Casablanca was beginning to feel particularly apt: we were alone in the barren sand dunes of Morocco, and there was no oasis in sight.

9

The Germans Are Coming!

Help arrives—The first subsidiary—Payroll service in Vegas—Lenny and Buddy—Neil's coup d'état—Sponsorship with Gibson—*Dressed to Kill*—The big Beacon gamble—Ménage à trois

November 1974
Casablanca Records Offices
1112 North Sherbourne Drive
Los Angeles, California

The oasis appeared on our horizon in the form of Trudy Meisel. Trudy was a slim, very professional-looking woman, who—with her husband, Peter—had had some success in Germany with experimental mood music along the lines of Tangerine Dream. She came to our offices on Sherbourne one day to meet with Neil, Cecil, Buck, and me, and she explained that she was representing Giorgio Moroder, an Italian-born musician. Moroder had established a small but loyal following in Germany through a string of releases. On some of these, he was the artist; on others, which were by a collection of now largely unknown artists, he'd served as producer. He was especially strong in the then-burgeoning field of experimental electronic music, and he would go on to become a pioneer in the disco and new wave movements. Trudy had already inked deals for Moroder in Germany, France, and the UK, but she was looking for a partner in the US. The five of us sat in Neil's office and listened to portions of the three Moroder projects that Trudy had brought with her: two electronic rock albums named *Schloss* and *Einzelgänger* ("Castle" and "Lone Wolf"); and a record by a dance artist named Donna Summer. We liked all three projects, which was a shame, because we couldn't afford any of them.

Trudy departed without a deal, leaving us to spend the rest of the afternoon listening to Giorgio's projects over and over and over again. We tried to convince ourselves that we liked them enough to figure out a way to make the deal work. By the next morning, Neil had hit upon a solution: we would offer Giorgio his own US label, and he would give us the three albums at no upfront cost. Neil contacted Trudy and asked her to come back to the office that day. We pitched the idea to her and she liked it. She called Giorgio directly from Neil's phone and explained the offer. In a matter of moments, we had a handshake deal. The details were finalized in short order—it took no more than two weeks—and Casablanca had its first subsidiary label. Moroder's one request was that his new US label have the same name as the small label he had started in Germany. That name was Oasis. A company called Casablanca with a subsidiary named Oasis? You had to love the karma.

So we had our first subsidiary label, and the only expense we would incur was the small cost of developing the artwork. The downside was that the label had no established acts. The two electronic albums didn't even feature an artist—they were nothing more than experimental studio projects done largely by Moroder himself. Even Donna Summer's album was unimpressive—just a few rough tracks of Donna singing Giorgio-penned-and-produced songs. Frankly, she was nothing more than a well-trained session musician.

The Moroder signing would become one of the most important moments in Casablanca's history, but we didn't know that yet. We were still a new label with a limited roster, a colossal bust that was the joke of the industry, and, most importantly, no money. Our financial liquidity was awful. One Monday morning, Neil, who was looking unusually downcast, walked into my office, sat in a rattan chair, and said, "Larry, we need ten thousand dollars to make payroll for the week. We're out of money, and I'm out of ideas." This was the guy who could walk through the eye of a hurricane saying, "How about that wind at our backs!" I wasn't surprised that we were out of money, but to hear Neil say it out loud was sobering. "My dad has some money," I said. "I'm sure he'd offer the cash if I asked." Neil rejected the idea immediately: "No way. I like Uncle Oscar a ton, and I am not going to put him in that position." Neil felt weird accepting money from my father for something he was not sure would be successful. He had no idea when the money would be paid back, if ever. Casablanca could fold at any second.

Neil tried various money sources, but he found no takers. On Thursday of that week, he ducked into my office, said "I'm going to Vegas," and disappeared. I assumed he was going to gamble at the casinos to try to win enough to cover payroll. I was only partly correct. Unbeknownst to me, he had a line of credit at one (or more) of the casinos. He cashed in the line and flew back to LA on Friday to pay our salaries.

Cashing in a line of credit sounds like a simple financial move, and it was. But it was also a big gamble, because in the 1970s Las Vegas was still largely a Mob-run town. The casinos would not become comparatively clean corporate entities until the late 1980s. Neil was able to pay back his line of credit before anyone knew what he'd done. When I asked why he hadn't gone through Arnold Feldman's contacts and borrowed directly from

- October 30, 1974: Muhammad Ali knocks out George Foreman in "The Rumble in the Jungle" to regain the heavyweight crown.
- November 13, 1974: Ronald DeFeo kills six members of his family in their home in Amityville, New York. The victims' ghosts would allegedly force the Lutz family from the same house a year later. These events would inspire a book and a movie, both titled *The Amityville Horror*.
- December 30, 1974: After years of wrestling with lawyers, The Beatles legally disband.

the Mob, he told me that once you'd dealt with the Mafia on that level, you would never get rid of them.

Despite our tenuous financial situation, Neil drove us forward, pushing us to look for new acts and new deals. In a move born mostly out of frugality, we bought the rights to Lenny Bruce's *What I Was Arrested For*, a landmark comedy album that had been released in 1969 by Douglas Records, a company Neil knew from our Buddah days. On its release, the album had had minimal exposure, and the deal to rerelease it was incredibly cheap. Bruce's name, despite the fact that he'd been dead since 1966, still had cachet in the marketplace, and the album, which came out in February 1975, was a decent seller for us.

Two other acts that we'd added to our roster by fall 1974 were Buddy Miles (famous for his stint in Jimi Hendrix's Band of Gypsies project) and Peter Noone, of Herman's Hermits ("I'm Henry the Eighth, I Am," "Mrs. Brown, You've Got a Lovely Daughter," and other 1960s pop hits). Peter and Neil had met when Neil was a singer, and they'd spent some time traveling together doing rock road shows. Peter was a gem. His fame as a major English influence on popular music in the 1960s had not gone to his head at all. Unfortunately, we could do nothing for his music career, mainly because we were just trying to survive. And, with almost all our eggs in the KISS basket, we had little time for other artists, especially one who was no longer considered hip and cool. Peter had the name recognition, but the music he was recording in the mid-1970s just wasn't what radio or consumers were looking for. We released a single or two, but we never even thought about a full LP for Peter.

When the Buddy Miles album was being recorded, we didn't have enough money to pay Buddy much of an advance, but he needed cash to rent a place to live. Out of kindness, Neil put Buddy up at his rented Beverly Hills mansion. Neil and Buddy seemed to get along really well, and for a little while they were fast friends. When we were finally able to pay Buddy some money, he found his own place. But soon afterwards his drug problem reared its ugly head. We would find him passed out on the floor of the office, and his music began to suffer. His behavior got so bad that Neil hired a security guard just to keep him out of the office. Years later, we ran into Buddy at a Parliament show at the LA Forum, and he threatened outright to kill Neil, throwing a knife at Neil before security hauled him away.

KISS was still our key act, even though we'd had no breakthrough success with them. I was continuing to work the band through my radio contacts, but I was becoming frustrated. Any success I had was intermittent. All of us—me, Neil, everyone at Casablanca, Bill Aucoin, and certainly KISS themselves—knew that they should be superstars. Their look, their energy, their spectacular performances just were too good to fail, but where were the sales? Why weren't promoters lining up to book them in the big venues? This should be an easy sell, dammit. Why wasn't it working?

To their credit, KISS never stopped moving forward. To hell with poor sales and indifferent concert promoters, they weren't quitting. They'd spent most of 1974 touring with almost no break at all. I would go on the road with them for a few days at a time, acting as an advance man of sorts, lining up promotion, schmoozing with my radio contacts and any other local media that would talk with me. These trips were never very long. While I didn't have to deal with the rigors of performing or sleep on tour buses, I was still exhausted after just a few days of touring. KISS had done this for months on end, and they showed no signs of fatigue. The band seemed to feed off the grueling lifestyle rather than letting it feed off them.

Their commitment inspired everyone at the label, helping to ease our frustration with the band's lack of album sales and radio airplay. If this band was willing to tour nonstop to help promote themselves and their albums, which would put money in our pockets eventually, how could we not want to work just as hard for them?

By the end of January 1975, KISS's second album, *Hotter Than Hell*, had slid off the charts, and Neil was itching for them to get back into the studio to do another. However, before recording could begin, a more pressing problem came to a boil. With the split from Warner and the debacle of the Carson album draining our bank accounts, we had yet to pay the band any royalties on their albums. And not just for that sales period—ever. Bill Aucoin and KISS were not pleased with us, and we didn't blame them. KISS's producers, Kenny Kerner and Richie Wise, as well as Bill and Joyce (who was still comanaging the band at that point), held a meeting to discuss their options. Kerner and Wise allegedly suggested moving KISS to another label. No sooner had the meeting ended than Joyce, in her clearly conflicted position as Neil's girlfriend, blabbed all the details to Neil.

I was not privy to any of these discussions, but at this point, Neil attempted to convince KISS to part ways with Bill. KISS held firm. They were loyal to Aucoin to a fault. Based on the insight into the KISS camp's mindset he'd gained through Joyce, Neil may have suspected that Casablanca would have an easier time breaking KISS as a best-selling act if Aucoin was out of the picture. I speculate that had he succeeded in his efforts, he would have handed management duties directly to Joyce, whose copartnership with Aucoin was about to end.

Joyce's split from Bill, coupled with his failure to remove Bill from the equation, left Neil looking for another way to gain more input and control within KISS's managerial circle. He decided to fire Kerner and Wise as KISS's producers. Neil was none too pleased with them already because of the conflict over the "Kissin' Time" single nine months earlier, so he didn't need much more of a reason to get rid of them. If they were part of a discussion, any discussion at all, that involved KISS moving to another label, that was grounds for immediate divorce in Neil's eyes. So Kerner and Wise were dismissed. Even prior to this, Neil had felt that Kenny and Richie had stabbed him in the back more than once, and he had lost all trust in them. Another major consideration was that their production was not a good match for the band, and their work had resulted in no KISS hits.

Neil's coup attempt hadn't escaped the band's notice, and I felt the repercussions when I traveled to New York shortly afterwards. During my entire time at Casablanca, I had focused almost all my efforts on KISS. When I'd caught up on my various KISS projects, I'd sit at my desk, bored, with nothing to do; or I'd go hang out in Neil's office and bother him while we smoked pot. At this point, if I wasn't working on KISS, I wasn't working on much of anything.

One of my projects was getting Gibson Guitars to sign KISS as an official sponsor. I'd successfully signed the band to a contract that provided them with free guitars in exchange for featuring the Gibson logo on all of their albums and promising to use Gibson instruments exclusively onstage. KISS had liked Gibson even before this, and they already owned several Gibson guitars, so I knew they'd have no problem complying with the arrangement. I flew from LA to New York with three electric guitars and one acoustic, courtesy of Gibson. I couldn't wait to tell the band that I'd signed them with the legendary guitar maker. When I arrived, Gene Simmons said to me matter-of-factly, "I am not allowed to talk to you, per Bill Aucoin's instructions." Even so, I gave the three electric guitars to Gene, Paul, and Ace. I'd planned on keeping the acoustic for myself, but Peter Criss looked so forlorn that he hadn't gotten a present too (we signed him to be a sponsor for Pearl Drums not long after that) that I felt sorry for him and gave him the acoustic. He told me years later that he had used it to write songs like "Beth," though I suspect he was just bullshitting me.

When it came time to record KISS's third album, rather than look outside our circle to replace Kerner and Wise, Neil decided that he would produce the record himself. He thought that KISS needed a fresh approach, and while a record company exec stepping in to produce an album could be seen as a meddlesome and ego-driven move, Neil had more than enough recording studio experience to pull it off. Recording for the album, titled *Dressed to Kill*, began at the end of January in Los Angeles, though most of the work was done in February at Electric Lady Studios in Manhattan. I attended some of the sessions, but I don't remember much more than the constant haze of pot smoke that drifted around the control room. The weed smoking was primarily Neil's doing, as Paul and Gene were notorious teetotalers when it came to drugs, and Ace and Peter tended to drink or take drugs only when they weren't with their bandmates. The album was finished in a blur, both literally and figuratively. It was released on March 19, 1975 with the words "KISS uses Gibson Guitars because they want the best" printed on its jacket.

Two nights later, KISS was scheduled to appear at the Beacon Theatre in New York, a gig I'd booked myself. Ron Delsener, a big New York promoter, didn't want to book KISS in the city at all. I told him that if he put them in the Beacon—which had only about three thousand seats— we'd repay him any money he lost. We had worked with Ron a lot at Buddah, and our relationship was solid. He agreed to the deal, and he put the first show on sale, despite the fact that everyone, himself included, thought I was crazy. The only local airplay we were getting was on WNEW, plus a smattering on WLIR in Long Island and on shows such as John Zacherle's and Alex Bennett's on WPLJ. But, guess what? The show sold out in a day.

Ron called me in LA to share the good news, and I told him, "OK, put on a second show." Neil, who had just walked into my office, said, "What the fuck are you doing?" After I got off the phone with Delsener, I told him, "Neil, relax. The second show will sell just as well." He didn't say another word, he just let it go. Neil was brilliant about letting you do what you did best, gambling that you'd do the right thing. The second show sold out nearly as fast as the first.

These were KISS's first gigs in Manhattan as headliners, and we made huge, nightlong soirees of them. Along with the usual suspects from the local industry and media, Neil's parents, my parents, and lots of our friends attended a big after party at a restaurant near the gig. The show, of course, had been great, but you couldn't tell that to my dad, a staunch Sinatra and big-band guy. He couldn't stand the music or the volume and had spent most of the show in the lobby. I was especially looking forward to this night not because of the show or the party. A girl

I knew had told me that she and another girl would come up to my hotel suite and we would have a three-way, my first. For me, all else had faded to the periphery. I saw her at the party, and she could not keep her hands off me. She just kept telling me how she was looking forward to our get-together. I said my obligatory hellos to various party guests, said goodbye to my parents, and then headed off to the hotel to prepare for what I hoped would be a fantasy come alive. The girls never showed, and I spent the rest of the night alone feeling guilty for abandoning my parents at the party.

Almost two months later, on May 10, KISS did a show in DC. Afterwards, Paul Stanley and Gene Simmons met up with *Rolling Stone* writer Gordon Fletcher, who insisted that they all go to a local club to check out a band called Angel. Gene was so impressed with the group that after their set he called Neil from a pay phone at the back of the club to pitch them.

Angel was the anti-KISS, but the band shared KISS's sense of energy and showmanship. This five-piece band had a look that was as pure as the driven snow. They all had flowing, immaculately styled hair and perfect features. In a word, they were beautiful—at least compared to KISS. But, in contrast to their appearance, their music had a hard, progressive edge; it was laden with experimental synthesizer and keyboard sounds. Gregg Giuffria, the keyboardist, was completely surrounded by the damned things onstage—organ, piano, synths, Mellotron—at least half a dozen of them.

I am not sure what effect Gene's late-night phone call had upon Neil, or if it had any effect at all. I'm not even sure that Gene actually made the call. I could easily imagine him going through the charade of calling Neil to impress Gordon Fletcher or Angel. It also seems unlikely that Gene would have been inclined to help Casablanca out at that point, considering that just weeks before he'd told me he wasn't allowed to speak to me. Furthermore, I don't think Neil would have considered Gene's opinion for more than a moment; he still wasn't anybody, yet. I think that the real impetus for our interest in Angel came from their manager, David Joseph.

David was a native Australian who also had Gary Glitter on his client list. He worked with David Bowie as well. We had met David the previous summer, when we signed the Hudson Brothers, whom he also managed.

Neil and I both liked him, so we trusted his judgment on Angel; but the fact that they were close to signing with Capitol really got us off our asses. I've no memory of how many albums were written into the contract, though I can say with confidence that any advance that Neil would have given Angel was probably just enough to cover coffee for David and the band. That's the catch-22 we were constantly facing. We needed money. To get money, we needed acts. To sign acts, we needed money. And so it went.

Things would have been a lot easier if we'd known that we were about to do the album that would finally give the company the perception of success it needed, both internally and externally. A hit would have magic powers in terms of inspiring confidence, not just in others but also in ourselves—it would make us feel like the promotion and marketing geniuses we always thought we were. The next album would be our first step toward securing financial freedom.

10

Alive to Love You, Baby

Check is in the mail—KISS re-signed—*Creem* and *Circus*—
The fifth KISS—Coming alive—Twelve thousand voices
can't be wrong—The "Love to Love You" accident—
A seventeen-minute single—Duel with Aucoin—The
impossible happens—Donna at JFK—A flying cake—
Two breaks for one—The Top 10

May 1975
Casablanca Records Offices
1112 North Sherbourne Drive
Los Angeles, California

In April 1974, we had rushed KISS into Bell Sound Studios to record the single "Kissin' Time" for our big national kissing contest promotion. It had all worked out well enough except for one thing: thirteen months later, we still hadn't paid Bell the $1,718 we owed them. They had sent a collection agency after us, which was harassing us constantly for the money. They threatened legal action and claimed they were going to report us as delinquent debtors to the national credit agencies.

This wasn't an unusual circumstance for Casablanca. Over the course of our first year in business, our dire financial situation had forced Neil to become a master staller. His key tactics were to bargain with our creditors for a reduction in the amount owed or to hold them off until we had the money to bring the account current. He told Bell's collection agency—London Credit Associates—that we had credits with Bell that would reduce the bill by half (which I doubt was true, but that wasn't the point), and if they would accept half of the amount, then the issue could be resolved immediately. Alternatively, Neil suggested, London could redo the entire ledger, figure out the appropriate amount owed (he didn't tell them what he thought the "correct" figure was, because that would have derailed his attempt to stall), and contact him when they were ready to proceed. In this case, as in most others, his ploy worked, even though London Credit Associates saw right through his ploy. We had not yet entered the age of e-mail and FedEx, so even if a collection agency didn't buy your line of BS, it took a week for you to exchange letters, and this bought you some time. We stalled for another couple of months and ended up settling for half.

In the weeks after Joyce quit as comanager of KISS, the turbulent relationship between Neil and the KISS camp began to stabilize. On May 1, 1975, a new recording contract was drafted. This contract voided the original (November 1, 1973) agreement between Casablanca and Rock Steady, and it was directly between the label and the four members of KISS (using their legal, not stage, names: Gene Klein, Paul Frehley, Stanley Eisen, and Peter Criscuola). KISS guaranteed that they would deliver two new studio albums to us within the next year, and there were options for two additional contract periods—the first twelve months, and the second six months.

The agreement not only helped solidify our position with the band, but it also helped to alleviate our financial crunch. There was a point in the contract that allowed us to defer our first royalty payment to the band until October 20, 1975. We were also allowed to front our biggest independent distributors, Heilicher and Handleman, more royalty-free albums and singles than our other distributors. Our standard percentage of free product was 20 percent of albums and 30 percent of singles. With both Heilicher and Handleman, we were allowed 30 percent of albums and 40 percent of singles. Because these distributors moved as much product for us as all the others combined, this significantly decreased the royalties that would be due to KISS. This, and the fact that our first KISS royalty check wasn't due for another six months, finally gave us some breathing room.

The contract points weren't as lopsided in our favor as they might seem. Because we had no money to help finance KISS's touring, for the past several months Bill Aucoin had underwritten most of the band's tour expenses with his personal credit card, and he was now deep in debt to American Express. Bill insisted that the new agreement stipulate that Casablanca would provide forty thousand dollars in promotional money for each of KISS's tours during the term of the contract. The forty grand might seem like a large payout for Casablanca due to our cash shortage, but it was a drop in the bucket compared to the royalties we owed, and it at least gave the appearance that we were contributing something to the equation. Fronting KISS tour money (which we'd done before, anyway) in exchange for deferring royalty payments was a quid pro quo arrangement, and it seemed to satisfy everyone. At least for the moment.

While Neil held our growing list of creditors at bay, Cecil, Buck, and I persisted in our increasingly desperate drive to bring Casablanca some money. KISS-related projects still dominated my days, though I'd begun to shift my attention to different promotional possibilities. Thus far, I'd sold heavily to my network of radio contacts. It was what I knew, and I'd used the strategy successfully for several of our artists at Buddah, but with KISS, it hadn't really worked. While they were becoming very well accepted as a concert act, they hadn't sniffed the Top 40 with their singles.

- **March 26, 1975: The film version of The Who's *Tommy* premieres in London.**
- **June 20, 1975: Steven Spielberg's *Jaws* is released and quickly becomes the first $100 million movie, ushering in the age of the summer blockbuster.**
- **August 25, 1975: Bruce Springsteen releases *Born to Run*.**

Their albums were doing somewhat better, but sales were spotty—the LPs sold in some markets, while in others the results were dismal. We needed a way to bypass the traditional route of driving an album with a Top 40 hit single. We needed a drastic halftime adjustment to our game plan. With the radio approach stalling, I decided to give print media a try.

I began with the teen magazines *Creem* and *Circus*. They were appealing targets: we could work them as often as we wanted and did not need to have a new single to get exposure. *Creem* was owned by Barry and Connie Kramer, who were running their fun and very influential magazine out of a small suite of offices in Southfield, Michigan, a short drive from Detroit. Barry and Connie, who were both about my age, made no effort to be hip and trendy, despite helming one of the hippest music publications out there. They were casual and naturally cool.

The *Creem* offices, which had a separate photography studio, were a disaster. The rooms were filled with desks; paper, mimeographs, photos, and thousands of back issues littered every square inch of floor and desk space. But this is exactly what most magazine offices looked like, and Barry and Connie ran a pretty tight ship—professional but loose, and free of drugs and sex, at least during my many visits. Today, a magazine of such influence would be far more corporate and impressive looking. In the mid-1970s, it was a mom-and-pop operation, quite literally, and I think that's the way Barry, Connie, and their staff liked it.

The editor of the magazine was Ben Edmonds, and the main writer was the legendary Lester Bangs, an opinionated, talented, brusque gorilla, so well portrayed by Philip Seymour Hoffman in Cameron Crowe's brilliant 2000 film *Almost Famous*. Bangs was a towering presence in the music world, but at the office he was treated like any other member of the staff. I was introduced to all these key people by Mark Parenteau, who was still the driving force behind the city's big rock station, WABX. I hung out at the *Creem* offices whenever I went to Detroit, and we all partied together with the WABX people.

Working in Lester's shadow was a young writer named Jaan Uhelszki, the real life and energy of the magazine. Jaan was adorable. She was about five foot seven, with dark hair and an effervescent smile. She had a great natural enthusiasm for music and immediately ingratiated herself to Gene Simmons. Since she was close friends with the magazine's photo editor, Charlie Auringer, she was able to influence the selection of pictures to be published in the magazine, and she did so to our advantage.

Jaan was so infatuated with KISS and Gene that she would frequently call me with ideas for stories. The most intriguing one (and I could easily see Gene behind this) was for her to be a KISS-ette for a day. She would dress up as a female member of the band and perform with them. She asked if I would help coordinate the event and pay for her travel expenses. I loved the idea and told her to run with it, although in the article she eventually wrote, titled "I Was Onstage with KISS in My Maidenform Bra," she claimed that I had been nervous about it. She must have misread my reaction, because nothing could have been further from the truth. If the Beatles could have a fifth member (Murray the K), why couldn't KISS? Besides, Jaan was much better looking than Murray. I agreed to cover her expenses to go to a show and write about being a KISS-ette. She flew to Johnstown, Pennsylvania, on May 17, where she briefly joined the band onstage near the end of their set. The result was a major story in *Creem*'s August 1975 issue.

In the meantime, I had come to an agreement with Barry Kramer that if he helped us break KISS, then I would buy a lot of advertising from him and also supply him with thousands of free albums to give away with new *Creem* subscriptions. This was the only way we could advertise in *Creem*, since we still couldn't afford to buy ads in the traditional way. Our actual outlay would simply be the cost of the albums, and since they would be royalty-free, we could manage it. We'd also frequently offer concert tickets and periodically stage a contest where the winners would be sent to a KISS concert.

We struck a similar agreement with Gerald Rothberg, the publisher of *Circus*: he would give KISS extra print coverage in exchange for advertising and free albums as well as various contests and promotions. With *Circus*, I borrowed a trick that WMMS in Cleveland had pulled off using a *Rolling Stone* magazine readers' poll. WMMS had purchased hundreds of copies of the issue that included the poll. The station then had its employees fill in WMMS as their favorite radio station and sent the questionnaires to *Rolling Stone*. The stunt worked: WMMS was voted best rock radio station in America for many years in a row. This raised many eyebrows in the industry, as Cleveland was not the largest market in the country, and WMMS, although very popular, didn't have the most listeners.

We could have attempted something with *Rolling Stone*, too, but our relationship with the magazine was odd. I had almost no experience with them, because during the Buddah days, the press department had handled such relationships. Any overtures I made would have had to go through Neil, whose dealings with *Rolling Stone* ran hot and cold. His relationship with Jann Wenner, the magazine's owner and publisher, was icy. However, Neil was fast friends with *Rolling Stone* writer Lisa Robinson, whose husband, Richard, had worked under Neil at Buddah. Neil still had a lot of pull with Lisa, and she and Richard were always invited to our soirees. Why Neil had not yet exploited that friendship, I cannot say.

In any case, *Circus* also conducted a readers' poll. We bought up hundreds of issues and sat around the Sherbourne offices filling in the poll cards, voting for Ace as best guitarist, Peter as best drummer, and KISS as best group (we thought that voting for Gene or Paul as best vocalist would be stretching it a bit). We were exploiting the age-old perception-is-reality concept. To change Neil's mantra just slightly, we were "grease-painting the building."

Almost without exception, the critical reception of KISS's music and concerts had been awful. The negative reviews bothered us a little at first, but we quickly got used to them, and Neil was always reminding us (and himself) that any publicity was good publicity. And the fact that the music press so reviled KISS seemed to galvanize KISS's audience. To many, this just made KISS *the* antiestablishment band. Using print media to build up, if not outright fabricate, KISS's stature felt a bit cathartic and ironic to us.

After a while, kids began to believe that Peter was as good a drummer as any and Ace was the world's greatest guitar player—although this wasn't even close to the truth. Based on the perception created by the annual *Circus* poll, they started to buy up KISS albums. I also believe, although it went unsaid, that Gerald Rothberg was helping us behind the scenes. He thought that this whole KISS phenomenon could be beneficial to his magazine and actually helped us sell more copies. Even though the band wasn't yet a national success, having their picture on a magazine's cover increased circulation.

In conjunction with these efforts, I was soliciting independent photographers like Barry Levine in an effort to place photos of KISS in as many publications as possible. A handful of professional photographers had close ties with the rock magazines, and, given the right circumstances, they would use their pull to get coverage for the bands whose pictures they had taken. This was all done according to some loose-knit, wink-wink exclusivity agreement. We would periodically send some of these photographers on all-expense-paid trips to shows or events involving KISS or some of our other artists. We did not pay them; they would be paid by the magazines on a per-picture-published basis. So the photographers, in effect, worked as lobbyists for the band.

It was important for Casablanca's cash flow to have a new KISS album to promote every six months or so. This also helped the band keep their image alive and fresh in the press, and it fed the audience's growing demand for more KISS, although the band members were not happy that their tour schedule was frequently interrupted so they could record. Casablanca's near-constant need for new KISS material placed a creative strain on the band; we never gave them enough time to write and record new songs. *Dressed to Kill* was so rushed (recording had started only three months after the release of their previous album, *Hotter Than Hell*) that the band had been forced to dredge up songs for it that they'd written before KISS even existed, and even so, the final product was less than thirty minutes long. And here we were, barely two months after *Dressed to Kill*'s release, with Neil looking for yet another album.

Rather than force the band back into the studio to write more new material, we hatched the idea of doing a live album. In the mid-1970s, live albums were more prevalent than they are today (now they're largely nonexistent), but they were far from a no-risk, slam-dunk option. The band had so far released only three albums, and there was no monster hit attached to any of them, so releasing a greatest hits album—which, when you get right down to it, is what a live album is—was not an engraved invitation to success. Still, KISS was such an incredible spectacle in concert that a live album seemed like a logical next step.

Neil had no experience producing a live album, so we brought in Eddie Kramer, a veteran who had Jimi Hendrix and Led Zeppelin on his resume (KISS were huge fans of both), to guide the recording. The first and largest of the five shows recorded for the album happened on May 16 at Detroit's Cobo Arena. It was by far the most important concert of KISS's career to that point. This was a major venue, in the Motor City—arguably then the rock and roll capital of America—and they'd sold it out to great fanfare. The local promoter, Steve Glantz, had been trumpeting the sellout to the media, and both Neil and Bill were doing everything they could to turn the concert into an event. We all flew to Detroit days before the show—me, Neil, Joyce, Bill, the band, and the crew—and we were later joined by a huge entourage of family and friends from around the country. Aucoin rented the Michigan Palace, a Vaudeville-era theater, where he staged the photo shoot for the album cover and filmed the band performing for future promotional use. The footage included full-length music videos (which were then called "promotional films") for two singles from *Dressed to Kill*—"C'mon and Love Me" and "Rock and Roll All Nite."

The night before the show, I was eating an Italian dinner with Paul backstage at the Michigan Palace. We were in the middle of a conversation when photographer Fin Costello burst in and started taking pictures. Without missing a beat, Paul pretended to stuff sausage links and dinner rolls into his mouth, and then he posed with a can of Vernor's Ginger Ale (which was invented in Detroit). The second Fin was gone, Paul resumed our conversation, even though I had already forgotten what we were talking about due to the distraction of the flashing camera. Those iconic pictures would be published all over the world in various music magazines, and I always laughed when I saw them.

The next night, as the band began their show in front of over twelve thousand fans, Neil and I remained backstage, literally and figuratively the men behind the curtain, talking about what a rush it was to see all that we had worked for come to fruition. Over the course of the previous year, the skeleton of KISS's show had remained essentially the same, but it had grown in size. The backline of half a dozen speaker stacks had become an entire wall of Marshall cabinets. The altitude of Peter's drum riser had doubled, and during "100,000 Years," flamethrowers created the illusion that the band was surrounded by a curtain of fire. KISS and their crew were given free reign to indulge their production fantasies, and as a result of their ingenuity and Aucoin's and Casablanca's money (seemingly produced from thin air), the show just grew and grew.

For the Cobo gig, Neil and Bill both knew we had to swing for the fences. KISS's already oversized production had been amped up. The band was sporting new outfits, their lighting and pyrotechnic displays had been enhanced, they'd significantly shuffled and lengthened their set list, and the show was being projected onto a giant screen above the stage (a commonplace setup nowadays, but relatively rare in 1975). Instead of their usual opener, "Deuce," they started off with a little-performed song called "Rock Bottom," chosen for its shimmering acoustic guitar introduction. While a tape of the lengthy intro played over the house PA, a video camera followed KISS from their dressing room to the stage; the images were broadcast on the overhead screen. The gimmick was a spectacular success. The audience's shrill screaming ramped up to jet-engine volume as the band approached the stage.

Throughout the gig, Neil and I moved from the left side of the backstage area to the mobile recording studio outside. There, Eddie Kramer was hard at work putting the show to tape. Many of the WABX and *Creem* people were there, too—Jaan, Dan Carlisle, David and Linda Perry, Dave Dixon, John Detz (general manager of ABX), and Mark Parenteau—along with Joyce and Bill. The audience was borderline electric throughout the concert, even though there was a host of production problems. The new lighting company we'd hired was ill equipped to handle the production, and Peter's drum riser malfunctioned at the end of the set. Still, everyone said they were thrilled with the evening.

After taping four more shows over the next two months, Kramer and the band sifted through the material and, following quite a bit of over-dubbing, Kramer edited the final cut. Neil was not pleased that so much of the album had to be redone, but the downside of KISS's high-energy show was that the musical performances suffered. Vocals were often missing (as band members ran around the stage), the musicianship was sloppy, and so on. Most of the material from the five shows was unusable, and the finished record contains little original recording except for Peter's drum tracks. In essence, recording the Cobo show had been an enormous waste of money and time, and we had a surplus of neither. But, despite all this, the result-ing record spectacularly re-created the feeling of a live KISS show.

It was with this album that we began to become more conceptual, not only in developing KISS as four superhero-ish personalities but also in packaging our LPs. *Alive!*, a double album, had a gatefold sleeve, and its inner jacket had handwritten notes from the band to their fans, which really played up their four personas. This was the brainchild of Dennis Woloch, a creative young guy on the staff at Howard Marks Advertising. While KISS's makeup and loose identities had been in place since very early on, this was the first concerted step toward developing those iden-tities into full-fledged characters, a concept that opened up a world of marketing possibilities that KISS would explore to absurd degrees in the coming years. The album also contained an eight-page glossy booklet with a full-page shot of each band member and a centerfold collage of in-concert photos. This was an effort to establish Casablanca as a com-pany that gave fans something extra. We would greatly embellish this concept and use it with many of our other artists.

As the end of August 1975 drew near, we ramped up for a September 10 release date for the new KISS album. We were also heavily involved in the three Giorgio Moroder projects. We had issued the first of his albums, *Einzelgänger*, on the Casablanca label back in March. It was a largely experimental electronic album, which was easy enough for us to pitch to progressive rock radio, and it had an initially favorable recep-tion—we scored a "most-added" mention in *Record World*. But it died quickly. There was nothing to promote, nothing to sell to radio or the press: the album featured no group or image. Most of the music had been made by Giorgio with the help of some session musicians, and Giorgio lived in Europe, so even if we'd wanted to promote the LP using him as the face of the album, he wasn't available to do it.

The other project was an album by one of Moroder's German artists, American-born singer Donna Summer. It had its origins in a party Neil had thrown earlier in 1975. One night, Neil had one of our big blowouts at a house he was renting on Sunset Boulevard, not far from our offices. I don't remember the occasion—although we never really needed an excuse to party—but, as usual, there was no shortage of drink, weed, coke, and the like. At some point, someone bumped into a turntable, bouncing the needle back to the beginning of the track and turning a four-minute song into an eight-minute song. Everyone loved the experience. I don't know why, but they clearly did. The record was "Love to Love You Baby," a demo that Giorgio Moroder had given to Neil. It featured Donna Summer on vocals.

I doubt that Neil understood the crowd's reaction any more than I did, but he didn't care about the why. He focused on the what, and the what was that people liked it, and that's all that mattered. Making a creative (and crazy) leap, he insisted that increasing the length of this song by two or three times was the key to its success. He dialed Giorgio to share his thoughts. After some convincing, Giorgio agreed to redo the single to Neil's specifications, though I'm not sure the idea ever made sense to him. I'm not sure the idea ever made sense to me, either, but I'd long since learned to trust Neil's instincts.

Giorgio told Neil that he needed time to find the right vocalist and record the track again. He had used Donna Summer for the demo because they had a good working relationship (she'd done an album for his German Oasis label in 1974), but he wanted another singer to do the final version. Neil insisted that the song wouldn't work unless Donna sang it. Giorgio and a befuddled Donna (she didn't understand the need to extend the song any more than Giorgio or I did) rerecorded the song, and then Giorgio looped it several times to create an epic version—it was nearly seventeen minutes long. We released it as the A side of an album with the same title, *Love to Love You Baby*, on the Oasis label on August 27, 1975. The same day, also on our Oasis subsidiary, we released Giorgio's album *Schloss* and rereleased the Einzelgänger LP, which we'd previously issued on Casablanca.

While we waited to gauge public and industry reaction to this border-line lunatic idea of a seventeen-minute pop song, our royalty issue with KISS erupted again. We weren't in any better position to cut them a check than we'd been six months earlier, when we signed the new contract with them. They knew it, and we knew it. The May 1 agreement had felt like a small victory, but in terms of royalty payments, it was nothing more than a delay tactic. Neil and I knew that KISS's patience would soon run out. On September 15, 1975, he showed me a letter of termination from Bill Aucoin. KISS was leaving Casablanca.

Aucoin had all the leverage on his side, and he soon played his next card. For two weeks we heard rumors from several sources that Bill was shopping KISS to all the heavy hitters: Warner, Atlantic, and Capitol. Even more troubling was that Bill was bankrolling demo sessions with Alice Cooper producer Bob Ezrin for the band's next studio album, which would give him a big carrot to dangle in front of the record companies as he attempted to negotiate a new deal for KISS. But Neil, despite having every reason not to, remained confident, and in early October he filed an affidavit with the New York Supreme Court accusing Aucoin of attempting to sign KISS with our competitors. Then, a few days later, he blinked and cut KISS and Aucoin a check for two million dollars. This not only fulfilled our guarantee to pay them by October 20 (the date for the first royalty payment listed in our May 1975 agreement), but it also eased tensions between us and the KISS camp. Aucoin and KISS were happy, for obvious reasons, but Neil was physically drained. The stress of the past year was beginning to take its toll on him, and I could occasionally see chinks in his armor. Having to make such a huge payment was a severe financial blow, and it would contribute to the harrowing ride that awaited us in the coming months.

Despite the occasional flare-up, I never felt that there was any genuine animosity between us and KISS and Bill Aucoin. We all liked one another, and we shared the same great enthusiasm for KISS's future. But the risk we were all taking, and the financial struggles that ensued, did sometimes conspire to create some tense situations.

I would have given any takers hundred-to-one odds against what happened next, but it happened just the same. "Love to Love You Baby" began to break. Yes, a seventeen-minute song was getting some buzz. But it wasn't radio that broke the song. Discotheques, first in Florida and then in the Northeast, gradually began to play it. Club people were having the same reaction to it as the guests at Neil's party. There was something infectious about Donna's airy, sexy cooing layered over Giorgio's incessant, driving music. Neil could sense the impending breakout and pestered Giorgio to fly Donna from Munich, where she was living, to the US for some promotional appearances, which he felt would push the buzz to the critical level where we'd have a major hit on our hands. It took him the better part of a month to convince Giorgio, partly because Donna was recovering from a relatively severe heart infection, but in early November, she traveled to New York to start a six-week promotional tour.

While we were coordinating the details of her tour, Cecil, Buck, and I worked to get the song on Top 40 and R&B radio. Cecil quickly took care of the R&B side of things, Buck worked on the Top 40 stations, and I helped out where I could. Frankie Crocker, a DJ at WBLS in New York who would release a couple of disco albums through us, was one of the first to give the record some airplay, spinning the song in its entirety every night after midnight. Like most hit songs, it grew exponentially once the hype had begun. The momentum carried it forward. Shortly after Donna's arrival in New York, the record hit the charts.

Until this point, we'd barely acknowledged the existence of disco. Sure, we knew about it, but to us it was an arcane niche market that appealed only to a select few. We had no disco artists (and no money to sign them or time to promote them, either); very few radio stations, no matter what format they ran, were playing disco; and it simply didn't seem like a viable genre. Why bother with it? We didn't sign Donna and Giorgio because they were doing disco: we signed them because we liked the demos we'd heard—and we'd gotten "Love to Love You Baby" for free, anyway, as part of the deal to release *Schloss* and *Einzelgänger*.

But how would we control our emerging superstar? Having an insider in the KISS camp early on (Joyce, when she was the band's comanager) had been advantageous in many regards. Sensing a similar opportunity with Donna Summer, Neil positioned Joyce as a sort of comanager to work with Dick Broder, Donna's existing manager. Although she had not yet completed her move to LA, Joyce was living with Neil more or less full time. With her in Donna's camp, Neil would have a great deal of control over Donna's career without her management getting in the way. Giorgio, who not only wrote much of Donna's material but also served as her de facto producer, was living in Germany, so he would not be around to interfere either. It seemed like the perfect arrangement.

Coinciding with Joyce's new assignment was our hiring of Susan Munao as head of publicity for Casablanca. Susan had worked with us as a publicist for Gibson and Stromberg in New York. She was a firebrand. A dark-haired Italian barely five feet tall with her stilts on, she had a heavy, heavy New York accent, tremendous energy, and incredible tenacity. She was an outstanding publicist and took her job very seriously.

One of Susan's first tasks was to prepare for Donna's arrival. Neil would say to us, "It's a four-color world out there, boys. Don't live it in black and white." That was definitely the edict when it came to Donna. It had to be red carpet treatment all the way—nothing should be considered too good for Donna. Susan didn't disappoint. She was there, with Joyce, to meet Donna when she arrived at JFK. After making quick introductions, they escorted Donna to a waiting limousine. As they settled into the car, "Love to Love You Baby" began playing on the FM radio. Of course, it's possible that this was simply a coincidence—after all, the song was getting some serious airplay at that point—but, given Susan's drive for excellence, I think she got in touch with one of her legion of New York radio contacts, called in a favor, and arranged for the station to start playing the song on her cue. When Donna entered her room at the Park Lane Hotel, which overlooked Central Park, she found nearly two-dozen floral displays. Susan had laid on every bit of pampering she could muster. This was how impressions were made, and Susan knew it.

Buck certainly knew it, too, and so he came up with this ridiculous, harebrained stunt. He had a cake made for Donna's homecoming appearance in her native Boston. It wasn't just a cake. It was a huge cake that had Donna's likeness emblazoned on it with icing. Buck had ordered it from Hansen's Bakery, because Hansen's was the only bakery that would agree to decorate a cake with the image of a sexy reclining woman. But, oh, by the way, Hansen's was in LA—three thousand miles from Boston. How do you get a four-foot-long cake from LA to Boston without destroying it? Buck arranged for an ambulance to pick the cake up at Hansen's and chauffeur it to LAX; then he booked three first-class seats to Boston (two for the cake, one for him). Of course, there were photographers in place at both ends of the trip. Never let a good photo op go to waste.

Donna was floored. The poor woman hadn't been to the US in nearly seven years, she had been bedridden for the better part of several months with myocarditis, and she was now on the receiving end of the full Neil Bogart superstar treatment. And the promo tour had barely begun.

Her six-week excursion was launched in New York with a short performance and an extravagant after party at the Pachyderm Club. Her three-song set was plagued with production problems, mostly stemming from the fact that Donna could not hear herself sing. But the audience didn't seem to mind, and the evening was a blowout success. The quick tour that followed hit a host of cities across the country, where Donna performed minishows at small discotheques for the very people who were helping to lift her to superstar status. The promotional tour also included high-profile appearances on *Soul Train* and *The Mike Douglas Show*.

The first time I would meet Donna was several weeks later, when she came to our offices accompanied by her Casablanca retinue. At the time, this entourage consisted of Susan, Joyce, and Cecil, but then it grew rapidly and exponentially. Donna greeted us all warmly—me, Dick, Mauri, and the rest of the staff—and she expressed her gratitude for all of our help with her career. The meeting was pleasant and very low pressure. One thing that struck us was that Donna did not look a lot like the woman in the picture Trudy Meisel had given us nearly a year earlier; but you could see a resemblance. She was very pretty, but she looked a bit heavier than she had in the picture, and her hair was not the flowing mane of her album covers and press photos. It was very, very short, and not at all in keeping with the diva status that she was pursuing. This is why Donna would always be photographed in a wig.

Quietly, during the very early stages of the "Love to Love You Baby" hurricane, the daily sales reports from the distributors began to show that the KISS live album sales were far surpassing those of any of the previous KISS efforts. I spoke with reps from each of our twenty-six distributors several times daily, and the phone was constantly ringing with the news: "There were 1,951 units moved today in Chicago—you got a real smoker here!"; "There were 4,081 in Detroit—your new LP is on fire, Larry!"; "Another 2,949 in Los Angeles—this one's got long legs, Larry!" But the most exciting news came from the rack jobbers, who began placing orders in excess of one hundred thousand units for the big box stores.

The scent of blood was in the water, and we began calling the distributors and urging them to buy more units in the days leading up to KISS appearances in their markets. They did it without blinking, because they knew a hot album when they saw one; plus, the product was returnable, so there was no appreciable risk in it for them anyway.

This was how touring and promotion were supposed to work, and it was finally happening the way we'd envisioned it. Mainstream America was about to find out why KISS was our first signing. We watched with growing anticipation (and pride) as the album began to scale the charts. It was at No. 24 on the *Billboard* chart, and it had been steadily climbing for a month. "Great, first KISS, and now a hit for Donna, too," we all thought. The distributor reports on KISS kept getting bigger, and the album kept climbing. It hit No. 19 the next week, then 15, then 12. And then it cracked the Top 10. Our first Top 10 album!

11

The New Casbah

**Angel doesn't fly—The Mothership—8255 Sunset—
The billboard—Decorating the digs—Sharell
declines—Life in the big office—Pockface—All demand,
no product—Close to the end**

November 29, 1975
Sunset and Whittier
Beverly Hills, California

Was this it? Had we really arrived?

We had spent most of 1975 fending off creditors and desperately trying to keep our marquee act, KISS, on our roster. We'd barely managed to release one album per month. Every day, I would arrive at the office with the same question in my head: How much longer before it all ends, before everyone realizes we're just deluding ourselves with drugs and parties and expense accounts that we can't afford?

Now, in November 1975, after nearly two years of either sitting around bored with nothing to do or scrambling in a mad panic for artists and money, we saw that everything was happening at once. KISS was finally on fire; Gold status was imminent. The Donna Summer album, with its absurdly long dance number, "Love to Love You Baby," was blowing up, and what was to become a groundbreaking Parliament LP was about to drop.

The Sherbourne office was a mess. The original five-person Casablanca staff had quadrupled, and the place was a nest of people, desks, and tangled phone cords. We desperately needed to move, and we were making arrangements to relocate just down the block to the building formerly occupied by A&M Records on the Sunset Strip. The only way I could have made my life more complicated was to get married. So I did that, too.

On Saturday, November 29, 1975, after dating for about a year, Candy and I were married. Neil and Joyce insisted on throwing the wedding, offering us the house they rented at Sunset Boulevard and Whittier Drive (next door to Tony Orlando) for both the wedding ceremony and the reception. Joyce attended to every detail, ordering the invitations, selecting the colors for the decorations, hiring the valet parking attendants. It was, I'm sure, a heartfelt gesture, and I appreciated the generosity she and Neil showed us, but Candy felt that she didn't have a hand in planning her own wedding. She was also a bit uncomfortable because she knew that Neil would insist that everything be tied in with the business, which meant a guest list filled with industry contacts whom neither Candy nor I had ever met. KISS and Donna Summer were invited, but they were touring and couldn't attend. Gregg Giuffria, the keyboardist for Angel, whom we'd signed about six months prior, was one of only a handful of Casablanca artists to attend, though all of the staff were there.

My elder sisters, Arlene and Pat (who are identical twins), their husbands, Fred and Bob, and their children, along with my parents, flew out for the occasion, and we all had a nice Thanksgiving dinner together at the rotating restaurant atop the Hollywood Holiday Inn. Candy wasn't quite so lucky with her family. Her younger brother, Jimmy, who had come with their parents, passed out before the ceremony, and her father had to take him home, leaving her mother (who had MS and was confined to a wheelchair) behind with relatives from the Midwest.

Among my industry friends in attendance were: Mary Turner (KMET); Norm Winer (WBCN); Mike and Carol Klenfner (Columbia Records and Gibson-Stromberg); Mike and Sharon Harrison (*Radio & Records*); Richard Kimball (KMET); Alison Steele (WNEW); David Perry and his wife, Linda (from WABX and KWST, respectively); Jeff Franklin and Wally Meyrowitz from ATI; and act managers Roy Silver (Fanny) and David Joseph (the Hudson Brothers and Angel). Many others were invited but either couldn't afford the trip or couldn't get away during the Thanksgiving weekend.

The idea to have the wedding on the Saturday following Thanksgiving was mine. The compulsion to devote attention twenty-four/seven to Casablanca was all but part of my DNA at that point, and having the wedding on Thanksgiving weekend meant that I would not miss any work. In fact, from the time Casablanca was formed until I got married, I do not remember ever doing anything that was not work related—unless it had to do with women, and even then I often blended work into the equation. Even my relationship with Candy had fallen under that umbrella, as we shared the Casablanca gig.

Neil was the best man, and Candy's maid of honor was her sister, Christy, who I later found out had told Candy not to marry me. Christy wasn't alone in that regard: Neil's young daughter, Jill (about six or seven at the time), had gone into the room where Candy was getting ready and said to her, "You can't marry Larry. My daddy is going to," which underscores how close Neil and I were. For the ceremony, I was dressed in a rust-colored suit, and Candy wore a flowing gown, though it had no train to speak of. The guests were dressed in an assortment of styles, from formal to casual. There were even a few people in jeans.

The ceremony took place in the main house, with a justice of the peace presiding (Candy was not Jewish). The reception was held outside in the pool and cabana area, and it was catered by an older African American woman to whom Neil was very loyal; he always hired her to do our parties and events. The pool was left uncovered, although we had entertained the idea of covering it and using it as a dance floor. A tent had been erected over much of the reception area, and there were video games inside (Neil and I loved the things). Space heaters were placed through most of the outdoor dining area; even in LA it can get chilly in November. Jerry Sharell, our old friend from the Buddah days, sang Cole Porter's "So in Love," with Neil accompanying him. I thought the wedding was fantastic.

Candy had a completely different take. When she first joined the company she had expressed her dislike for Neil. He was very smooth, and most people found his perpetual enthusiasm enjoyable, even contagious. I was sure Candy would grow to love him like I did once she really got to know him. Was I ever wrong. She was (and is) very down-to-earth and had trouble dealing with people who fawned over the latest hip styles and fads. Despite my efforts to point out his good qualities, and Neil's own attempts to curry her favor, Candy never warmed to him, his style, or his methods. She and I would fight about it, because she was reluctant to hang out with Neil and Joyce.

I tried for a long time to broker some sort of peace between Candy and Neil. I knew that the key to this was getting Candy to go along with the program Neil believed in—that is, she should never utter a negative thought (although this was just about impossible for her), and she should express complete faith in his decisions. After a year of playing Henry Kissinger, I resigned myself to the fact that the best I would achieve was some fragile level of civility.

Not long after the wedding, we moved into a modest house in Studio City, which had once been owned by Bud Abbott. The house was small, with only two bedrooms, but it had a huge pool and a guesthouse. The walls in one room were paneled, or at least they seemed to be. I had assumed that the paneling was wood until I looked closer and saw that the knotty pine texture had been painted on. Asking around, I found out that the faux paneling had come courtesy of the art department at Universal Studios.

While the KISS and Donna Summer albums were certainly garnering most of our attention, they weren't our only ongoing projects. Two of our other acts, Buddy Miles and Hugh Masekela, had also issued albums, and they were selling well. These two releases and the KISS album combined to give us two million-dollar months: September and October 1975. This was the first time we'd risen to the seven-figure plateau, and the fact that it was in consecutive months made it seem less like an accident and more like a trend. Or so we told ourselves.

Angel, whom we had signed in the spring, had completed their debut album after forty-five days of recording with producer Derek Lawrence, of Deep Purple fame. I was pleasantly surprised at the result—a hard-edged blend of progressive melodic rock. We were all bullish on the band, and despite the fact that their sparkling appearance was the antithesis of KISS's, we planned on using the KISS blueprint to break them: we'd marry frequent albums with nonstop (and flamboyant) concerts and hope that something would stick. We had released Angel's debut effort on October 27, and just before Thanksgiving they were in Chicago for the start of the tour to support the album. They were scheduled to kick things off as an opening act for Robin Trower at the Aragon Ballroom.

The show was plagued with production problems from the start. Angel's crew was not yet comfortable with the setup process for the stage show, and, in the tight confines of the Aragon (an old 1920s dance hall), this delayed the show's start time quite a bit. Jerry Michaelson, owner of Jam Productions, was steamed, and he went backstage to pull the plug on Angel while they were still playing their set. Angel's tour manager, Bill Schereck, stepped between Jerry and the power source, and the two argued for a few minutes. Bill lost the battle but won the war: he'd delayed Michaelson long enough for Angel to finish their set. With that crisis averted, Schereck took the crew to Akron, Ohio, where he rented a theater and organized what amounted to a tour boot camp. He had the crew run through the show setup again and again and again, timing their efforts until everything was to his satisfaction. Then he had everyone switch positions and learn the process again, so that the entire crew knew one another's jobs. They hated him for it, but it worked; by the time they were finished, they were one of the most efficient crews touring.

Our final album of 1975 was Parliament's *Mothership Connection*. Unlike our other artists, Parliament never seemed to need our help: they just needed our money. The band's driving force, George Clinton, may have been the most musically creative person Casablanca ever signed, and he was never at a loss for wildly out-there ideas. He had, through sheer force of will, carved out a niche unto himself, and his output was all so uniquely Parliament that it may as well have been trademarked.

- September 26, 1975: *The Rocky Horror Picture Show* premieres in US theaters.
- October 11, 1975: *Saturday Night Live* debuts on NBC-TV with George Carlin as host.
- December 25, 1975: Queen's epic song "Bohemian Rhapsody" goes to No. 1 on the UK singles charts.

Between KISS and Parliament, we had the two most absurd acts in the business, and they were both just so ridiculously entertaining to watch.

Parliament's first two albums for us, *Up for the Down Stroke* and *Chocolate City*, had done well, but not spectacularly well. The group had a highly loyal following, but it wasn't enough to sustain an album; it just provided a nice sales surge upon release. With so much of our attention focused on advancing KISS, as well as on pushing the Angel, Buddy Miles, Hugh Masekela, and Donna Summer albums forward, it was somewhat of a relief to us that Parliament was propelled by its own creative power. We never had to light a fire under George—a joint, yes, but not a fire.

It's hard for me to distinguish one Parliament album from another, because they all left me with nothing to say but "What?" and "Wow!"

However, if there was a musical pinnacle to Parliament's career, I'd say that *Mothership Connection* was it. How can you not love an album with song titles like "Night of the Thumpasorus Peoples" and "Supergroovalistic-prosifunkstication"? George and his assembled funksters, including the legendary Bootsy Collins, had crafted a unique and completely mad masterpiece, and its impact over the years has never ceased to astound me. Current artists, especially hip-hop and rap ones, are still influenced by it. Dr. Dre, for instance, sampled "P-Funk (Wants to Get Funked Up)" and the title track on one of his CDs in the 1990s.

George was certainly an integral part of the black music community, but he was also into a host of other things that usually aren't associated with black culture. For instance, he was a huge fan of *Star Trek*, and this led him to create a cover for *Mothership Connection* that looked like Huggy Bear flies the Starship Enterprise: it featured a pimp in a spaceship. George was something else. He had an imaginative way, to paraphrase George himself, of putting black people in situations that were new. I'll stop short of calling him an out-and-out activist (he always seemed to be more interested in having fun than in political saber rattling), but he definitely broke down stereotypes with every move he made.

Our Sherbourne offices had never been designed to house more than six or seven people, but, with the staff we'd hired over the past twelve months, we were now sitting on top of one another. Offices that had once been for the private use of Cecil, Buck, or me were now home to four people. Most of us were sharing desks, if not chairs and phones. Never one to think small, Neil had found space for us at 8255 Sunset Boulevard. Not only had he bought the building, but he had also purchased the entire block. He had put together a small investment group, and with the help of Richard Trugman's close banking relationships and his own good credit, he'd raised enough money to buy the block as a real estate investment. He offered me the opportunity to join the group. I appreciated the invitation, but I declined because I couldn't afford it.

One perk of owning this block of offices was that it came with its own billboard overlooking Sunset, and we made good use of it. Each month, we would promote another artist with it, and soon those who thought they had the clout were angling to get the billboard for their new product. This led to some heated arguments with artists over whose album was going to be hanging over the Sunset Strip that month. We'd defuse these blowouts with a bullshit excuse: an artist had to sell over half a million units to be on the billboard. This was totally arbitrary. Anyone who was paying attention would have noticed that any number of our pet projects, all of which had sold very little, ended up on the billboard. We would do everything we could to make sure Hollywood knew we were big players.

To decorate the new digs, Neil hired Carol Eisenberg and Lynda Guber. They were both into the LA scene, and both had husbands in the motion picture and television businesses. "Ah, there's the rub," I thought: this wasn't as much about decorating as it was about networking with players. In Hollywood, the motion picture business is king, and the music business is a distant tenth on the list. Even though the music business generated double or triple the revenue of the motion picture business, it just doesn't have the same prestige, and it never will. Neil was friends with Lynda Guber's husband, Peter, who had a five-picture deal with Columbia and was a major Hollywood power broker. But the ladies were the decorators from Hell. Everything with them was "fabulous" this and "fabulous" that—it was like dealing with Zsa Zsa Gabor, dahling. They had a certain Hollywood flair that no one but Neil enjoyed, but we lived through it.

Hollywood operated according to some strange mathematics. The bigger your office, and the more important people thought you were, and the harder you were to reach, the more power everyone assumed you had. Being from New York, we tried not to fall into this Hollywood mentality, and we developed (in truth, stole) this line to live by: "Assumption is the mother of all fuckups." It's hard not to make assumptions based on appearances, but we did try.

I had the same interest in office decor as I had in fashion, which is to say none. I couldn't have been more indifferent to what my office looked like. I just needed a phone to call radio and retail, and a turntable and cassette player to listen to albums or demos, and I was a happy puppy. I wound up with an office furnished with a couple of cane chairs and large desk that had cane embellishments along its edges. I guess it looked good, but the decoration made it difficult to write on the desk top unless you used a thick pad.

The decoration scheme was, yet again, Moroccan. Where was the creativity in that? There were pillows, cane, and bamboo everywhere. Buck and I had similar rooms on the second floor. Cecil was on the other side of the floor from us in a little suite of offices that he shared with his secretary, Fran. He also had on his staff Renny Roker, who came from a very talented family. His cousin was Al Roker, and the late Roxie Roker (of *The Jeffersons* fame), was his sister. Renny was a robust guy, much like Al, and he would pester Cecil to demand more for their department. In the long run, his passion was a good influence, even if his constant requests were a pain in the ass.

Neil's office was also on the second floor. It took up half the front of the building. It had a bar (though it was never really used as one), faux-stucco walls, a large desk, and a huge conference table (it could seat about twenty people), all with bamboo accents. But the thing that immediately drew your attention upon entering the office was the speakers. They were enormous—maybe five feet by four feet—and they were as loud as they were big. In a Moroccan-style armoire, Neil kept his stereo equipment: record player, reel-to-reel tape deck (a big one), amplifier (the biggest), cassette player, receiver, TV, Beta video player, and professional three-quarter-inch video player. Neil would frequently change his office decorations just to impress visitors. He'd swap the artwork out, or he'd put up funny signs, like "All bad news is due by 4:00 p.m. tomorrow." Anything to make a positive impression. He had a separate office for his secretary, as well as a waiting area, complete with a table, chairs, and a white canvas couch.

Adjacent to Neil's office was another large room. The two rooms were linked by an adjoining door. The question was: Whose office would it be? Neil, impressed with the job I was doing, decided to give me the adjoining office and make me executive vice president. He had initially offered the job to Jerry Sharell, but Jerry declined. He wanted to stay where he was, at Elektra. I was happy to be the beneficiary of Jerry's decision. I actually had my choice of titles, and I chose to be called "senior vice president," not knowing that "executive vice president" was a more prestigious title—but, what the hell, everyone knew what I did, and the title meant little. I moved into the big office and had the same sound system as Neil's—an exact duplicate—installed. This was living.

I was running all the day-to-day operations of the company except accounting and legal. Trugman, who'd joined us after he helped close the Carson deal and found someone to lend us money after we left Warner, was running legal. Neil was overseeing the accounting department (which was run by our controller, David Powell), as it seemed that every day there was another major cash flow problem. Even though Trugman was ostensibly running the legal department, nothing was done without Neil's approval—especially anything to do with artist contract negotiations. Neil was thus able to use Trugman to help him play a good-guy/bad-guy routine for managers and attorneys.

Neil and I controlled the outer doors of our internally joined offices with buzzers under our desks. Most of the senior management staff would eventually have similar devices installed. Often, Neil and I would get so messed up on Quaaludes in the middle of the afternoon that we'd both take naps in my office. The corner of the office had been taken over by a couch, massive mirrors, and tons of throw pillows courtesy of our delirious decorating team. Neil usually crashed on the couch, while I'd grab half a dozen pillows and create a makeshift bed on the floor. When we wanted to get high, we would go into my office and close the door; we'd go back into Neil's office for meetings. We thought we were fooling the entire staff. Of course, everyone knew. They could smell the grass on our clothes, hair, and breath, but we thought we were really putting something over on them. I'm sure the smell coming out of my office was responsible for more of the legendry surrounding Casablanca's drug use than anything else. It probably didn't help that Neil and I both loved to run the air conditioners in our offices at arctic levels, circulating the smoke throughout the entire building.

I don't believe that we at Casablanca did more drugs than people at any other company. The difference was that at Casablanca, the executives (except for Cecil), not just the employees, did the drugs. In the 1970s, everyone seemed to be doing drugs of some kind. For instance, in his autobiography, Walter Cronkite mentions that after CBS sold their record division to Sony and no longer occupied a few floors at Black Rock (CBS headquarters in New York), the one thing that changed for the better was that he could enter an elevator without fear of getting a contact high.

I had a very seedy drug dealer in LA who had the worst complexion you could imagine. His name was Tom, but I nicknamed him Pockface. He would come to the office with three or four kinds of pot for me to choose from. There was Panamanian red, Hawaiian gold, Mexican, Thai sticks, and sometimes hashish. Quaaludes or cocaine—whatever you needed, he could deliver. He would come to see me at the office maybe once a week or once every two weeks. Selling drugs out of the office was never OK, but acquiring them for others at the going rate was just fine. I was brought up in the drug culture, so I knew that you did not try to make a profit on others. If you could help someone out by giving something to them for the price you paid, then you did it.

Tom would bring bottles and bottles of Quaaludes. There were usually five hundred pills per bottle, and the cost was only twenty-five cents per pill. We went through them like they were M&Ms—not just me, but Neil as well. I recall that one evening a dozen or so of us were celebrating something in a private room at the Palm restaurant in LA when someone mentioned Quaaludes. No one had any on them. Neil fished around in his pockets and brought out a set of keys. "Someone drive over to my house and go into my closet. In the inside pocket of my brown suit you'll find a big bag of 'ludes." With Howie Rosen, one of our promotions guys, I drove over to Neil's house and rummaged through the bedroom looking for the brown suit. When we finally found it, I stuck my hand into the pocket and pulled out a gallon baggie filled with 'ludes. Everyone floated out of the Palm that night.

I collected dozens of empty bottles and proudly displayed them at my house, like a kid lining up his Matchbox cars to show to his friends. Quaaludes were eventually outlawed, and the price jumped to one dollar, five dollars, even ten dollars a pill. An ounce of really good pot was maybe $350. It all went down on the expense reports. An ounce of weed was steaks and a nice Bordeaux with Alison Steele. A bottle of 'ludes was surf and turf at Roy's with the sales department.

Blow put me to sleep, and Quaaludes made me want to stay up and talk, which is the opposite of what these drugs do to most people. Same with Neil. He did not smoke as much grass during office hours as I did. I started smoking most days after lunch. I kept the 'ludes and grass in an unlocked drawer in my office. Just about anyone could go to the desk when I was not there and take what they needed. The atmosphere at Casablanca was open and loose, and I usually left my office door unlocked and open unless I was in there stoned, taking a nap, or doing drugs with a visitor.

Despite the prevalence of drug use in the office, to my knowledge we never sold drugs to people or used them to buy airplay. We did invite radio people or artists to join us while we did drugs, but we did not exchange drugs for spins. While I say that, I do admit that I would have given drugs for airplay if Neil—or, for that matter, a DJ—had asked me to. But the fact that we simply did drugs instead of selling them alleviated any worries we might have had that the cops or feds would come crashing through the door and bust us for possession. Actually, we never thought about it. Bankers were doing it with us. Lawyers were doing it with us. Even doctors. In those days, it was expected. It was very much a part of everyday life in our world.

The only time I worried about the police was when I went to the acupuncturist. Sounds weird, but, believe it or not, acupuncture was then against the law. The acupuncture therapist we used had a house in Laurel Canyon that was fifty steps above the street. These steps were on what seemed like a seventy-degree incline, and I nearly had a heart attack every time I had to climb them. Bobby Klein was the acupuncturist's name, and he had been recommended to us by Evelyn Ostin, Mo's wife. (Before taking up acupuncture, Bobby had been an album cover photographer, and he may have met the Ostins via that pursuit.) He had a guru-ish way about him. His house was open plan, incense burned everywhere, and bees buzzed around inside, but they'd never sting you. Bobby was a very calming influence. During the sessions, he'd stop every fifteen minutes, walk over to a window, and look down at the street to see if the cops were there. He was very paranoid about it, and the paranoia soon rubbed off on me.

But when it came to drugs, I never worried, because I figured everyone was doing it. There was safety in numbers. I even did drugs in front of Alison Steele's husband, who was an assistant district attorney in New York. He didn't join me, of course, and neither did she, but this just goes to show how accepted and commonplace drug use was.

While pot, hash, 'ludes, and coke were prevalent, we steered clear of the really heavy stuff. I tried mushrooms once, and they did nothing for me. I never took acid, and I don't think Neil ever did either (except once, when Tom Donahue from KSAN-FM spiked the punch at a get-together), and we never did heroin. If anyone brought a needle within twelve feet of Neil, he'd start to sweat. I took him to my acupuncturist once because he had a problem with his knee. It was so bad that he'd be walking along, the joint would buckle, and he'd lose his balance and fall. Bobby started the treatment, and Neil screamed like a stuck pig. I was receiving treatments every week, and knew it didn't hurt anything like his level of screaming would suggest, so I told him to calm the fuck down. After the treatment, his knee didn't bother him again for months. But Neil never saw Bobby again.

As 1976 began, *Alive!* was selling faster than anything we'd ever released, and the Donna Summer album was not far behind. Parliament's *Mothership Connection* had also landed in stores, and it was exploding right out of the gate. Buddy Miles and Hugh Masekela still had some legs. This was all great news, right?

Not really. The sudden jump in sales began to cause some major problems for us. When we'd had no money—which was almost all the time until late 1975—we would pay the record manufacturing plants in credit to press our albums. Now we had used up so much credit with these plants that it was getting difficult to find one that would trust us enough to press the large quantities of albums we needed to keep up with consumer demand. The manufacturing plants were comfortable pressing twenty thousand units on credit for us; this wasn't that big of a risk for them. But half a million or a million units? No way—not gonna happen.

Neil got on the phone with the manufacturers and begged and cajoled them to extend us more credit. Only because of his personal relationship with many of the manufacturers and his unbelievable tenacity were we able to keep our product in the stores for the duration of the 1975 holiday season. Neil finally made a deal with an LA plant called Rainbow to extend us the credit we needed to fill our orders. Rainbow became our saviors, and I am sure they were happy they took the chance.

It felt awfully good to have hit product that was selling huge numbers, but our joy was eroded by the fact that we could be making so much more money. Had we been a large corporation with supporting infrastructure, like Warner or Capitol, we likely would have had twice the sales. We faced the worst problem a small company can have: too much success too soon. The public wanted our product, but we couldn't get it to them fast enough. Our distribution system was too small. It was imperative that we keep this a secret. If anyone found out, then our artists would go crazy on us and all of our creditors would demand that we bring our accounts current, thus forcing us out of business. Neil's approach was to spend every dollar that came through the door, but that meant that we couldn't build up enough cash to improve our infrastructure, which we desperately needed to do to keep pace with the exploding demand for our product. With each passing day, the pressure grew, and we inched closer and closer to bankruptcy.

12

Breakthrough

**A two-hundredth birthday party—New label—Buck
departs—Helming promotions—Gold and Platinum—Scott
Shannon—*Destroyer*—Rock Steady—Billy Squier—The
arrival of Glickman/Marks—Million-dollar contract—Lost
in England—Rosalie and "Beth"**

January 1976
Casablanca Records Offices
8255 Sunset Boulevard
Los Angeles, California

As 1976 opened, America began the yearlong celebration of its two-hundredth birthday. Sounds dull now, but it had a profound effect on business: bicentennial sales, bicentennial advertising and marketing plans, bicentennial special editions—it was everywhere. As for Casablanca, we were lagging 198 years behind, but that didn't stop us. We'd just moved into prime real estate on the Sunset Strip, and the fact that we were about to turn two seemed like a good reason to change our logo. More painting the building, you could say.

At Neil's behest, Chris Whorf drafted a few versions for us to look at, and after a couple of passes he hit upon the right look. The logo, literally just "Casablanca Records," remained faithful to David Byrd's original neon tube design, but the rest of the artwork had been completely overhauled. The dark-blue background, the white skyline of Morocco, and the Humphrey Bogart icon were gone, replaced by a more natural Moroccan scene with camels, a casbah, and palm trees in a palette of desert colors. The new artwork was completed early in the year, but we had only a few pending releases, so it didn't make its debut until May, for Angel's sophomore release—*Helluva Band*.

Just after the year began, Buck Reingold told me he was leaving. He'd been offered a position at Chelsea Records, a new company founded by

Wes Farrell. Wes had made a big splash with the Wes Farrell Organization, a music-publishing company famous for a string of hits in the late 1960s and early 1970s like "Hang on Sloopy" and "Knock Three Times." Buck told me that I should come with him, as Wes had far more pull in the industry than Neil (which was true) and I could make more money (also probably true). There was no way I was going to go anywhere with Buck, for numerous reasons, not least of which was that Neil was my mentor and I owed him everything.

Buck's relationship with Casablanca—and Neil, in particular—had been eroding for a long time. After Neil and Beth's marriage had crumbled, Buck started complaining about Neil spending company money on things like renting a house in Beverly Hills, and later buying a house in the equally affluent Holmby Hills. This house was a magnificent four-acre estate with a pool, a tennis court, ten-foot-high wrought-iron double gates, and a guesthouse the size of a normal family's main abode. Neil had purchased the house for about seven hundred and fifty thousand dollars, with the company footing the bill. Richard Trugman's brother, Marty, a big-deal Hollywood real estate agent, had found the property for Neil (nearly a decade later, it would sell for a reported $7.5 million). Buck felt that Neil was taking money right out of our pockets. I don't know what the hell Buck was thinking, because were it not for Neil, Buck would still be slinging hash. Plus, Neil had given up all his stock in Viewlex to launch Casablanca in the first place. He had taken tremendous personal and professional risks, and it was his reputation that would be ruined if things didn't work out. Neil was the one who'd gone to Vegas to get the payroll money. He was living this every hour of every day, and he was under more stress than all of us put together.

Buck made the same offer to Cecil, who also turned him down. The next day, he broke the news to Neil, who was livid that Buck had tried to take Cecil and me with him. Neil never allowed people to work through the standard two-weeks'-notice period, and Buck was gone within twenty-four hours, taking Nancy Sain, A.J. Cervantes, and Nancy Reingold with him. Nancy Reingold would return to us later that year, after she had divorced Buck.

Even though Buck was one of the original four musketeers—along with Neil, Cecil, and me—his departure was a great relief to everyone. Candy, in particular, was thrilled to be rid of him. Buck would often come up behind her and lick her neck as she sat at her desk, and I'm sure she wasn't the only victim of his stunts. We were all tiring of his shit, his boorish behavior, and the constant parade of sex partners he would bring into the building. He was loud and pushy and determined (all good qualities in a promotions man, to a degree), but he dressed like a redheaded, white pimp, and it was clear to everyone that he was a huckster with no real passion for, or understanding of, the business. Some radio station people liked him a lot because he supplied them with women and drugs and (possibly) money, but just as many would call Neil and ask him to ensure that they never saw Buck again. In the end, I think Buck was simply the wrong man for the times. Had it been the 1950s, his look and demeanor may have made him a big success. As it was, he had become an embarrassment to us.

With Buck gone, I had to run Top 40 promotion by myself. This was a big stretch, because it was so different from the FM progressive radio promotion I'd been focusing on. I had done Top 40 in my early days at Buddah, but it was never really my thing. My feeling was that if you loved the music and wanted it to change the world for the better in some way, FM progressive promotion was a much more effective road to travel. Becoming a successful promotions man is an intuitive process. It requires a keen feel for the marketplace and a sense of how to play a network of connections. I just didn't have the network or the name recognition in Top 40 to do the job well, nor did I know where all the bodies were buried, or who to pay off, or when. As good as I was with FM, I was wrong for this niche. I was able to hold it together for about ten minutes, but I knew I was kidding myself. The time was going to come when we had an important single to get played and I wouldn't be able to do it justice.

Fortunately, we had only four albums coming out in the first quarter of 1976. With no one to attend to promotion full time, not to mention our ongoing cash crunch, we were in no hurry to push any more releases forward, so we kept the pace slow. Both Hugh Masekela and Buddy Miles had issued follow-ups to their 1975 successes with us: Masekela released *Colonial Man* at the end of January, and Miles released *A Bicentennial Gathering of the Tribes* a month later (see, there's that bicentennial thing creeping in again). Margaret Singana, a South African musician, released an album with us on the same day Miles released his: February 24. And KISS, too, was working on a follow-up, a studio LP called *Destroyer* that

KISS during their August 1973 Casablanca audition at the Henry LeTang School of Dance in New York. (Eddie Solan)

KISS, sans makeup, outside the offices of *Creem* magazine in Southfield, Michigan, in June 1974. (Charlie Auringer)

Cecil Holmes, Curtis Mayfield, Neil Bogart, and Art Kass circa 1970. (Michael Ochs Archives/Getty Images)

Publicity Director Nancy Lewis and Larry Harris give George Burns a tour of the Buddah offices in 1973. (Collection of Larry Harris)

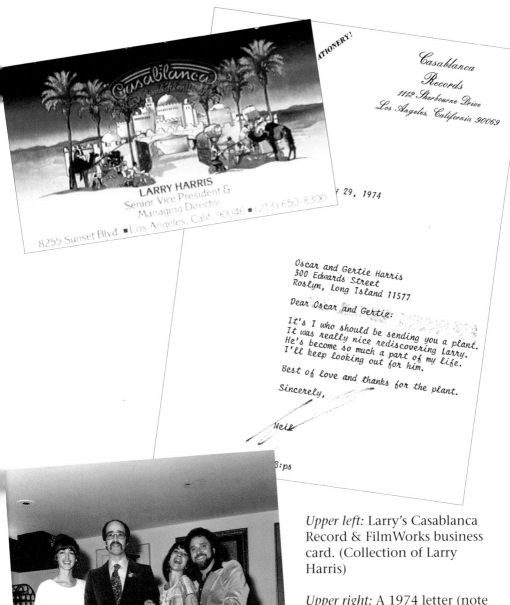

Casablanca
Records
1112 Sherbourne Drive
Los Angeles, California 90069

LARRY HARRIS
Senior Vice President &
Managing Director

8255 Sunset Blvd ▪ Los Angeles, Calif. 90046 ▪ (213) 650-8300

STATIONERY!

29, 1974

Oscar and Gertie Harris
300 Edwards Street
Roslyn, Long Island 11577

Dear Oscar and Gertie:

It's I who should be sending you a plant.
It was really nice rediscovering Larry.
He's become so much a part of my life.
I'll keep looking out for him.

Best of love and thanks for the plant.

Sincerely,

Neil

B:ps

Upper left: Larry's Casablanca Record & FilmWorks business card. (Collection of Larry Harris)

Upper right: A 1974 letter (note the early Casablanca stationery) from Neil Bogart to Larry's parents. (Collection of Larry Harris)

Left: Larry and Candy Harris getting married on November 29, 1975, at the Bogarts' residence. Earlier in the year, this same living room hosted the party where "Love to Love You Baby" was discovered. (Barry Levine)

Early Casablanca promo photo of Parliament from 1975. (Echoes/Redferns)

KISS driving them wild in New Jersey, during their first U.S. stadium show, on July 10, 1976. Less than three years earlier, they were a local club band. (Vintagekissphotos.com)

Larry Harris backstage with Gene Simmons moments before KISS recorded their *Alive!* album in Detroit, Michigan, on May 16, 1975. (Fin Costello/Redferns)

Trade publicity shot from Winter 1976–77 promoting Casablanca Records and Casablanca ArtWorks. *Left to right:* Donna Summer, Neil Bogart, and Donna's then-boyfriend Peter Mühldorfer. (Michael Ochs Archives/Getty Images)

Larry Harris onstage at Detroit's Cobo Arena on January 25, 1976, to present KISS with their first Platinum album, *Alive!* (Vintagekissphotos.com)

Neil Bogart onstage at the infamous Casablanca Records launch party, February 18, 1974, introducing KISS to the shell-shocked West Coast music industry. (Michael Ochs Archives/Getty Images)

Above: Neil in June 1977, hard at play in his office. (Brian Leatart)

Following page: Donna Summer onstage during the 1976 leg of the Love to Love You Baby promotional tour. (Fin Costello/Redferns)

we hoped would sell even a fraction as well as *Alive!*, which was still a runaway sensation.

Alive! had won Gold status in early December 1975, and we'd received the plaques marking this achievement soon afterwards. This was a first for KISS, and I don't know who was more thrilled—us or the band. It was our first legitimate Gold record, too; Carson's album had technically qualified for that status, but I don't think there was a soul alive who didn't know that was a sham. KISS was on the road when the plaques arrived at the office. (When weren't they on the road?) To surprise them, I flew to New York on New Year's Eve and went to Nassau Veterans Memorial Coliseum, the big arena out on Long Island, where the band was playing. Just prior to the show, I gave them the awards backstage, and we made a little photo-op of the impromptu event.

A matter of weeks later, the album passed the one-million mark for units sold. Again, it was a first for KISS and us. The RIAA, the industry association responsible for tracking sales and handing out awards, had created a Platinum award at the beginning of the year for albums that had sold one million units. Prior to that, no matter how many units you'd sold, you would

- **January 21, 1976: The first commercial Concorde flight takes off.**
- **April 1, 1976: Stephen Wozniak and Steven Jobs found Apple Computer.**
- **April 23, 1976: The Ramones release their first album.**

never get anything other than a Gold award. So, it seemed that *Alive!* would be our first Platinum album. However, the new award was not retroactive: it only applied to albums released after January 1, 1976. There was no way Neil was going to let the occasion go unheralded just because of some arbitrary RIAA rule, so we had Platinum awards made up and I again flew out to a gig, this time at Cobo, in Detroit, on January 27. We made a big event of it. I arranged with KISS's road manager, J.R. Smalling, to present the awards onstage just before the group did their encores. The record industry was often a glamorous gig for me, even just sitting behind a desk in the office bullshitting with distributors or artists could be a rush, but there's nothing quite like walking onstage in front of twelve thousand screaming people and a battery of spotlights to raise your heart rate. The event was an even bigger thrill for me than it was for the band. I left the stage with the most intense high I'd ever experienced. No matter what drugs I'd experimented with in the past, none of them ever had that effect on me. Kinda makes you understand why people become entertainers.

Being head of promotions can be fun, but to pull it off you need to be a full-timer, not a pinch hitter. We needed a permanent replacement for Buck, and I took it upon myself to find him. In early February, I was browsing through one of the many trade publications that came my way each week when by chance I read that Scott Shannon, a fairly influential Nashville program director, had been let go. I knew Scott reasonably well. He had been heavily involved in getting the kissing contest promotion off the ground back in the spring of 1974, and Buck had maintained our relationship with him. Scott helped promote our product and got it on the air whenever he could. I had met him a few times through Buck and was impressed by his line of bullshit, so I gave him a call, and, with Neil's blessing, I offered him the job of director of promotion. It wasn't a tough sell. Scott was working promotions at an influential industry publication called *Radio & Records*, which to me sounded like a fill-in-the-gap gig. I offered him double the salary he'd made as a PD, an unlimited expense account, and a Mercedes convertible. He gladly accepted, and we had our man.

I was thrilled to have Scott on board. He brought something to the table that I could not: solid relationships with PDs nationwide. Scott had been in radio for a long time, mostly in the South. He'd had great success in places like Mobile, Memphis, Nashville, and Atlanta, often increasing ratings for his stations. The name Scott Shannon carried some weight in radio circles and beyond. The other program directors in Top 40 radio knew him by reputation, if not personally, and they took his calls, which was not always the case when I rang them. He was smart and ambitious, but he was still out of his element somewhat, and Neil and I provided him with extra support during his first months on the job. I called in favors from a couple of our distributor reps—namely, Brian Interland and Bruce Bird (both of whom we'd hire before long). I asked them to help Scott in whatever way they could. It was a great hire for us and for Scott, and within a matter of months, he would play an integral role in cementing KISS's superstar status.

KISS, in the meantime, had completed *Destroyer*, and we were ramping up for a mid-March release. The record was an ambitious project for the band. It was produced by Bob Ezrin, who was in his mid-twenties and already renowned for his successes with Lou Reed and Alice Cooper; later in the decade, his work with Pink Floyd on *The Wall* would push him into the pantheon of elite producers. *Destroyer* showcased a grand level of production and musical arrangement. It was far more nuanced and complex than anything KISS had ever done. We sent the initial single, "Shout It Out Loud," to radio stations and stores at the beginning of March, and it received good airplay in some markets. Despite some pans from critics (including our friends at *Creem*), the album sold well, but not as well as we'd hoped—which is to say that it wasn't doing *Alive!*-like numbers. A second single, "Flaming Youth," followed at the end of April, and it was one of only a handful of singles we'd ever issue that featured a picture sleeve.

May was a tremendously hectic month for KISS—even more hectic than usual. First, they took their nonstop touring brigade to Europe for their debut performances overseas. Aucoin had attempted to book them in Europe in the fall of 1975, but he hadn't managed to solidify an itinerary. We were eager to see it happen, as it gave us the opportunity to do copromotes with our overseas affiliates. While KISS was on the verge of becoming a superstar band in the US, European fans, especially those in the UK, looked upon them as a curiosity. Only in Sweden had a substantial fan base developed, and there would be some major stumbling blocks for us to overcome as we attempted to repeat KISS's domestic success in the European market. West Germany, for instance, refused to let the band use their trademark logo because the double lightning bolt "S" in their name bore a striking similarity to the Nazi SS insignia. Oddly enough, this wasn't even a German law, but rather an edict issued by the Allies at the end of World War II. We finally worked it out by changing the logo slightly. The other factor that slowed our development efforts in Europe was that the distributors and licensees with whom we had a loose association all hated one another, so there was little cooperation going on. This is another instance in which having the clout of a major label would have been beneficial.

The international music business was not something we could ever grasp. In some markets, we had great distributors who would go out of their way to make things happen; in others, it was one fiasco after another, and nothing got done. Neil never cared very much about the international market anyway. He was happy to get the cash advances, and anything else was gravy. He'd never seen much international money at Buddah—why should things be different at Casablanca? As it turned out, the worldwide success of Donna Summer, KISS, and, to a lesser degree, Parliament would change Neil's tune and our fortunes.

Things were similarly unsettled for KISS in terms of business infrastructure. Bill Aucoin had split his management company in two, retaining Rock Steady and opening AMI (Aucoin Management Incorporated), which was headquartered in a dazzling Madison Avenue high-rise. Bill's confidence had reached new heights with the success of KISS, and he began to look for other artists to sign. One of those he signed was a singer named Billy Squier, whose girlfriend was Maxanne Sartori, a DJ on WBCN radio in Boston. Maxanne was about the only person there who would play KISS. Because of this, I had introduced her to Bill Aucoin, and Maxanne, in turn, had introduced Aucoin to Billy Squier. The two got along very well, and it wasn't long before Aucoin was managing Squier. Bill offered us Squier, but we thought it better not to have all of Aucoin's eggs in our basket and also wondered what KISS would think if Casablanca had another Aucoin act. We passed on inking Squier, mostly because we were leery of getting involved with someone Aucoin was having a personal relationship with, and we were under the impression he was *with* Billy in a physical sense—Aucoin was and is openly gay. Aucoin eventually signed Squier to Capitol Records, where he had several hits.

While KISS had always been very loyal to Aucoin, they were troubled that they were selling concert tickets and albums as fast as they could be printed, but there was still no money to be had. Part of this, or most of it, could be ascribed to the fact that the money they made was funneled back into touring, which was an expensive undertaking, considering how elaborate their production demands were. Still, KISS felt that their money could be better managed. So, in May 1976, they hired Glickman/ Marks Management as their business managers. Carl Glickman was a big real estate tycoon out of Cleveland, and Howard Marks was an advertising guy in New York. Aucoin had known Marks for years, as Bill's old company, Direction Plus, had produced commercials for Howard Marks Advertising. I found the hiring somewhat odd, as Carl and Howard were both way past understanding rock and roll: Marks was forty-seven, and Glickman was fifty.

We soon found ourselves on the receiving end of a demand for a new record contract. Keep in mind that one of Neil's greatest fears was that we would lose a band and then see them have a hit with someone else. Neil loved music, and he loved success, but he had an obsessive, abject fear of failure. For him, the style of the music was largely irrelevant; if it was good, he liked it, no matter what the genre, and he was usually excellent at second-guessing the public. But the fear of losing out on the opportunity for a hit consumed him. It had happened with Melanie. After she left Buddah, she had a big hit with "Brand New Key," and Neil felt that this reflected badly on him—he had worked so hard for her, and he'd committed so many resources to making her a star. Numerous people in the record biz later told me that Neil had made a Herculean effort on behalf of Melanie's career and that for a while her name seemed to be the only thing coming out of his mouth. I thought that Neil had taken the entire thing far too personally. I subscribed to the shit-happens school of thought. My take was that Melanie had had the right song at the right time, and she'd never had another. It was no one's fault. Neil's fear was something I could not understand, and it would be the source of several arguments between us over the years.

KISS was big enough to be a very attractive jewel for a major record company to add to its crown, and the band could easily have left Casablanca for a more lucrative domain—Capitol, Warner, or any of the other big houses. To their credit, and to our relief, they decided to stay with us. I'd like to think it was partly out of loyalty, but an important motivation was the fact that even if they signed with another label, Casablanca would retain control of their back catalog, and that made them uncomfortable. Additionally, they still believed in Neil and his ability to market them better than anyone else. Their contracts always contained a clause citing Neil as the key man. This meant that if the company was ever bought, or if anything ever happened to Neil, they were free to do what they wanted. We were going to pay through the nose to keep them, and it would be one of the main reasons for Casablanca's downfall.

The contract Glickman/Marks brought to us called for half a million dollars per album as an advance, and another half million for advertising. A million dollars per album! In 1976, this was a ton of money for any band, though the ratio between advance money and advertising was perfectly reasonable. The cash outlay for advertising would help us as well as them, but seeing the price tag on paper nearly made us choke. Again, if they had trusted us, we would have spent the money anyway, but they didn't, and they had decided to take control of their own destiny. Marks's advertising agency had almost complete discretion as to how that advertising money was spent; the only fail-safe was that we had to mutually agree to all expenditures. But, in the end, while I would argue with them about certain points, they would usually prevail because they were the so-called advertising experts. I took to reminding myself that we had other things to do, and we couldn't concentrate all our energies on one group. I won a few battles, but as time went on, I began to pay less and less attention to the hundred-page advertising schedules they sent me. Marks's firm was to receive the typical agency commission on advertising: 15 percent of gross. This translated into a guaranteed minimum of seventy-five thousand for Glickman/Marks's advertising agency fee, plus their fee for acting as KISS's business managers. Aucoin was still their manager, as well, and his fee was 25 percent, so the total of fees incurred by the band was significant.

We knew that KISS would eventually become so big that they would sell at least two to three million units each time out. Cutting a deal for one million dollars per album was therefore not out of the question. The band deserved the money, and we knew that with the strong fan base they had cultivated, they would be selling large amounts of product for years to come.

Glickman/Marks got so heavily into the band's finances and advertising that Casablanca became almost superfluous to the operation, simply handling sales and a minor bit of promotion. We were used to being involved in planning tours and controlling the press. Now we would step back and let the new KISS organization do the work, unless they interfered with our plans, and then a fight would develop. We were on the brink of getting a KISS single on few major stations when things suddenly fell apart because the KISS promotion team had butted in and ruined everything we'd set up. The KISS promo guys—they actually worked directly for Aucoin—had offered a concert exclusive to a rival station without consulting us. Neil hit the ceiling when he found out. We were all frustrated, because we felt like we were dealing with amateurs.

But there was an upside to this situation. With the growth of the company, and with all the other major artists we were developing (like Donna Summer and Parliament), it was probably better that we had less to do for KISS. While it would have been nice to use the celebrity of the band we'd worked so hard to establish to boost other up-and-coming artists, KISS was not about to let that happen. Neil and Joyce (who very quietly married on May 28, in an extremely atypical ultra-low-profile Justice of the Peace ceremony, which none of us fellow Casablanca people attended) did maintain their strong personal relationship with Howard Marks, and he and I always got along great. So the communication between the company and group improved, and soon it was running very smoothly.

For both political and practical reasons, we began to hire Howard Marks Advertising to do campaigns for other acts. We had them place advertising for Donna Summer and Parliament product and tours; they also took on various projects that we did not feel we could develop properly without using a full-service advertising agency. In any case, keeping Howard Marks happy was a strategy that we had come up with to keep KISS grief to a minimum. If we could convince Howard that his fortunes lay with us as much as they did with KISS, then he would be more amenable to working with us as partners on equal footing. We grew closer to Howard and one of his execs, Rosanne Shelnutt, through all the contact we had with them. With these deals, I paid very close attention to the agency's advertising buys, and I often asked that buys be changed to reflect our approach to marketing many of our artists, not just KISS.

As the dust was settling from Glickman/Marks's arrival on the scene, KISS left for Europe. They headed to England first. Wally Meyrowitz (who was still KISS's booking agent at ATI) and his wife, Lorie, along with me and Candy, made the trip to London. The band was scheduled to rehearse for a few days at Shepperton Studios in Surrey, just outside the city. After rehearsals concluded, the entire contingent trekked to Manchester for the first show of the tour. Following the concert, Wally, Lorie, Candy, and I headed back to London, while the rest of the group moved on to Birmingham. With no one to guide us, we quickly got lost. After wandering around for a while, we made our way to a railway station, and Wally spotted a train that we thought might be headed back to London. The train had already begun to pull out of the station, so we ran after it and leapt aboard like a group of vagabonds. We landed in what looked like a cattle car—no seats, no tickets required. We rode the train for what seemed like hours before finally arriving in London. At the time, the terror campaign of the Irish Republican Army was particularly active, and people were paranoid about suspicious-looking strangers; we got back to our hotel so late and looking so disheveled that we were subjected to a strict and very thorough search before we were allowed to enter.

The response to KISS's European tour was hit and miss. Worse, as far as we were concerned, *Destroyer* was not maintaining the tremendous momentum established by *Alive!* Not a good sign. Neil and I knew that failing to recapture the kind of hype and sales that *Alive!* had generated could lead to the band being labeled with three words we avoided like the plague: one...hit...wonder.

Upon returning from Europe, the band immediately geared up for another tour of North America. They would have new costumes and a completely new stage show. Glickman/Marks was turning this into a business and had hired the Jules Fischer Organization (whose experience ran toward Broadway shows) to design and manufacture a new set and production.

Much like Casablanca, KISS seemed to be operating without a budget—their only constraint was the limits of their imagination. Taking their cue from the *Alive!* liner notes (the first purposeful attempt to highlight the band mates' individual personas) and the *Destroyer* cover's postapocalyptic landscape, Jules Fischer drafted a set and production that was astonishing in its excess. Flights of stairs flanked the drum riser, which was guarded by two green-eyed demonic cats and rose more than twenty feet in the air at the show's end, unfurling an enormous cat-adorned tapestry in its wake. On stage left, another flight of stairs led up to something called the Moon Garden (in keeping with Ace Frehley's Spaceman character). On stage right, Gene Simmons's demon profile had its own platform, which held a structure of decaying bricks like an iconic castle from the old Hammer horror films and a towering bloody stake that rose behind the bassist during his now infamous blood-spitting routine.

The backline of speaker cabinets was decorated with pieces of a cityscape (again from the *Destroyer* cover), which fell off on cue. There was also a prop that looked like a desiccated tree, which didn't bear a resemblance to anything the band had done. It just sat there and looked strange. Above the stage were three huge lighting rigs designed to look like red-white-and-blue lightning bolts (you couldn't escape the bicentennial), and the main lighting rigs were constructed to look like high-tension electrical towers. Behind the drum kit was an oversized Van der Graff generator that shot out enormous arcs of electricity. In a set replete with all sorts of dangers, this forty-five-year-old prop trumped them all (it had been made for the 1931 film *Frankenstein*), and I can't imagine that Peter Criss was fond of sitting a few feet away from a rickety movie prop that shot out that kind of amperage. Even the stage floor and the band's front stage monitors were decorated. At one point, the idea of crashing a car onstage had been discussed. Too bad that never happened—I was looking forward to working over Ford, Chrysler, and GM for the rights to give us free cars to destroy every night.

By July, Neil and I knew that we needed to increase *Destroyer*'s sales. KISS was already touring, so that avenue of promotion was covered. We released *The Originals* on July 21, a multi-album set of KISS's first three albums, in the hope of exploiting the exposure *Alive!* had given us to revitalize KISS's back catalog. While the repackaging did well on its own, eventually reaching Gold status, it did nothing to boost *Destroyer*'s middling sales.

Another single seemed like our best option. The obvious choice was "Detroit Rock City," the album's hard-rocking opening number. The reason we chose this song was twofold. KISS was big in Detroit, and we would get an airplay assist from the AOR stations in the market. The other reason was Rosalie Trombley and CKLW. CKLW was a fifty-thousand-watt powerhouse AM station located across the river from Detroit in Windsor, Ontario, Canada. We knew that Rosalie had liked KISS back when Buck was pushing the group on her. When KISS had first played Cobo Arena, in May 1975, we'd brought Rosalie in for the show. Buck had picked her up in a limo, presented her with a dozen roses, taken her across the border to a fancy Detroit restaurant, and brought her backstage to meet the band. KISS, being forewarned about the visit, treated Rosalie like royalty. One of the things KISS (Gene, in particular) was good at was making someone feel comfortable, especially if it helped the band.

Scott Shannon made a special effort to get Rosalie an advance copy of "Detroit Rock City" and asked her to give us her opinion of it. We knew that if she liked the song and made a commitment to play it, then we would be well ahead of the game. After Scott had heard from Rosalie, he came into my office. His complexion was ashen and he was very subdued. Rosalie, he told me, did not like "Detroit Rock City." She liked the B side, "Beth." I immediately understood Scott's reaction.

You see, Neil hated "Beth." Months earlier, in February, when KISS and Bob Ezrin had first played *Destroyer* for us, Neil's divorce from Beth was just being finalized. His emotions were raw, and his wounds were reopened every time he had to speak with an attorney about the situation, which was often. Hearing "Beth" (cowritten and sung by Peter Criss), he jumped to the conclusion that the band was making fun of him by writing a song about his ex-wife. He blurted out that the song would never be a single, and he promised to bury it as a B side. It didn't matter that Peter explained to everyone that the song was about his own wife, Lydia; when he couldn't find anything to rhyme with "Lydia," he'd switched to "Beth." (The true story, related to me years later, was that "Beth" was originally titled "Beck," and it had been written long before KISS was formed, not for Lydia, but for Becky, the nagging girlfriend of one of Peter's previous band mates.)

Still fairly new to the company, Scott was afraid of what Neil might do or say to him when he told him about Rosalie's reaction. Neil was on vacation in Acapulco and unreachable that day, so I had to make the decision. I had Scott tell Rosalie that we would back her up if she played "Beth," and that I would take the heat from Neil for changing the sides. From that point on, "Beth" was the single's A side and "Detroit Rock City" was its B side. Why was it necessary to make this switch if the single had already started receiving airplay? Because it gave us the opportunity to reintroduce the single to the marketplace and resend it to radio stations (many of which may have already tossed out the original issue); it also made things easier for the chart makers at *Billboard*, *Cashbox*, and *Record World* and for retailers, who would have been at a loss as to where they should place the single in their display bins.

Rosalie began to play "Beth." Scott had also called in some favors from a few buddies at stations in the South, and they obliged him by adding the song to their playlists. The single began to break, appearing on radio add lists, breakouts, and hot lists in all of the radio trade publications. This was another of those serendipitous occurrences—common then, but impossible now, with the advent of the CD and the demise of the 45rpm record. Today, no music director or program director at a major station would take a chance on a new record from a still-unproven group. A record now has to be tested to death, and numerous consultants have to agree that it's worthy. This is a prime example of radio's contribution to the stifling of creativity and excitement in music. Today's record company reps can't talk to most music and program directors without going through the station's independent promoter.

By September, "Beth" had begun to climb the charts. Then this unlikely song—the B side of the third single from an album that had been panned by some and had thus far fallen well short of building upon its predecessor's momentum, a string-laden, melodramatic ballad from a band that had established itself by breaking ribcages with three chords and by shooting flames across the stage—became a runaway, crossover, adult contemporary hit. And, as the weeks scrolled by, the song so hated by Casablanca's owner, the song that had turned our otherwise upbeat promotions guy into a defeated zombie, shot up the charts and became KISS's first Top 10 single.

I cannot overemphasize how important that song was to KISS's eventual achievement of superstardom. And it shoved Casablanca several rungs up the prestige ladder in the process. In fact, without "Beth," it's entirely possible that KISS would soon have found themselves in the "Where are they now?" category. Up to that point, they had created great buzz as a live act and had broken through in a high-profile way with *Alive!* (which was still comfortably positioned on the charts). They were clearly a band that many in the industry were watching, but the bottom line was that they couldn't sell singles with the big boys, and their appeal as recording artists and as live performers was still limited to a fairly narrow demographic. "Beth" changed all that. The single surfed the charts for months, peaking at No. 7 on both *Billboard* and *Cashbox*. Suddenly, middle-aged moms carting their kids to school were crooning along with KISS on their favorite adult contemporary stations. With its crossover appeal, "Beth" hurdled demographic walls that we'd never dreamed of scaling. An entire new world now lay open to us. We only had to take that first brave step forward.

13

The Mothership Arrives

**Flying saucer dudes—The Group with No Name—
Long John Baldry—The casbah grows again—The Disco
Forum—Welcome, Mr. Guber—Casablanca Record &
FilmWorks—*The Deep*—The Alexander Calder art
gallery—*Rock and Roll Over***

September 1976
Hangar E
Stewart International Airport
Newburgh, New York

"You want to land a *what*?"

The conversation between George Clinton and me had been surreal. Then again, most of our conversations were strange. And the few that weren't strange were incredibly strange. This was one of the latter.

"Wait a second, George—you want to land a what? A mothership? Onstage?"

Through a haze of pot smoke, Clinton's unmistakable head was nodding up and down. I could have argued. I could have listed a hundred reasons, starting with the fact that it defied common sense, why landing a life-sized spaceship onstage on a nightly basis was not going to work. I could have quoted numbers and margins and returns on investment. I could have, but I didn't. I'd learned not to bother trying to talk George Clinton out of something when he had his mind set on it. Hell, George always recognized his own absurdity: "Larry, when you're funky, you don't make any sense," was something I'd heard a dozen times. And, considering the success his creative inspirations had brought Casablanca so far, maybe choosing not to argue was the smart move.

That was months ago and three thousand miles away. Now George and the boys were on an air force base in upstate New York, in a big, echoing hangar, watching a life-sized spaceship (that cost two hundred and seventy-five thousand dollars to construct) landing on a massive stage set. Wow. They were in production rehearsals for an upcoming tour. The facility was owned by Theatre Techniques, the stage construction company that had built the set. Both the Rolling Stones and KISS had rehearsed here, KISS as recently as three months before. The KISS connection did not stop there, as the Parliament stage and production had been designed by the Jules Fischer Organization, the company that had provided a similar service for KISS's new tour.

Parliament's concerts were out of this world, even without the expensive mothership production. The show revolved around the history of funk on our planet. Funk had been brought to Earth by aliens aboard UFOs and stored in the great Egyptian pyramids. About halfway through the set, during "Mothership Connection," guitarist Glenn Goins would repeatedly sing the line, "I think I see the mothership comin'." The other band members would point toward the back of the house, just as pyro ignited. Then the silver mothership would begin flying over the arena floor above the lighting rig.

The mothership was shaped more or less like a flying saucer—round if you looked at it from below, from the audience's perspective, and tapering to a point like a pyramid if you looked at it in profile. There were lighting cans circling the perimeter of the mothership's base. As the saucer flew overhead, the lights would glow, a torrent of sparks (from Roman-candle-like effects called gerbs) would arc downward, and plumes of dry ice would flow into the air; all of this combined to create the illusion of exhaust and flight. After completing the trek to the front of the house, the mothership would hover briefly, and there would be a short blackout, during which a quick switch would be made: the mothership was obscured in the lighting rig, and a much larger version of it was lowered slowly to the stage floor; clouds of dry ice billowed out from underneath it, cleverly mimicking powerful thrusters shooting down into the dust, as 120 decibels of rocket power ripped through the PA. Four glass orbs, which were lit from within, were mounted on the corners of the scaffold-like frame that supported the prop.

Then, after a two-second blackout and a single burst of exhaust from the ascending mothership, George Clinton would rise from beneath the multilevel set to the top of a staircase. As the fog abated, he would begin his classic pimp walk down the stairs while the band launched into their next number. It was a very effective production, and Parliament would continue to use it throughout most of the decade.

Neil, Joyce, and Cecil flew out to New Orleans for the inaugural landing of the mothership on October 27, and they came back with reports of the crowd's ecstatic reaction. Clinton was equal parts Sly Stone, Pink Floyd, and Billy Graham, and the concert experience he created was a euphoric revivalist celebration, a religious communion. I reminded myself that this was why we didn't argue with George. Parliament stayed on the road for months, taking the mothership to tens of thousands of mesmerized concertgoers.

With two of our biggest acts, KISS and Parliament, on tour, we turned our attention to others. Even at this point, a full two and half years into the Casablanca adventure, and with quite a few successes on our résumé, our release schedule and our artist roster were still sparse. Just before Labor Day, on September 3, we released a self-titled album by a group with no name—literally, that was what they dubbed themselves: The Group With No Name. We'd tried and tried to figure out a name for them, but no one could come up with one. Their album had been nearly a year in the making, and it was a pet project of Neil's.

- **April 24, 1976:** *Saturday Night Live* producer Lorne Michaels proposes on the air to pay The Beatles $3,000 for a reunion on the program. Among the viewers are Lennon and McCartney, together in New York, who consider walking to the studio to accept.
- **July 29, 1976:** The Son of Sam (David Berkowitz) murder spree begins.
- **December 8, 1976:** *Hotel California* by The Eagles is released.

The quintet consisted of two singing waiters and three singing waitresses from the Great American Food and Beverage Company in Los Angeles. From what I recall, Gene Simmons was an old college buddy of one the guys in the group and had brought them to Neil's attention. Gene also had something going on with one of the waitresses, Katey Sagal, who, eleven years later, would play Peggy Bundy on the hit Fox sitcom *Married with Children*. Katey and the rest of the group had been hanging out with us for the better part of a year, since we were back on Sherbourne. They were nice kids and everyone liked them a lot. I felt that their LP had the potential to turn into something special, but, again, it was Neil who really loved this band. Since all five members could sing lead, he believed they had that magic something that it takes to become a supergroup. The band eventually hired Joyce and Donna Summer's manager, Dick Broder, to represent them, and they did a live appearance on the syndicated TV show *Don Kirshner's Rock Concert.* They opened with their first single, "Baby Love (How Could You Leave Me)," and they were quite impressive. Despite this high-profile appearance, a second single ("Get Out in the Sunshine"), and continued print support in the trades, no one could figure out how to market the band, and the LP went nowhere.

The Group With No Name wasn't the only act we struggled to develop. Another was Larry Santos, a blues/soul singer who'd penned a No. 3 hit called "Candy Girl" for The Four Seasons in 1963. We'd released a self-titled album for him in June of 1975 and a follow-up in early October 1976. We all loved Larry, and his voice was just haunting (he has since done a multitude of commercial voice-overs), but we'd no idea how to market him. His material was wonderful, but its produc- tion—featuring lush orchestral accompaniment—morphed his blues/ soul vibe into something unmarketable. The music was too progressive to be blues, and too bluesy for the progressive radio stations to touch. Try as we might, MOR (middle of the road) radio was the only place where we could find a home for it, and MOR was such a catch-all category that landing it there meant nothing. Larry fit into no existing format, and because of that, his albums flopped in terms of sales.

Another project we were spearheading was an album by Long John Baldry. John was an extremely tall, thin guy who is probably best remembered for his association with other, more successful musicians: he shared a stage with Jimmy Page, Rod Stewart, and Elton John at various points during the 1960s. I was very much aware of his pedigree, recognizing him as royalty on the English music scene. I met him a few times and found him brilliant and interesting to talk to. His only album for us, *Welcome to Club Casablanca*, did not do well. It was mostly a case of bad timing; with Parliament, KISS, and Donna Summer skyrocketing simultaneously, plus the constant influx of new people at Casablanca, our plate was too full to give his album the attention it needed. There was also the problem of his back catalog: John had so many past releases that there was little demand for new material. He eventually launched a suit against us for not marketing his product, and I wanted to fight it. Neil cautioned me, "If you want to, then fine, but sometimes it's cheaper to settle and bite the bullet." I considered this and weighed it against the cost of giving John what he wanted. We settled for ten thousand dollars, which was a lot less than the lawyers would have billed us to fight it.

Between the successes and failures of our various releases, Casablanca's personnel file grew and grew and grew. It's not much of an exaggeration to say that I could walk into the office on any given day and meet someone new. Entire departments seemed to sprout up overnight, like weeds through cracks in the pavement. To give you an idea of the volume of our promotions, hirings, and firings, in the space of seven days in September we: promoted Susan Munao to VP of press and artist relations; promoted Al DiNoble to director of singles; hired a guy named Eliot Sekuler to be director of creative services; and rehired Nancy Reingold, now divorced, to handle MOR radio (she'd championed Larry Santos, which is why he'd landed on MOR). And we weren't done yet: we promoted Phyllis Chotin to director of advertising; promoted Peggy Martin to national tour director; hired Nellie Prestwood as publicity tour coordinator; and hired Elaine Cooper to be our artist relations coordinator. That was just one week. I had little idea if the promotions were even merited. Not that I thought people were doing a poor job per se, but it was mind-boggling to watch promotions being handed out like hors d'oeuvres. We were growing rapidly and needed more resources, so we hired more people. That made sense. But doing so forced us to shuffle the people already working for us into new positions and/or give them new titles, and it all felt like a big game of massage the ego.

Our publicity department consisted of three or four people, including Susan Munao. We needed that department to grow quickly to support other areas of the company, including promotion, sales, accounting, and the art department. I think the only area that did not see substantial growth was the international department, which was headed by Mauri Lathower, whose assistants were Scott Bergstein and Candy's sister, Christy. We began to expand the press department by hiring Soozin Kazick as a publicist. She had worked for Neil at Buddah as early as 1969 and then gone on to Capitol Records; she was now living with Howie Rosen (I had introduced them), who would soon be tapped for our promotions department. Susan Munao wasn't crazy about Soozin—she knew her from New York and did not like her reputation or the way she worked, but she had little choice in the matter.

Neil and I knew that Soozin was a very good publicist. I remember a night that Neil and I spent with Soozin and her close friend, *Creem* writer Lester Bangs, at her apartment in New York. Lester was in New York for business, and we all got together for dinner and schmoozing. We did not do many drugs that night, we just sat around talking. Lester was probably the most opinionated writer in rock, especially when he was among other critics, and he wielded a great deal of influence in his professional circle. The night was great, and from then on we never had to worry about Lester verbally destroying any of our rock artists. He was never kind to our disco artists, but we didn't care.

Having Soozin at the company made things a little awkward for Candy, as many years before, Soozin and I had had a brief affair. I was forthright with Candy about it, and eventually she and Soozin became the best of friends. They went through their first pregnancies together. When our son Morgan was born, on June 21, 1978, Howie and Soozin were in the room next to ours—they'd had their daughter the day before. We turned the maternity ward into a Casablanca satellite office.

Part of successfully navigating Casablanca through the waters of the music industry was attending a seemingly endless string of conventions. As a young record company, it was especially important for us to make our presence felt at every opportunity. Next on the convention itinerary was a trip to New York at the end of September for *Billboard*'s second Disco Forum at the Americana Hotel. It was a four-day affair that ran from September 28 through October 1. On the final evening, an awards banquet was held at which twenty-six winners were presented with various accolades. Largely, if not exclusively, on the strength of Donna Summer's "Love to Love You Baby," Casablanca was named disco label of the year. I remember accepting the award in person, but I can recall nothing else about the convention, which says something about how many of these get-togethers I attended and what a blur my life had become. We took out a full-page ad in the next issue of *Billboard* heralding the award. The ad was in the form of a letter from Neil praising disco and emphasizing the genre's glowing future. It was a nice little award, the first of many disco-related achievements Casablanca would claim in the next eighteen months.

By far the most significant development came later in October. Neil completed negotiations with Peter Guber to merge Guber's film production company, FilmWorks, with Casablanca. Peter was a tall, thin, good-looking guy, always well dressed, with an engaging personality and an easygoing smile. He was pure Hollywood. He'd spent some time at Columbia Pictures as an executive VP in charge of worldwide production, leaving in 1975 to form his own company. He knew the movie biz inside and out and had a great brand of bullshit, to boot. Guber navigated the film industry with the same natural ease that Neil navigated the music world. The two had known each other for years, and together they formed a very dynamic duo. They were either Batman and Robin, or Abbott and Costello—I'm not sure which.

Entering the motion picture business gave Neil the opportunity to become more of a player in Hollywood, and this was of utmost importance to his long-range plans. He had been working on the deal for quite some time, probably close to a year, and he'd always kept the Casablanca ownership group of Cecil, me, Richard Trugman, and even Buck apprised of developments. In order to make the deal happen, we would each have to grant Peter 20 percent of our stock. This was one of the many issues Buck had had with Neil that eventually led to his departure. Buck was so stuck in the here and now that he never seemed to grasp the big picture. If he'd had any foresight, Buck would have seen that the deal Neil had struck was particularly lopsided in Casablanca's favor. Considering Guber's success at Columbia, I was very surprised that he wanted to join a company that had spent most of the past two years peering into the abyss of bankruptcy without ever making a profit. Guber could easily have made much more money producing movies on his own than with us, but he was hedging his bets. He bet against himself, and it turned out to be a bad gamble for him.

Casablanca would own the profits from a five-picture deal Guber had in place with Columbia. In exchange, Guber got 20 percent of a company that was in the red and that, despite all its successes, real and apparent, had never come close to being profitable. But in some ways it may have been a good move for Peter to make: if he had stayed with Columbia, I have no doubt that they would have amortized all of his movies against each other and eventually, through creative accounting, showed that he owed them money and his firstborn.

The newly merged company was renamed Casablanca Record & Film-Works. We retained our Sunset location as our headquarters and built out the first floor to accommodate the new film division. We owned three buildings at the site (over fourteen thousand square feet combined), and we still had plenty of room for expansion. Neil kept the title of president, while Peter was named chairman of the board.

The first picture, an adaptation of Peter Benchley's follow-up novel to *Jaws*, titled *The Deep*, was already in production in Bermuda by the time the deal was inked. Development of the movie had begun under the Columbia banner, and Columbia would serve as our domestic distributor on the deal. The merger was certainly a coup for us, and I was especially blown away by the size of the first movie. It had been barely a year since the *Jaws* phenomenon had exploded into theaters—the film had single-handedly created the concept of the summer blockbuster. The property and anything associated with it was still red hot. Peter Benchley's name gave the picture instant cash-cow status, and with an impressive cast (Jacqueline Bisset, Nick Nolte, Lou Gossett Jr., and Robert Shaw) included, I couldn't see how it could fail. Guber had also finalized a deal with Bantam Books to release a behind-the-scenes documentary paperback, tentatively titled *Inside the Deep*, which he would pen himself.

Another film was listed in the initial agreement. Titled *Six Weeks*, it had a certain cachet to it as well: the script was to be written by David Seltzer, who was hot due to the success of his screenplay for *The Omen*. However, unlike production on *The Deep*, production on *Six Weeks* went nowhere, and the film wasn't released until years later, in 1982.

The glitz and glam of having big names on your roster comes with a price—it demands that you coddle egos and deal with hypersensitive personalities. In November, we were forced to confront a growing problem related to Donna Summer's boyfriend, Peter Mühldorfer. A lanky fellow, Mühldorfer had established himself as an up-and-coming artist in European surrealist circles. He had come to LA to spend time with Donna, and we all bent over backwards to make him feel comfortable, but all the luxuries and the hospitality we bestowed upon him had no effect. He could see no reason to stay on in the US. He felt that he was the artist, not Donna—she was just his "woman." He had also grown

tired of looking after her young daughter, Mimi. We needed Donna in
LA, but getting Donna stateside on a permanent basis required getting
Mühldorfer stateside.

Neil backed into the solution when he was in Europe with Joyce
attempting to garner Casablanca a better distribution deal with some
European record companies. (Our distribution arrangement with EMI
had been terminated, and an arrangement with RCA to step into the
fold had collapsed as well.) While there, Neil got a chance to buy some
works by the great artist Alexander Calder—enough to fill a shipping
container, and all for a steal. He and Trugman decided that if they had
all of these Calder pieces, they could open an art gallery in LA and sell
the work; they could also show the work of Peter Mühldorfer, thereby
giving him a reason to live in Los Angeles. This would allow Donna to
be in LA full time to work on her publicity. It was a win-win situation for
everyone, and thus the short-lived Casablanca ArtWorks was born.

Preparations for the opening of the ArtWorks Gallery were accelerated
when the seventy-eight-year-old, terminally ill Calder passed away, on
November 11. Not to be ghoulish, but the timing could not have been
more ideal in terms of business: nothing increases the value of art like the
passing of the artist. Neil and Richard had more invested in the gallery
and inventory than anyone else, and they thought that this would be
their road to riches. Casablanca's press department worked on a big opening for ArtWorks, which Candy and I attended, though not necessarily
willingly. In fact, Neil decreed that attendance was mandatory; furthermore, we were pressured into purchasing a few Calder prints. The Art-
Works Gallery failed almost immediately. Calder had hired many people
to work on his stuff, so even if it bore his name, a Calder work might
never even have been touched by the artist. The market was flooded with
Calders as soon as he died. But, even though it was a miserable failure as
a business, ArtWorks did get Donna Summer over to the US permanently.

Our work wasn't finished on that front. We found out that Peter beat
Donna when he was feeling down or depressed. She was the focus of
attention, the star, not him, and this was very difficult for him to take.
We marshaled a campaign to help her build the courage to leave him.
Eventually, she saw the light, and they split up. The breakup devastated
her, but I believe that her musical success and her new support group
helped her to get through this difficult part of her life.

Meanwhile, KISS was ready to release yet another studio album. In the 1970s, when the biggest acts only released albums on a yearly basis, at most, KISS was churning out material at a breakneck pace. It had been a little over two and a half years since their debut release, and they were completing their sixth album. Much of that output had been directly supported—if not outright demanded—by Neil. The album, titled *Rock and Roll Over*, was scheduled to ship on November 1, and to get some national exposure for it, we booked the band to appear on *The Paul Lynde Halloween Special*. The hour-long program aired on October 29 on ABC Television, and it created a nice sales spike for us. It was a great opportunity to feature some of KISS's material, especially "Beth," which was in the middle of its successful ride on the charts; the band lip-synched three songs on the show. The national exposure was likely responsible for "Beth" peaking on the charts: it entered the Top 10 a few weeks after the special aired.

14

The Skyrocket Takes Flight

**Bird flies in—Shannon flies out—Howie, Brian, and
Don—Managing the asylum—Fire!—Blow job—
Machine guns—Spinal Tap: The prequel—Angel at
Midnight—Douglas Records—Millennium and
galactic funk—"The CIA Report"**

January 1977
Casablanca Record & FilmWorks Headquarters
8255 Sunset Boulevard
Los Angeles, California

Casablanca released sixteen albums in 1976. In 1977, that number
would triple. This type of growth is exactly what the owners of every
young business hope for, but steering a company through such expansion
is more challenging than creating it to begin with. One of the major
factors behind our accelerated growth rate was Bruce Bird, whom we
hired as vice president of promotion in January 1977. Bruce ran a successful independent promotion business out of Cleveland, and we'd
used him to help market our product in that region. He was happy
where he was (his mother and his children from his first marriage lived
nearby), and he made an excellent living, but he was also developing a
relationship with Nancy Reingold, Buck's ex-wife. They had known each
other for many years—in a purely platonic way—until their relationship
took a different turn at a convention in 1976. The news of their budding
romance was not well received by Neil. He was desperate to keep Beth
and their children in LA. If Nancy, her twin, moved to another city to be
with Bruce, then Beth could decide to follow her, taking the kids.

Nancy had finally ended her marriage to Buck earlier in 1976. He was
lying to her and cheating on her every hour of every day. He was
absolutely shameless about it—it was almost as if he wanted to get caught.
He was so brazen that among his shack-ups was a woman who lived

across the street from them. He would even cheat at the office while Nancy was in the next room. But her loyalty to him was so strong that it took a sledgehammer to the head to get her to recognize his infidelity.

Early in her relationship with Bruce, Nancy (who had begun to spend a great deal of her time with Bruce in Cleveland) had decided that it would help ease Neil's angst if she and Bruce were to visit him in LA. So she and Bruce came to town, but they spent most of their visit with Candy and me, and a lot of that time Nancy and Candy just hovered over lines of coke complaining about Neil. Of course, word of these bitching sessions ended up getting back to Neil (Nancy had trouble keeping her mouth shut), leaving the Bruce-Neil relationship in an even worse state than it would have been if Bruce had just stayed home, which is what he'd wanted to do in the first place.

One afternoon a week or two later, after Nancy and Bruce had left LA, I heard Neil on the phone through our adjoining office door. The volume of the conversation was so loud that I could hear what he was saying with the door closed. "You're going to do what?!" Neil sounded incredulous. "No! Nancy, you can't . . . I won't stand for it." I shifted uncomfortably in my chair, realizing that Nancy was trying to explain her feelings for Bruce. Neil spun into a tirade. "How could you? How could you possibly marry that complete slob?! He's going nowhere! He's a nobody!"

I absolutely hate playing the middleman in personal conflicts. I'd tried acting as hall monitor between Candy and Neil and gotten nowhere—I'd always thought that two adults shouldn't need some outside moderator to broker a peace treaty for them anyway. And if I had thought that this particular conflict would have no impact on the company, I would have simply let Neil and Nancy hash it out, but as vice president I had a responsibility to protect Casablanca.

I let it play out for a few more minutes before I rolled my eyes, sighed, and trudged off to talk Neil down. I opened the adjoining door and shut it behind me. I'd learned that the key to coaxing Neil back off the ledge was a mix of calm, quiet, and resolution. "Look, I know you want Nancy to stay here in LA, but screaming at her and calling the man she loves a slob is going to get you absolutely nowhere, and you know it." Neil looked at me intensely, eyes popping out more than usual. Then he exhaled and said, "Yeah, I know, you're right. I'll get it together." "OK, then," I thought, and then I went back to my desk.

Not five minutes later, I received a call from Bruce, who must have been listening to Nancy talk to Neil. Bruce was every bit as livid. He told me that he and I would always be friends, but he would never do promotion work for Casablanca again, and he would certainly never speak to Neil. Later in the day, after I knew that Neil's emotions had settled and I had given myself time to think, I went back into his office to talk things over. I was blunt: "If you ever want to have a relationship with Nancy again, you better find a way to apologize and make it up to her. And to Bruce, too." Although his emotions were easily stirred, Neil was a smart man, and he finally admitted that he wasn't really mad at Bruce at all; he just desperately wanted to maintain his contact with Nancy, he valued it so much. After a few days, he spoke to Nancy and Bruce and invited them back to LA. Bruce was apprehensive about returning, but he would grin and bear it for Nancy. During their visit, Neil had them over to his house and did a real sales number on Bruce, offering him the position of vice president of promotion. Bruce accepted, even though it would cut his salary in half. Neil assured Bruce that he would take care of him—wink, wink. To my knowledge, he never did, but for the moment, Neil was happy, Nancy was happy, and Bruce was happy.

I was fine with the resolution, too, but only because this is what Neil needed to do to keep Nancy in LA. But the collateral damage caused by Neil's move was now my problem—that is, I had to figure out a way to tell Scott Shannon that someone had just taken his job. That would have been relatively easy had Scott been doing poorly, but he hadn't. I was very satisfied with Scott as head of promotion; he was doing a good job, and we had had some major hits under his watch—"Beth," in particular. Since Neil had gotten me into this mess, he would damn well help get me out of it. The next day, he and I huddled to figure out what we could offer Scott that would seem like a lateral move or, better yet, a promotion. I called Scott into my office and explained to him that with the company growing so fast, we wanted to give him a promotion and a raise. He was to be our vice president in charge of special projects. He would help out in various areas of the company, including the motion picture division. Scott went along with this for a time, but I suspect he always resented it, and that showed up later when he was back in radio running a big station in Miami; he refused to help any of us out—me, Neil, or Bruce. He wouldn't play our records or even take our calls. Years later, I ran into him in a restaurant in New York. By that time, he was a fairly famous DJ on Z100 with a nationally syndicated show. The chance meeting was pleasant enough, and we greeted each other cordially, but that was as far as it went.

When Bruce moved to LA, he started to build the promotions department, luring some of the best promotion guys away from other companies with perks like a Mercedes, first-class airfare everywhere, and a big salary increase, plus full coverage of moving expenses and, in some cases, the down payment on a house. By March, the department was staffed by three guys talented and experienced enough to be running national promotions by themselves: Howie Rosen, Brian Interland, and Don Wasley.

Don was entirely new to me, but I'd known Howie and Brian for years. We knew Brian from the Buddah days, when he had worked promo for the local Boston distributor. We'd always liked him a great deal, plus he was still tight with all of my friends at WBCN, so that was another point in his favor. All three had different strengths, and Bruce efficiently captured and directed those strengths to give us the strongest promotion team in the country. Brian was close to the northeast programmers, Don ran in San Francisco circles, and Howie had programming friends scattered along the eastern seaboard. The lineup didn't last for long. Don Wasley became head of our artist relations department, which meant hanging out with KISS and other artists. Brian was in LA only a short while before his failing marriage forced him to return to Boston, though he retained his position with us after the move. This left Howie as the lone in-house national promotions guy.

Another Bruce Bird hire was T.J. Lambert. Everyone in the promotions department was married except for T.J., so the rest of the promo guys tended to live vicariously through him. T.J. would come in after a rough night and have the rest of the guys on the edge of their seats with his war stories about entertaining the female population of Los Angeles. Twenty-five years old and working for Casablanca, T.J. was already living the dream—but when two girls moved in with him, everyone in the office, at least everyone with a dick, was even more impressed. One morning, he came to work looking particularly wrung out and collapsed into his chair. He had that running-on-no-sleep look we all knew so well. No one could resist the bait for long. Someone asked him what had happened. T.J. sighed heavily and mumbled, "Well, the girls had six or seven of their friends over last night, and one thing led to another, and . . . " Then he lapsed back into the semiconscious state we'd aroused him from. The guy had had an orgy with nine women, and he'd regaled us married stiffs with all the joy and enthusiasm of someone doing a line reading of the Sunday classifieds. He stopped talking, stared for a moment (if it's possible to be asleep with your eyes open, then he was), and pondered out loud, straight-faced and monotone, "I don't know if I'll be happy with just two women ever again." The poor bastard.

It was fun to work surrounded by such an assortment of characters and lunatics, but, due to Casablanca's rapid growth, maintaining a sense of managerial presence or control was becoming a real challenge. The feeling of teamwork that had been such a part of the culture at Buddah and at Casablanca in the early days was beginning to disappear. Departments were establishing their own cliques—sales didn't know what was going on in marketing, legal barely spoke to accounting, and so on. This slow fracturing undermined the sense of family that Neil so cherished, and he was determined not to let that go. As the company grew, Neil, whose first love was always promotion, would periodically walk down the hall to the promotions department and shout out things like, "OK, first person to get me the Parliament single added anywhere west of the Mississippi gets two hundred dollars. You've got sixty minutes . . . go!" or, "Anyone adding a single on a major Top 40 station by the close of business can come to my office and take a C-note out of my hand." The promotion team members were thrilled when he came into their area of the building, and his visits helped bolster spirits and foster unity. When Neil walked through the offices, he left awe in his wake. He was the Man, and everyone knew it. I made a point of walking the halls every day, too, but with me there was more joking

- January 23, 1977: The landmark miniseries *Roots* debuts, scoring the highest ratings of any miniseries in TV history.
- February 4, 1977: Fleetwood Mac's *Rumours* album is released.
- July 13, 1977: A twenty-five-hour power blackout hits nine million New Yorkers, leading to rampant looting and riots.

around. My presence certainly did not carry the weight or inspire the same feelings as Neil's did, which was OK with me, because not long before that I had been in awe of Neil myself.

Casablanca was big business. Important decisions were constantly being made, and millions of dollars and the careers of hundreds were on the line every day. Still, more often than not, we acted like a bunch of sixth graders. One day, a fire broke out in Howie's office. Neil had taken a bottle of lighter fluid, poured it on Howie's desk, and ignited it just to show everyone how hot we were. A few miles away at Warner, or over at Capitol, they would have been content with a nice interoffice memo to pass on the news. Not us. We set the furniture on fire.

That wasn't the half of it. We played games, too, like Bruce Bird's "hit the hooker with the Frisbee." An infamous strip joint, the Body Shop, was located directly across Sunset from us, and it wasn't all that uncommon for hookers to pace on the sidewalk in front of the club. When he was bored or looking for something to do, Bruce would open his window wide and chuck Frisbees across Sunset, trying to hit the hookers. From time to time, you'd hear the screech of tires—some driver slamming on the brakes when a toy disc zipped passed the windshield.

Even the parking lot wasn't immune from our decadence. For instance, Al DiNoble, our director of singles, wasn't Al. His first name was Fuckin'. As in, "that fuckin' DiNoble." Employees had their names painted through stencils onto their parking slots in the lot behind the building. Naturally, Al's parking space had "Fuckin' DiNoble" painted onto it. We loved it because it so obviously offended the occasional conservative stuffed shirt who came to visit.

For his part, Neil would conspire with Phyllis Chotin (our director of advertising) on a practical joke that would leave visitors with stunned expressions. Phyllis would crawl under Neil's desk before he met with a client and then climb out in the middle of their conversation, like she'd just given Neil head. It was all in good fun, and Phyllis thought it was hilarious, but today we'd be sued into oblivion for it. Howie had his own stunts—one was playing a recording of machine-gun fire at full volume or repeatedly striking a very loud gong every time a record was added to a major station. Even though my office was a good fifty feet down the hall from him, if I was on the phone, the person I was speaking to would ask me what was going on. Neil couldn't hear the gong unless I had both my doors open, but when he did hear it, he loved it, and he would ask Howie to do it again. I enjoyed these antics, too, and when we had VIP visitors we would sometimes tell Howie to bash the gong just to impress upon them how crazy we were.

With the pop promotions department growing, the R&B side of the company was clamoring for attention. Spurred on by Renny Roker, Cecil insisted that his department needed to be expanded. This made sense, since Parliament, Donna Summer, and others were being played heavily on R&B radio. Cecil hired Jheryl Busby to be vice president of R&B promotion, Eddie Pugh and Ernie Singleton to handle national promotions, and Ruben Rodriquez to be promotions VP for the East Coast. Once again, we had a team of men so talented and experienced that each could have handled national promotions at the company of his choosing.

Busby was everyone's favorite. He handled himself well with radio people and artists, and he would later become the head of Motown Records, which he brought to a greater level of success than it had previously enjoyed. Jheryl became a major player in the biz. He would frequently credit Neil with mentoring him and claim that Neil had made him a better record executive.

Ruben, too, was a consummate promotion person. He had a simple MO: when it came to working records, there would be no drugs, no payola, and no women. Instead, he would be the Flower Man. He would send flowers to anyone—flowers to all the girls in the office, flowers to the girls he met on the road, flowers to the receptionists at radio stations. And it worked, big time. Ultimately, he did it to get airplay by scoring face time with the bosses: "Oh, you should take a meeting with that Ruben from Casablanca. He's so nice." Ruben had his own perception-is-reality gimmick, which involved establishing what a nice guy he was. The flower bills that he sent in could have floated the debt of a Third World country, and I would lightheartedly protest them, but what he was doing worked, so he was allowed to keep doing it. You couldn't argue with the results.

Eddie Pugh, who had brought the kissing contest promotion to my attention in 1974, stayed with the company for only a short time. He did not get along very well with Bruce, and the jockeying for power among Jheryl, Ernie, Ruben, and Eddie came to a head. But he did leave on a good note and went on to run the R&B department at CBS.

Then it was sales' turn to ask for more people. We needed someone who had the contacts among the major one stops and rack jobbers to get more attention for our product. The person we chose was a well-liked and savvy salesman named Pete Jones. Pete brought us a respect that we were lacking. Not that department head Dick Sherman was held in low regard, but he was not comfortable applying the pressure when we needed it. Dick played the joker/nice-guy role much more naturally. Pete could put the screws to people in such a way that they never felt he was being pushy. He also had a good grasp on how to do major promotional tie-ins with retailers and often came up with fresh ideas to market bands at the retail level. I remember a photo of Pete and his family standing in the snow on the East Coast and holding a banner that said, "Thank you Neil and Joyce, Larry and Candy, and Bruce and Nancy"—we had just put a down payment on a house for them in LA.

Without question, all of these hirings helped Casablanca, but there was little doubt in my mind that Bruce was the major reason we began to grow so rapidly. Bruce understood how the game was played on Top 40 radio, and Neil and I gave him carte blanche to go out and do whatever was necessary (we didn't ask for any details, because we didn't want to have to swear to anything on the stand). Casablanca now appeared—especially to people in the industry—to have all the trappings of success, and there is nothing like success to breed success.

Along with Bruce's obvious talent came a temper to match. On a few occasions, he came close to engaging in physical combat with Renny Roker or Eddie Pugh, and I had to rein him in. Bruce had grown up in an atmosphere that was less than conducive to getting along with minorities, and he had mentioned to me several times that in Cleveland, black people and white people kept to their own areas. Much of this anger would disappear when Bruce was not doing drugs, but when he mixed certain substances, he would become extremely belligerent and refuse to back down from a fight (the man could certainly handle himself in a brawl).

In January, right on the heels of Bruce's hiring, we released the debut album of a band called Stallion. I had signed them to the label late in 1976, convinced that they sounded exactly like the Eagles. Another factor in their favor was that my friend Ken Kohl had a piece of their management. Ken was in need of a gig and some money, so it was no big deal to sign them. To this day, Ken and I get kidded about this band, because their finished album sounded nothing like their demo tape. I did not do my homework thoroughly enough and neglected to check out the band up close. I figured the problem was their producer and guru, Dick Darnell. My first clue should have been that when I asked him to make the band sound more like the Eagles, he looked nonplussed and asked who the Eagles were. But by the time this happened, it was too late. The band was already in the studio in Colorado, and I could not pull the plug on the band of one of my best friends.

Because they were my signing, I put a lot of pressure on our AOR guy, Dick Williams, to get airplay for Stallion. I probably shouldn't have given him so much grief, as I doubt I could have gotten much airplay for these guys either. I even went so far as to make some phone calls to help promote the band myself, something I hadn't done in a while. By pressuring some of my old radio friends, I got some airplay, but it was not enough to make a difference.

My other pet project, Angel, was doing somewhat better. Angel's first two albums had done OK for us, but Neil and I always felt that they could do more; we fully believed they would become the next KISS, and we spread that perception in the rock press. Neil and I had met with the band's manager, David Joseph, as early as September 1976 to plan Angel's third LP, *On Earth as It Is in Heaven*, and we collectively agreed to pull out all of the stops. It was time to make Angel the next supergroup. After all, we'd done it with KISS, so doing it again would be easy, right?

Neil agreed to hire Eddie Kramer (the man whose touch with *Alive!* had broken KISS) to produce the album. We also planned a heavy point-of-purchase and print-marketing campaign and paid for thousands of elaborate press kits and mobiles. As we did our annual filling in of *Circus* readers' poll cards for KISS, we also voted for Angel in the category of best new group or artist. To everyone's surprise—except ours, of course—they won, receiving over forty thousand votes and beating out Boston and Heart in the process. To capitalize on the momentum, we built the marketing campaign for *On Earth as It Is in Heaven* around the poll result.

Another major addition to our Angel project was their famous visual palindrome logo. As the story goes, a seventeen-year-old fan named Bob Petrick showed up backstage before one of the band's East Coast shows. His persistence finally won him an audience with Angel's tour manager, Bill Schereck. Bill (whom Wally Meyrowitz and I had made an honorary

Jew and nicknamed Bill Schereckwitz) listened politely as Bob explained that Angel needed a logo, so he had designed one. He showed the drawing to Bill, who told him that he couldn't promise anything but he'd see what he could do. Going into a dressing room, Bill put the drawing down on a table and accidentally glanced at its reflection in a mirror. He noticed something very interesting that Bob had neglected to mention. When it was turned upside down, the logo was still right side up. Bill was blown away and ran off to find Bob, panicked that he might have lost him. He finally found him, and he bought the logo from him that night for five hundred dollars and an album credit.

The band members, David Joseph, and everyone at Casablanca loved the logo, too, and when Neil and I were stoned, we'd sometimes amuse ourselves by flipping it back and forth, over and over. We figured if it worked on us, the kids would really think it was magic.

Speaking of magic, David Joseph wanted Neil to fork over an obscene amount of money for Angel's tour support. I sat there in disbelief as he laid out his reasoning. He wanted to integrate "high-art illusions" into the band's live show. As he ran down his idiotic list of magic tricks for the band, I felt embarrassed for him; David was actually pitching this to Neil, and he was 100 percent serious and sober. I waited for him to finish this absurd sales job, knowing Neil was doing his best to suppress howls of laughter.

And then Neil agreed to every item on the list.

This was my band, I had signed them to Casablanca, nobody wanted them to succeed more than I did, and even I wasn't buying this. I decided to keep my opinions to myself, as you never wanted to be negative with Neil, especially in front of a client. After David left, Neil, sensing my hesitation, explained that both Parliament and KISS had huge productions and were beginning to reap the rewards. So why shouldn't Angel?

Angel's stage show was, depending on your perspective, either the greatest or the worst thing you ever saw from a rock band. For those of you who have never attended an Angel concert, here's how it went down. The house lights would go out, and a lengthy taped introduction based on the end-credits music from *Ben-Hur* would begin to play over the PA. A huge 3-D prop of a hollow-faced Gabriel (the angel from Angel's debut album cover) would rise into place atop the backline of the stage. Reaching his zenith, Gabriel would seemingly come alive and begin to address the stoned audience in a booming, God-like voice. Everyone thought the angel's face was a hologram, but it was actually a rear-projection film of the face of Warren Entner, former guitarist for The Grass Roots, in gold makeup. The voice-over was provided by famous voice actor Paul Frees, who would solemnly intone:

> And it came to pass one day in Heaven that Gabriel summoned his flock of angels unto him and spoke thus, "I have watched my children on Earth at play, and I am saddened that they know not the pleasures of our music. Who of you will go forth and let the music of Heaven echo throughout the lands on Earth?"

While this was going on, roadies above the stage dressed in black jumpsuits were setting up five mirrored Plexiglas cubes downstage. These were maybe two and half feet wide by two and a half feet tall. They would then stack three additional cubes atop the first one, which created futuristic portals that looked like mirrored doorways. As each band member was introduced, smoke from a fog machine would be released, a spotlight would hit the mirrors, chaser lights would begin revolving around the doorway, and each of the five musicians would seem to materialize inside his cubicle.

> And the first Angel stepped forward and spoke thus, "I will go to Earth," and Gabriel rejoiced and said, "Go forth my son and sound your drum throughout the land, and from this very day be known as Barry Brandt."

Angel drummer Barry Brandt would emerge from the lighted doorway, go slap some quick high fives with fans in the first row and then run over to join his drums as similarly imposing scripts were spoken for Gregg, Punky, Mickie, and, finally, lead vocalist Frank DiMino.

"And thus it came to pass that there was music on Earth as it is in Heaven." As Gabriel finished speaking to the crowd, the band members would take their places and start the show with their signature song, "Tower." Of course, if you had an amazing entrance, you had to have an even better exit. So a giant Angel LP cover would descend from above the lighting rig to the center rear of the set. The five Angels would walk into it and begin beating on the sides so you could see they were actually inside. Suddenly, the giant LP would begin to rise above the stage, as if it were ascending to Heaven. And then . . . BOOM! It would explode into pieces. All the spotlights would then go black and, with the crowd clamoring for more, the houselights would go up. By then, the band would already be miles away from the venue. Pure showmanship: always leave them wanting more.

When the illusions worked, they were effective, but it seemed more often than not at least one of the Angels would get stuck in his cubicle. If that sounds eerily similar to a scene in *This Is Spinal Tap*, that's because Angel's ridiculous cylinders were probably the inspiration for the translucent plastic egg in which Harry Shearer's character, Derek Smalls, gets trapped. Between KISS and Parliament, I was more than comfortable with over-the-top shows, but I was flat-out embarrassed by Angel's. In my opinion, the grandiose *Ben-Hur* music paired with the overblown band introduction wasn't dramatic, it was silly, and it caused me to question my faith in the band's prospects.

The biggest problem we faced was far more practical: Angel wasn't a headliner in most markets, so they often had to scrap their costly production because the acts that were headliners wouldn't allow an opening act full use of the PA or lights, much less approve anything approaching the rest of Angel's elaborate requirements.

In December 1976, as we were preparing for the release of *On Earth as It Is in Heaven* (January 24, 1977 was the target date), we had the band do their first promotional films, videotaping performances of two tracks from their back catalog ("Tower" and "Feelin' Right") and two songs from the new album ("That Magic Touch" and "You're Not Fooling Me"). *Don Kirshner's Rock Concert* eventually broadcast "That Magic Touch," and it would turn out to be (if my memory serves me correctly) the only national airplay any Angel video would ever receive in the US, although the clips did appear to help the band in some foreign territories, especially Japan.

David Joseph continued to work his act both with us and overseas. Going against everyone's advice (the band wasn't big enough to justify it), he sent Angel to Japan in early February to officially inaugurate their new stage show. The tour was a disaster. They'd sold out a few of the shows, and the overall turnout was respectable, but the sheer number of problems that arose during the tour was enough to make me wonder if this group wasn't living under a bad sign. Angel had, quite accidentally, offended the promoter and some members of the public: while visiting several local attractions to do photo shoots, they had climbed upon some hallowed structures. The promoter considered this to be an act of desecration. Another problem arose when the promoter (who allegedly had ties to the criminal underworld) took issue with the way the tour finances were being handled and hijacked Angel's entire stage production, refusing to give it back. Bill Schereck met with some heavies and arranged for the equipment to be returned. Then Japan Air Lines told him that the check the promoter had given them to cover the round-trip shipping costs had bounced. It was the band's first and last overseas tour.

Wanting to get the maximum return on our investment in Angel, we decided that our six-month-old FilmWorks division should produce a ninety-minute Angel concert movie. The thirty-five-millimeter film, which would cost one hundred and fifty thousand dollars to make, would showcase the band's new stage show and feature fantasy sequences of the band performing in Heaven. Fifty prints of the movie would be distributed to local radio stations in advance of tour dates. A single weekend screening in each market would begin at the stroke of midnight— the film would be titled *Angel at Midnight*. Given the recent release of *The Song Remains the Same*, the wildly popular midnight screenings of *The Rocky Horror Picture Show*, and the fact that we had an in-house film division, an Angel movie wasn't that hard a sell. Cleveland, one of the band's biggest strongholds, was chosen as the location for the live segments. WMMS-FM sponsored the event, which took place on April 6 at the Public Hall and cost patrons only $1.01 each. Attendees were strongly encouraged to wear white so that in the film it would look like they were in Heaven with the band. Then, in the second week of May, additional "beauty coverage" (close-up footage) of the band was shot in LA.

We hired Peter Lake, who had worked with Peter Guber on *The Deep*, as vice president of creative services in late 1976. Lake began editing the raw Angel footage at FilmWorks, downstairs at 8255 Sunset. But the film was never completed. There were several contributing factors to this decision. Neil was beginning to get cold feet about Angel (as was I); plus, Angel's original bassist, Mickie Jones, had been fired just before the final pickup shots were done. I recently ran across a blurb in a 1977 issue of *Circus* that said we were so pleased with the movie that we were thinking of doing a second Angel film in 3-D. Pleased? We'd never even seen the film. This just goes to show that we would put a shiny ribbon on a funeral casket.

As an interesting sidenote, before *Angel at Midnight* completely fell apart, we met with brass at MCA DiscoVision to discuss releasing the movie on an emerging videodisc format, which eventually became LaserDisc (if you're too young to recall the format, just imagine a twelve-inch DVD). At that point, the entire entertainment industry was eagerly anticipating the arrival of the home video medium, and, for a while, the low-cost videodisc looked like the way things were moving. Neil was well aware of its potential, and since Casablanca had such visual acts, we strongly believed that we'd have a serious advantage over our peers when the time came. With this in mind, Peter Lake was overseeing the future production of promotional films for our artists and tie-ins for our movies. I found out years later that Peter had infiltrated the Aryan Nation to write about the group. Peter was a tall, blond white guy, so I can't imagine he found it hard to work his way in. He eventually testified in the case involving the 1984 murder (allegedly by the Aryan Nation) of Denver radio host Alan Berg.

All record companies have subsidiary labels. We could not consider ourselves real players unless we had some smaller companies under our umbrella. Neil had always kept an eye open for these opportunities. Of course, our first subsidiary had been Giorgio Moroder's Oasis, which we'd acquired in 1975, but Oasis had been totally absorbed into Casablanca and had ceased to exist. In July 1976, Neil had begun to solidify a relationship with Douglas Records, an all-jazz label founded and run by longtime producer Alan Douglas. The deal had included the rights to rerelease twenty archive albums. Among the first were albums by The Last Poets and legendary jazz guitarist John McLaughlin. Both albums had been previously released, and I don't remember the reissues going much of anywhere. We renewed the deal in February 1977, but if the Douglas-Casablanca pairing is remembered at all, it is for a five-album set called *Wildflowers: The New York Loft Jazz Sessions*, which was released in March 1977 and to this day carries some weight in experimental jazz circles.

The next signing was Millennium Records, headed by Jimmy Ienner and Irv Biegel; Jimmy's brother, Donnie, was their only promo guy. Jimmy was the producer of the Raspberries, and Irv was a record guy who had been around a long time. He was also friends with Jeff Franklin of ATI, and Jeff helped strike the deal with Neil. Since we all loved Donnie, this looked like it might be fun.

In March, we opened up a New York office with Millennium at 3 West Fifty-Seventh Street. A matter of months later, Millennium was ready to deliver its first album, *Star Wars and Other Galactic Funk*, which was the brainchild of Meco (Domenico Monardo) and an obvious attempt to ride to success on the back of the *Star Wars* phenomena, which was then sweeping the nation. The young musician was enamored of the film, and he'd decided it would be a great idea to create a disco version of John Williams's score. Today it's easy to recognize *Star Wars* as a cash cow, but at the time Neil had to talk Jimmy Ienner into putting the Meco album on Millennium, as Jimmy didn't like it. We'd have been more than happy to keep Meco on the Casablanca roster, but it was important for the new label to establish itself as a bona fide presence in the biz, and nothing spoke louder than a Platinum album. Neil knew it was a guaranteed hit, and he gave Ienner little choice in the matter.

The LP was coming out at the same time as the official 20th Century Fox soundtrack set, and with John Williams and the London Symphony Orchestra on board, 20th Century Fox clearly had the upper hand. Our promotions department would have weekly conference calls late on Sunday afternoons to get everybody hyped up about the releases they'd be working that week. During the call related to the Meco release, Bruce made sure that everyone understood it was Casablanca versus 20th Century Fox, and that we were the underdogs.

When the promotion staff arrived the next day, they found an unwelcome delivery from Harvey Cooper, head of the promotions department at 20th Century Fox—a black wreath with a banner announcing that Fox was going to bury us with their *Star Wars* record. Needless to say, the promotions department went ballistic over the threat, redoubled their efforts, and got us our very first No. 1 single: Meco's "Star Wars Theme/Cantina Band," the biggest-selling instrumental single in the history of the music business. But it wasn't Harvey Cooper who had sent the wreath. It was Bruce Bird. He'd had Soozin send it to him to create a villain and thus motivate the promotions department. And it worked.

One of the things that stands out in my mind about Millennium, and especially Donnie, was that whenever he and Howie Rosen found themselves in a city at the same time, I would get a call from our accounting department. We would have to pay for the hotel rooms Donnie and Howie destroyed. They thought they were wrestling stars, and they would battle each other with little regard for the furniture and fixtures. Donnie became CEO of Sony Records, and I wonder if he put up with such shenanigans from his people.

Another of our subsidiary ventures was Parachute Records, run by Russ Regan. Russ was a legend in the music business, as he had discovered both Elton John and Barry White. He was president of MCA Records, and he'd had the foresight to sign Elton (he's kept in close contact with him to this day). MCA seemed to go through presidents like a shark goes through teeth. The company's primary focus was movies, not music, and for some reason they had a great deal of trouble finding or keeping people who knew what to do and how to do it in the music sector. Russ had started up Parachute after being dismissed as head of MCA.

Russ was a nice guy. We supplied him with offices in one of the buildings on our Sunset lot, which was a natural fit for him since between 1967 and 1972 he had headed MCA's Universal City Records at the same location. Again, it was very important to Neil that the new label had a hit, but no matter how hard we tried, we could not bring home the money for Russ. There was no new Meco with a disco smash for Russ, and we all felt bad that things weren't working out for him. The situation came to a head when Neil told me and Bruce to go over to Russ's office and tell him we were not going to re-sign him once his original contract was up (which was soon). I was not crazy about being the bearer of this news, as I hadn't had anything to do with signing the label in the first place, but Neil asked, so I swung the axe. Because I wasn't happy playing the role of executioner, I was fairly blunt with Russ. Bruce was no help to me—he liked Russ, too, and he wanted no part of the conversation.

Years later, I met Russ at a convention, and he told me that he had been under the impression that ending the relationship had been all my idea because when he went to say goodbye to Neil, Neil had told him that he'd known nothing about it and had only found out from me after it was all done. I explained to Russ that Neil would never have left a decision to drop a label, especially one that I'd had no hand in signing, up to me. Such a decision would come from the very top; my opinion might be solicited, but the final decision would always come from Neil.

Neil and I were no longer leading the charge with every single thing that was happening. We were now too busy running the company, which had expanded way beyond our ability to micromanage. Our interaction with much of the company was no longer on the level of intimate detail, and we had pulled back to weekly meetings of department heads in either my office or Neil's. We used these weekly get-togethers to disseminate information through the departments, which no longer managed to communicate with each other very well. Neil and I were still having fun, but this behemoth was growing at such a rate that it was hard to be as hands-on as we would have liked.

To boost company morale, we began a newsletter of sorts, called *Inside the Casbah*, to report on what was happening within the company so that everyone would be aware of what their colleagues were up to. It was produced by the press department and handled by writer Walter Wanger, a very bright guy who would become an integral part of our special products division. The newsletter, which came out every few weeks, began with a one- or two-page letter from Neil on company letterhead (the best-looking stuff in the biz, except that the Casablanca logo took up the entire top third of the page, leaving room for about two lines of text after the address and salutation); the letter related news on all upcoming releases and trumpeted the successes we'd had that week or month, all in typical Neil fashion: Great, great—everything is great! Following that were photocopies of the articles or blurbs on Casablanca that had appeared in the trades, along with copies of radio ad sheets listing our active singles and albums and a list of the radio stations that had added them to their rotations. At the end of each issue was a column called "The CIA Report," which stood for "Casablanca Informs America." It was written by Walter, and it made fun of all of us, including Neil and me. It spread all sorts of ridiculous, tongue-in-cheek gossip about various people. Cutting the executives down to size not only helped employees feel that we execs were people they could come and talk to, but it also ensured that we didn't take ourselves too seriously.

"The CIA Report" lasted only a short while, as Walter became preoccupied with more important projects and Neil grew more thin-skinned about the Dean-Martin-roast quality of the newsletter's jibes, many of them aimed at him. The daily pressures of wrangling with this monster we'd created were beginning to wear on him, and the loss of his sense of humor (one of his most upfront and likable qualities) was just the first of many changes.

15

The New Bubblegum

Two Frenchmen—The Casablanca test—Donna—
***I Remember Yesterday**—Love Gun—Dazzler—Genesis of*
a disco empire—Alec Costandinos—Paul Jabara—More
payola—The Frankie Crocker trial—A Year at the Top—
Two more strikeouts—In deep—Offer from Clive
Davis—PolyGram and the huge payday—
Bad tax shelters—KISS, George, and Donna

May 17, 1977
Casablanca Record & FilmWorks Headquarters
8255 Sunset Boulevard
Los Angeles, California

Neil was talking to me about a new project he wanted us to get into. We would be getting the official pitch in a few minutes, and he was pacing around my office giving me the details on the band and prepping me for the meetings that would ensue. He mentioned the players, but all that stuck in my head was the list of characters he described: guys dressed in leather, a construction worker, a cop, and some cowboys and Indians. "Great," I thought, "I'm now a casting director meeting with an overcaffeinated Hollywood producer."

These guys weren't cops or cowboys any more than George Clinton was an outer-space pimp. They were a newly created group who called themselves the Village People—a half-serious, half-tongue-in-cheek parody that had been assembled by two French producers and their novice New York music attorney. The producers, Jacques Morali and Henri Belolo, had been creating music in Europe for years with a modicum of success, but they were now concentrating on the US. They brought with them to our meeting a young lawyer named Allen Grubman, who was about to make the first deal of his long and storied entertainment career.

Morali and Belolo had recently relocated from France to New York in hopes of making their entry into the American music scene. Morali (who was openly gay) and Belolo (who was straight) started hanging out at Manhattan's hot nightclubs, and they noticed that many patrons showed up dressed in character—as cowboys, or Indians, or what have you. They hit upon the idea of creating a band comprised entirely of such characters; they were so taken with Americana that they wanted each band member to represent some aspect of the American dream—or, at least, the American dream as interpreted by two Frenchmen living in Greenwich Village. They figured that the act would have a built-in audience in gay nightclubs. But where to place them?

The two had picked up on Casablanca's maverick approach to the music biz, and they were impressed that we'd developed KISS and Parliament, two fairly out-there acts that many of the major labels wouldn't have looked at twice (remember that the Warner execs had initially hated KISS, telling us that the band should lose the makeup to be more palatable to the music-buying public). Morali and Belolo knew their vision for the Village People was likely to be met with ambivalence or derision if they pitched it to the likes of Capitol or Columbia. But with Neil they felt they'd found the perfect match. It didn't hurt that we'd broken the disco genre wide open with Donna Summer, either.

So, they flew out to LA to meet with Neil. As they walked into Neil's office, I saw that both Henri and Jacques were very cosmopolitan guys with a flair for fashion. Morali was energetic, flamboyant, and a bit prissy—definitely the salesman of the two. Belolo tended to hang back, was more subdued, and was the business force behind the project. After we exchanged some pleasantries, they got right to their pitch. They played us a recording of the Village People. The album, which was maybe twenty minutes long, was already a complete package, including artwork. This was a strong selling point for us: Casablanca would only need to manufacture and market the record; and with the cover done, we were already halfway home as far as marketing went. If the material was good, this would be an easy sell.

Neil immediately loved it, but he decided to let me put it to the "Casablanca test" first. This consisted of playing a song at such a high volume that everyone in the entire two-story building would hear it. If people came running to find out what it was, we knew we had something.

I played the record at ear-splitting volume, and the office quickly filled with people from sales, promotion, and PR—everyone was attracted to the music. Neil's eyes were glowing, and we both sensed that this crazy idea had the makings of a monster. The album cover was the cherry on top: we were the label of KISS, Parliament, and Angel, so this group of guys dressed as leather fetishists, Indians, and construction workers was right up our alley. We got it!

Neil sat down with Allen Grubman and signed the group on the strength of the finished album. We'd yet to meet or speak to a single member of the band, and we wouldn't for several months. The guys were cast members more than musicians or singers (though each could carry a tune), and the idea was for them to be entertaining, not create great music. None of us paid attention to the fact that the Village People and their vibe were blatantly gay. Frankly, not only did we not pay attention to it, but we didn't even realize it. Their music was so energetic that it demanded your attention. I don't think it was possible not to like it. But anything more than a five-second glance at the band revealed an array of obvious references to the homosexual lifestyle, which was the foundation of so much disco music.

This aspect of disco never bothered Neil or me. Again, the Village People's best songs were so catchy—you were instantly pulled into their hook-laden melodies, and that's all that mattered. This is precisely how (and the irony is laugh-inducing) many fundamentalists who regard the homosexual lifestyle with contempt can dance around shrieking "Y–M–C–A" at the top of their lungs along with the Village People, happy as clams, oblivious to any subtext or message. Great melodies hide lyrical meaning, which is why a song like Bruce Springsteen's "Born in the USA" can be considered a pro-American anthem when it's nothing of the sort.

With the addition to our roster of the Village People, disco became Neil's new bubblegum. Not everyone at Casablanca was unaware of the sizable homosexual presence in disco culture, and a fissure grew between the disco and rock contingents. As our disco department expanded, a few homophobes in the company—mainly in the pop department—began to reveal themselves. They mostly kept their mouths shut, but Neil and I could feel the tension. Some of them would refuse to shake hands with a person (an artist or a fellow employee) who was gay, or even breathe the same air. A few snide comments were made in meetings, but it never went beyond that.

Our first and still premier disco act was Donna Summer. But we just couldn't duplicate the huge breakout success of her initial album and single, released in 1975. The follow-up, which came out in March 1976, was titled *A Love Trilogy*, and it had gone Gold, but the buzz that surrounded "Love to Love You Baby" just wasn't there. Donna's *Four Seasons of Love* followed, coming out around Thanksgiving. It was a five-song concept LP based on the four seasons (spring had two songs). The second single, "Winter Melody," came out in January 1977, and it had the distinction of being one of the very first 12-inch singles ever released. (Disco clubs, which liked to play epic-length singles, were the prime movers behind the creation of the 12-inch single.) The same month, we had Peter Lake direct and produce a sixteen-minute Donna Summer promotional film, portions of which he shot at Donna's Benedict Canyon home. The primary footage for Donna's promo was lensed on a very warm day, which was all wrong for a "Winter Melody" (one of the tracks Peter was shooting). Peter came up with the idea to spray a semiopaque white material over the lens to simulate winter, and the stunt actually worked. The extra attention garnered us another Gold album, but again the record had no real legs, no hype sustaining it. Desperate to keep Donna from sliding to one-hit-wonder status, in February we released a two-track limited edition LP of *Love to Love You Baby* (not to be confused with the 1975 Oasis album of the same name), which was designed as a greeting card to capitalize on the Valentine's Day market.

> - **August 16, 1977: Elvis Presley dies of an apparent overdose at his Graceland mansion; he was 42.**
> - **October 14, 1977: Bing Crosby passes away on a golf course near Madrid at age 74.**
> - **October 20, 1977: Three members of Lynyrd Skynyrd are killed in the crash of a chartered plane near McComb, Mississippi.**

The promotions department came up with the idea of sending copies of the LP to radio stations accompanied by an oversized heart-shaped chocolate that complemented the LP's cover art. Karmen Beck, who worked in promotion for us, was working overtime to get 150-plus Jiffy

LP mailers ready to ship out, and yellow boxes of the chocolate were stacked in the hallway outside the promotions department. Neil walked by, noticed the huge pile of candy, and casually asked Karmen what she was doing. "That's a nice idea, Karmen, but what is this chocolate? It's not Godiva. Since this is Donna, and we're Casablanca, only the very best will do. Fix it!" Poor Karmen had to redo most of the packages at home in order to make her deadline. We then flooded the scene with advertising for what we thought was a cash cow. Same results: good sales, no buzz.

When something isn't working, an artist has to blame someone, and artists rarely, if ever, blame themselves. Donna decided that a change of management was in order, and Dick Broder was out. Her other manager—Joyce Bogart—remained, of course; and Jeff Wald was brought on board to oversee her affairs. The association was short and not sweet. Donna never got along with Jeff, and he found her diva-like attitude to be unprofessional—intolerable, in fact—a sentiment that he would later express publicly.

By mid-May 1977, we were ready to roll out yet another Donna Summer album: *I Remember Yesterday*. This was Neil's standard tactic, and we'd already used it with KISS: if the public didn't like an album or a song, then it was time for a new one, even if only six months had elapsed between releases. After three KISS albums had come out in rapid succession and generated moderate success, the band broke big-time with *Alive!* and quickly followed it up with *Destroyer*, which expanded upon what *Alive!* had done. But with Donna, panic was beginning to set in. Since her debut, she had won a tremendous amount of peer acceptance, as well as industry awards too numerous to mention. But those accolades couldn't save her flatlining career. *I Remember Yesterday* was the final LP we would do with Donna under the terms of our original agreement, and we knew if we didn't hit it out of the park, then Donna would be shopping for a new record company.

"Can't We Just Sit Down (And Talk It Over)" came out as the first single. Thirty- and sixty-second TV spots aired all over the place as the summer wore on, and still nothing. Then, echoing what had happened with "Beth" the previous summer, toward the end of July, someone (I don't recall who) turned the 7-inch single over and began to play the B side, which contained a hypnotic little song that would become Donna's first Gold single since "Love to Love You Baby." That single, "I Feel Love," not only rescued her and us, but, due to Giorgio Moroder's innovative production (most disco songs featured orchestral accompaniment at that point, but "I Feel Love" had an entirely synthesized background), it significantly altered the direction of club music and jump-started the techno and electronica genres. The song and its production were so brilliant that five years later, in 1982, it was lengthened, remixed, and rereleased, achieving hit status all over again.

By the summer of 1977, disco was beginning to drive the company, even though KISS was still our premier act and was continuing to scale new heights. Their June release, *Love Gun*, had contractually shipped Platinum, a first for us and them. The memos from Glickman/Marks that came across my desk detailing production costs for a new tour were eye-popping—this on the heels of the one hundred thousand dollars they'd spent to record *Love Gun*. Two hydraulic platforms were installed to lower the band at the beginning of the show from the top of their now towering backline of cabinets to the stage. The staircase concept from the *Destroyer* tour had been expanded, Peter Criss's drum riser now not only went up but also slid forward to the front of the stage, and two portions of the stage itself now rose more than ten feet into the air during and at the end of the show. And KISS wanted *two* of these stages so that while they were performing on one stage, the stage for the subsequent show could be assembled. The entire outlay for this mess, including having new costumes designed and made, was nearly two hundred thousand dollars. That didn't sound impressive enough, so we told the press it was a million-dollar production.

Shortly after *Love Gun* was released, Marvel Comics issued a KISS comic book. It featured the band members as superheroes, which gave Neil an idea: Casablanca could create a comic book for a female disco superhero. He presented the idea to Marvel. Given that the KISS comic was their largest seller ever to that point, they were very happy to develop it. Thus Dazzler was born. One day, I went into Neil's office and saw several panels that had been submitted for approval. I picked one up and was shocked to see that Marvel had actually drawn an image of Neil and introduced it into the action. The concept was tossed back and forth between Marvel and us for so long that it eventually lost its charm for everyone involved and evaporated. I had forgotten all about it until years later, in 1981, I happened to see the first issue in a comic-book store.

KISS was now becoming an anomaly for us—a white-hot rock band in a growing stable of disco artists. Since we'd released the first Donna Summer album and "Love to Love You Baby," we had been talking up disco. We hadn't been big believers in the genre before this; it had seemed insubstantial, a little too much like the flavor of the month, but once we saw that the genre had staying power at the clubs and recognized that the clubs could dramatically influence radio, we embraced it. It was a money-making product, and we were in the money-making business.

Even unknown disco artists, who may have cost us only twenty thousand dollars, were selling enough product to make a profit. Casablanca was becoming so irrevocably associated with the disco genre that we were called "the disco label," and artists from all over the world were coming to us in droves to make deals. It reached the point where people wouldn't go into their favorite record store to ask for the new album by a particular artist—they would ask what was new from Casablanca. We were able to sell product that had no radio play just because the word "Casablanca" was printed on it.

This wasn't an accident. Initially, we ran into a problem selling disco. In fact, the entire industry was afflicted with the same dilemma. The club DJs tended to play one disco song right after another without naming what was playing. Disco was a very formulaic genre, and it all sounded fairly similar, so clubbers were clueless about what songs they were hearing. Our solution was to flood the clubs with advertising. We had cocktail napkins and posters and coasters and matchbooks bearing images of our artists and logos made up by the truckload, and we distributed them through the network of discotheques. While all this promo material didn't help you figure out what song you were listening to, it did make the Casablanca name omnipresent, and we soon had ourselves a very successful brand.

To help market that brand, we scoured the landscape for disco artists, and we spent most of the first half of 1977 signing them as quickly as we could get a pen into their hands: Love and Kisses, Paul Jabara, Munich Machine, and many others. Most did not produce any huge radio or retail hits, but they were wildly popular at the clubs. That wasn't all bad, because it gave Casablanca a consistent presence on a grassroots level.

To this day, it still surprises me that most people don't really understand that the typical disco act was just a producer and a concept. The bands were (for the most part) merely a fancy logo on a well-designed LP cover, which often portrayed a female in some high-fashion sexual pose. This fantasy concept was mainly intended to help an ad agency to build a marketing campaign around the cover art. And perhaps the best example of the concept was found in the work of European producer-songwriter Alec Costandinos.

Alec was a slender, good-looking guy of Egyptian descent who had been developing acts in France for several years and had scored a decent hit in 1976 with *Love in C Minor*, an album he'd collaborated on with a French disco drummer named Jean-Marc Cerrone. Alec was a joy to work with; the man knew every aspect of his craft. He knew how to write and produce music very quickly, but he was also intimately involved in creating cover art, and he'd often sit in on marketing meetings or work on contractual details with Richard Trugman. He knew that we were spending more time and effort on our bigger acts like KISS and Donna Summer, but as long as we gave him what he needed (which wasn't much) he never complained. Of all the artists we ever signed, Alec unquestionably delivered the most for our money. He was a one-man assembly line of great disco: between June 1977 and September 1979, he would release eleven albums through Casablanca under six different monikers. The most successful of these was our first Costandinos acquisition: *Love and Kisses*. The debut LP, whose artwork featured a close-up of a woman's partially exposed breasts (her T-shirt was being ripped apart by several groping hands) had already been released in France, and both Neil and I felt it would do very well stateside. In no small part, this was due to the fact that both of the LP's two songs were sixteen-plus minutes long. We released the album, and everyone was very pleased with the success of "Accidental Lover" and "I've Found Love (Now That I've Found You)." Both songs were huge in the clubs throughout the summer of 1977. *Love and Kisses* was so successful that we also snatched up *Sphinx*, a project Alec had worked on with French arranger Raymond Donnez (aka Don Ray). Like *Love and Kisses* before it, *Sphinx* had already been released in France. It had been designed as a concept album that told the story of the betrayal of Christ. Again, the album contained only two tracks, both epic-length, each filling up one side. Jesus meets disco.

It was a match made somewhere south of Heaven. It sounded like a good idea at the time, but Neil and I should have known better. We had tried something similar at Buddah with Vaughn Meader, a comedian who in 1971 had released an LP called *The Second Coming* on the Kama Sutra imprint. The album depicted Christ coming back to Earth, getting a Hollywood agent, and doing the talk show circuit. I thought it was funny and wondered if it would open people's minds with its social commentary, but the public didn't buy into it, and the album bombed.

Munich Machine came courtesy of our original European disco import, Giorgio Moroder. It was another project Giorgio had developed with songwriter and producer Peter Bellotte. It, too, stuck with the prog-rock-length song idea—"Get on the Funk Train" took up the album's entire A side. The album was released in May, and it was quickly followed by another of the pair's Euro-disco experiments (bearing only Giorgio's name, however) called *From Here to Eternity*. Both albums followed the Casablanca disco trend: a hit in the clubs; not as much buzz on the air or in the stores.

Another signing soon became the favorite artist of almost everyone in the company: the pushy, very talented, very confused-about-everything (including his own sexuality) Paul Jabara. Paul began his relationship with Casablanca by hanging out with us at clubs and then endearing himself to us and many of our artists. Industry luminaries like Barbra Streisand, Donna Summer, and Cher all took a liking to Paul and recorded his songs. It didn't hurt that he was managed by Ron DeBlasio and Jeff Wald, both of whom (along with Joyce) were also overseeing Donna's career.

Paul would come into my office and dance and sing his latest song. He was a breath of fresh air. Though he was a funny sort of character, we initially didn't take him all that seriously. Paul released his first album for us, *Shut Out* (which we pressed on cherry-red vinyl), in May 1977. The album's title track featured a duet with Donna Summer. Despite his talent and the success other artists had with his songs, Paul never had a hit album of his own, but he was always humble and fun to be with. His manic energy and occasionally neurotic behavior sometimes grated on one's nerves, but he made coming to work fun. Thirty years later, I still love to listen to his albums.

Another of our disco albums originated in an entirely different fashion: *Frankie Crocker and The Heart & Soul Orchestra*. Frankie had been a DJ for years before landing the program director job at WBLS in New York. Black DJs and PDs got paid very little by their white bosses, who had little regard for black music or the black community; the bosses were just in it to make money, and they'd do it on the cheap if they could. Black radio employees in general were paid far less than their white counterparts. As PD at WBLS, Frankie had been involved in payola. You'd pay him three thousand dollars to play a new release for a specified number of weeks—if the record did well in that time, then he would keep it on; if not, it was off. All the record companies knew about this, and it was actually a cheap way to see if you really had a hit: if it worked on WBLS, then it would work throughout the country. This eliminated the hassle of testing a record all over the place, which could cost tens of thousands of dollars. One of Frankie's friends, Rocky G., turned state's evidence on him, and Cecil (among many others in the industry) was called in to testify. Though a federal court in Philadelphia later overturned the conviction, Frankie lost his job at WBLS, and after that everyone in the industry treated him as a pariah. Except us—Neil wanted to help him. In order to give Frankie some money to live on, we made a deal with him to do his own product release. Of course, Frankie was not a musician, but he did know R&B—he was one of the best ears in the biz when it came to that. The record he did for us didn't do great, but quite a few programmers, especially in the black community, played it because they believed that he had been given a raw deal.

When you sign that many bands that quickly, some are going to bomb before they even get started. David Joseph and Chris Bearde (whom we knew through the Hudson Brothers and Angel) brought us one of Bearde's acts, Greg and Paul, who had a new CBS Television show called *A Year at the Top*, which was about two musicians trying to get signed by a record company. Despite being backed by a production team that included Norman Lear (of *All in the Family* fame) and Don Kirshner, the show, slated for a six-week run, failed almost before it went on the air; it was canceled shortly after the pilot was broadcast on August 5. We'd already agreed to release a self-titled album by Greg and Paul, which featured songs from the series. The program flopped so badly that I don't think we ever mailed the album to radio. But Greg and Paul did go on to become famous: Greg Evigan as the star of *BJ and the Bear* and *My Two Dads*; and Paul Shaffer, who was already the bandleader on

Saturday Night Live, as David Letterman's longtime musical director and sidekick.

To capitalize on the disco revolution and help make something of all our new signings, Neil began to look for the best disco marketing/promotional person in LA. The name that kept coming up was Marc Paul Simon, a good-looking, very bright disco-marketing genius. Marc had his own company, Provocative Promotions, and it was so good that we eventually absorbed it into Casablanca so that we could have Marc's services exclusively. With Marc came two of his associates, Michele Hart and Ken Friedman. Ken worked out of New York, and his influence over the club scene there was so great that he practically owned it.

I worked with Marc and his company in planning and organizing our marketing and retail campaigns. Marc also had direct access to Neil, and they would dissect disco in great detail in an effort to distill the formula behind the hits. They would discuss things like beats per minute (most disco hits had almost exactly the same number of beats per minute, and the formula seemed to change every four months or so, keeping things fresh). I explained Neil's promotional philosophy to Marc and showed him how to implement it at the clubs. The clubs became our research and development labs; we would ask them to test our songs before we put them out for mass consumption. If a song kept club patrons on the dance floor, we knew we had a potential hit, but if they didn't enjoy the song, we didn't release it.

Neil took to disco like a duck to water. He began to establish the company as the genre's home. The competition was slim, as none of the major labels were embracing the music. Even when they did take a chance on disco, they had a hard time dealing with the gay mindset that pervaded the genre. Many also failed to understand that, much like bubblegum acts, disco artists usually had little to do with the music; they were just the drivers of the race cars built by the writers and producers.

The problem with having a glut of disco product was that our rock promotion department, which was second in size only to publicity, had little to work with. Seeing a department of two dozen people with nothing to do didn't sit well with me, so I went on a tear to get some rock product into the pipeline. This wasn't easy, because we only had one noteworthy rock group on our roster, so most others didn't consider us the best label to sign with—they only turned to us after everyone else had passed on them.

Not long after I started this drive to acquire more rock, Scott Bergstein from our international department brought me an exciting tape. The songs were great, and some tracks had the added bonus of including a saxophone—I'm a huge sucker for the sax. I got so excited that I ran into Neil's office and told him I had found the next great group, but it would cost a hundred thousand dollars to sign them, so I needed his approval. He said, "Why sign a band for a hundred thousand when we could sign four or five disco acts for that amount?" He never even asked to hear the group. I was disappointed, but there was nothing I could do, and so Casablanca lost out on signing Dire Straits. The band signed with Warner Brothers and released their first album maybe a year later, scoring a nice hit with the single "Sultans of Swing." Under the stewardship of Mark Knopfler, they went on to become a multi-Platinum monolith in the mid-1980s with the enormous hit "Money for Nothing," a touchstone moment in the history of MTV.

The Dire Straits strikeout wasn't our only big swing and miss. In 1976, not long after he'd left Genesis, Peter Gabriel came to see us. We met with him and his manager and had them looking for a pen in a matter of moments. They would have signed with Casablanca on the spot had it not been for a poison-pill, oh-by-the-way stipulation Gabriel threw in at the last moment. He wanted half a million dollars per LP. Had we been clairvoyant enough to see "Shock the Monkey" or *So* in our crystal ball, then the half million wouldn't have seemed so ridiculous, but at that point Gabriel wasn't much more than the ex-singer of Genesis who hadn't proved himself as a solo act. Neil felt it just wasn't worth the risk.

A host of new acts and dozens of new employees would seem to be the earmarks of a successful record company. But we were spending so much money on paint—placing full-page ads in the trades by the gross, racking up mind-numbing figures on our expense accounts, increasing our pay-roll several times over—that despite the successes (even the real ones) we were still nearly broke. We had no cash flow even when we did have hits. We were having record sales months: $5.8 million in May, followed by $6.3 million in June. In July, seven of our albums were on *Billboard*'s disco charts. And all that money was gone as soon as we made it. We spent so much time keeping the wolves from the door that it cut into our ability to run the company as we would have liked. That was just part of the game, and we were used to the wolves, but things were getting worse.

Our motion picture deal with Peter Guber had given us the appearance of being a rising player in traditional Hollywood. The first picture in the deal, *The Deep*, was released in June, and within three days it was apparent that it was going to be a big hit. It bolted out of the gate with a first-weekend gross of nearly seven million, on its way to pulling in over $125 million (adjusted for inflation) in ticket receipts. We kept the cast constantly in the public eye—they appeared on Johnny Carson, Merv Griffin, Dinah Shore, and Phil Donahue, as well as in the pages of *Time*, *Newsweek*, *Playboy*, and *Cosmopolitan*.

Just before the movie was released, Neil arranged a screening for all of our promotions people. Then he announced that we were not going to promote the movie in the traditional Hollywood fashion. Instead, we would have a heavy radio focus. The promotions guys, of course, had all appreciated the infamous and alluring scene at the beginning of the film where Jacqueline Bisset emerges from the water after a scuba dive wearing a transparent T-shirt. The publicity brainstorm was obvious: we organized wet T-shirt contests around the country (which must have been among the first events of their type ever staged) in conjunction with local radio.

The soundtrack album was released on transparent blue vinyl, and it came with a poster that featured an incredibly sexy image of Jacqueline in her wet T-shirt. The record featured original music by John Barry of James Bond fame, as well as songs by Donna Summer and Beckett, another of our recent disco signings. It was a decent seller, and we added to the din by releasing not only the making-of book, penned by Guber, but also a sixty-minute documentary film called *Making "The Deep,"* the brainchild of Peter Lake. The documentary aired as an ABC Television prime time special on September 11, nearly three months after the feature film had been released—a lag time that would never occur in today's marketplace. *The Deep* was the fourth-highest-grossing film of the year, so things looked rosy for Casablanca's FilmWorks division. That might have solved our cash flow issue, except that by September we'd yet to be paid by Columbia Pictures. They were trying to screw us out of our share of the profits—something *unheard-of* in Hollywood. Luckily, Guber, who had worked for Columbia, knew about their accounting practices and worked with Columbia chieftain Ray Stark to figure out a way for us to get paid. We were owed eight million, but we settled for five. However, the funds were not available when we needed them most, leaving Neil to face several courses of action, none of them appealing.

Neil and I, along with Richard Trugman, met in Neil's office. I sat on a barstool while Neil paced around the big conference table running over our options. He was trying to convince us that selling the company made sense, but he was just convincing himself. It was hard to watch. There seemed to be only one taker: Clive Davis at Arista. Clive had offered us two million, and Neil was seriously considering it. I wasn't all that worried about myself, about not having a gig if this went through. I knew Clive a little, and I'd heard from others that he liked me. To me, the problem was that Casablanca was much more successful than Arista: we had stronger acts and far better promo people. It would be like the Yankees being bought out by the Milwaukee Brewers. I could abide selling the company, if that's what it came down to, but to a smaller and less-talented one?

Neil also had an offer to run MCA for an annual salary of one million dollars with bonuses, and I knew that if he decided to accept the job he'd take me with him. But the MCA deal, as attractive it might sound, meant little or nothing to Neil. MCA was known as a crummy label to work for; they didn't care about their employees. The music end of the company had gone through a new president every year. Also, MCA was part of a huge corporation, which meant that Neil would be forced to run through endless bureaucratic gauntlets—a situation that had driven him away from both Buddah and Warner Brothers. Rumors of our sale to ABC, or Columbia, or Capitol—depending upon which source you believed—ran rampant in the trades, and Neil flatly denied them, even though they weren't far off the mark.

When Casablanca first signed with Warner, in 1973, the deal was set up for us to go out of business. After a specified period of time, the controlling interest in our label would be bought out and rolled into the Warner family. But our sentiments had changed by the time the 1974 split occurred, and we remained an independent company. Now we were really missing that big, warm security blanket. Like the cavalry coming to the rescue, Neil's close friend and ATI chief, Jeff Franklin, showed up with an offer. And this offer was so good that rather than cry in our soup over losing Casablanca, we were ecstatic. After failing twice to broker a deal with ABC Records to merge with Casablanca, Franklin had gone to PolyGram, which was co-owned by two old and very powerful Dutch and German corporations, Philips and Siemens. As early as 1962, both companies had begun expanding their international operations by acquiring several American music and film companies, including Mercury, MGM Records, and Verve, plus Robert Stigwood's RSO Records in the UK. It was an impressive list, to be sure. Talks between PolyGram and Casablanca went on for weeks, and when PolyGram seemed to be dragging their heels, Neil played them in the trades. Blurbs started appearing in *Billboard* with gossip-column copy like, "Is the gleam in Neil Bogart's eyes fading over the prospect of a PolyGram buyout?" It was pure propaganda. Neil was using the press to leverage negotiations in his favor. PolyGram finally offered us ten million for just half the company, with a guarantee to purchase the remaining shares of Casablanca within five years at five times earnings. Plus, they weren't experienced in our market niches and could probably be bent to our wishes. This wasn't the death of Casablanca: this was our lottery ticket. It was turn-off-the-lights-we're-flyin'-to-Bora-Bora-to-count-our-money time. It's not that PolyGram had bought into the vision we'd cultivated that Casablanca was the four-hundred-pound gorilla of the record world; in their eyes, our motion picture division, with its five-movie deal with Columbia, was a license to print money. The record company was nothing more than a shiny bonus.

Once the offer was made, Neil pulled the trigger quickly. Then Guber decided he could improve it, and that's when things got interesting. Guber waited for PolyGram's check to clear the bank, and then he told them that he was going to the beach—Hollywood jargon for "I'm not working for you unless you give me more money." Guber wanted an additional five million to cut short his vacation, so to speak, and he got it. The already lopsided deal improved by 50 percent when PolyGram caved and bought half of Casablanca for fifteen million dollars total. I never asked and was never told what Jeff Franklin got to put the deal together; but I do know that he didn't get any of the fifteen million, so I assume he received a finder's fee from PolyGram. Jeff often told people that he owned part of Casablanca, but he never did; the only owners were Neil, Peter Guber, Cecil Holmes, Richard Trugman, me, and Buck Reingold, who had relinquished his share when he left the company.

Soon after the deal was signed, Neil, Cecil, Guber, Trugman, and I gathered at the main branch of Security Pacific Bank, a major financial institution in LA. As a group, we were escorted to the room where the PolyGram buyout checks had been made out to each of us. We signed some legal documents, we each had our picture taken, and then the money was placed into accounts that investment firm Bear Stearns had already opened for us. Guber received 20 percent of the ten-million-dollar payout. Trugman and I each received about 8.5 percent, Cecil took about 10 percent, and Neil pocketed the remainder. Neil had made sure to retain a bit more than half so that he would never lose controlling interest in the company. The percentages on the additional five million Guber had been able to get for us were paid out some months later.

The room was filled with laughter and joking. After years of living paycheck to paycheck, we were all in a state of semishock due to this sudden windfall. We felt a great sense of relief and excitement over the fact that we did not have to worry about the company having money; we had what amounted to a blank check from PolyGram to sign acts, increase the company payroll, be creative, and have fun. With a very curious bit of rationalizing, Neil decided not to pay any taxes on his PolyGram money. He was convinced that because he'd given up his Viewlex stock when we left Buddah in 1973, he shouldn't have to pay taxes on the PolyGram payment. It was a fair trade, to his mind. Everyone laughed and told him that's not how it worked, even his accountant, but he still insisted that he shouldn't have to pay taxes on that money.

After we got the payout, we needed to minimize the taxes that would be demanded by the IRS and the State of California. Since the money from PolyGram was not a capital gain (to qualify for that status, we would have to have owned the stock for five years or more), our accountant, Arnold Feldman, came up with some tax shelters. When Neil had launched ArtWorks, Arnold had figured out that if you owned a lithograph (or any type of master print from which duplicates could be made), you could not reproduce it infinitely; the master would begin to show signs of wear, and you would have to stop making prints from it. An unusable master, Arnold reasoned, could be depreciated as an asset. This meant that the owner—in this case, Neil—could claim a deduction on all masters.

With that in mind, we thought that we could shelter the PolyGram money by purchasing master recordings—tapes or acetates used in the mass production of cassettes, vinyl, 8-tracks, and so forth. I therefore ended up owning some children's recordings that were absolutely terrible, and few of them were ever manufactured or distributed—maybe a dozen or so. After a few years, the IRS threw out the shelters and told us to pay up; California followed suit a year or two after that.

If I had been savvier about this stuff, I would have just paid what was due in the beginning and aligned myself with my own accountant, but we all considered Arnold a friend and thought he knew what he was doing. I had certainly never had this kind of money before, so I listened, and when Neil told me to trust Arnold, I did. Those decisions would haunt me for years; the State of California alone charged me over eighty thousand dollars in interest and penalties.

Bear Stearns also got us into some real estate deals that everyone but me knew would never show a profit. In most cases, only the principal players ever saw a profit, and—silly me—I did not stop to think that the principals here were the Bear Stearns account reps who were handling my stuff. I once called a rep and said I had a feeling about gold and wanted to buy some. He tried to talk me out of it, but I insisted, and I bought ten- or twenty-thousand-dollars' worth of gold at about one-hundred-forty dollars per ounce. I was ecstatic when it reached over eight hundred dollars. I later found out that Neil had also bought gold, but he knew what he was doing, and instead of hard gold, he bought some kind of contract for one hundred thousand dollars and made considerably more money.

Years later, in 1986, Bruce Bird, Richard Trugman, and I were called to be expert witnesses at a tax evasion trial that involved the masters of *The Deep* soundtrack, which were owned by the family of Sydney S. Baron (who had passed away after purchasing them). Baron had acquired the masters as a tax shelter, and he thought that since Donna Summer was on the album and the music was largely composed by John Barry, it would be a big hit. He'd made an initial cash outlay and backed the rest of the purchase price with a promissory note for more than half a million dollars. This was an instance of Neil cleverly hedging his risks by selling off an album that, according to our own projections, wouldn't recoup the sale price. When the album didn't sell anywhere near enough for Baron to break even, he'd written it off as a depreciation of an asset. The IRS nixed the idea and cut him to shreds. I am sure Donna and Giorgio never knew about this; if they read about it here, it may come as news to them.

The independent distributors who had saved us when we left Warner in 1974 were not at all pleased at how the buyout changed the distribution pipeline. It forced us to indemnify them for returns so we could have a fairly seamless transition to PolyGram. When product was returned, the distributors had to reimburse the retailers for the cost of the albums; Casablanca had been paid for that product when it was first released. But we could not let the distributors hold the bag for unsold product, so we agreed to reimburse them. Fortunately, returns were minimal, thanks to KISS and the disco craze.

I felt bad leaving some of the distributors. I had worked closely with many of them, and I recognized the vital role they'd played in our success. Without them, we would not have survived the departure from Warner in 1974. The major problem with PolyGram acquiring various record companies—the list included RSO, Mercury, Polydor, and us—was that they now had to establish their own distribution company. This proved more difficult than they had expected. They hired a guy from the trucking industry, John Frizolli, to head the distribution company, and he knew less than nothing about the music business. Casablanca was moving product at a good rate on several fronts, but aside from that, plus RSO's mainstay, the Bee Gees, and the soundtrack of *Grease*, nothing was really selling well for PolyGram. The company needed to establish a consistent flow of hit product if it wanted retailers to pay them and buy their new artists.

PolyGram had an issue with us from the beginning. Remember, we hated the stiff culture of the corporate world, in which you practically had to ask permission to use the toilet. We didn't like being managed; we didn't like bureaucracy; we liked acting like a bunch of delinquents with an expense account. On top of that, a number of our key positions were filled by Jews, and most of the contingent at PolyGram's corporate headquarters in Europe was German. One of them, in particular (his name was Kurt Kinkler), bragged that he had been a U-boat commander during World War II, which certainly did not endear him to us. This situation struck a discordant note in the relations between Neil, Peter

Guber, and numerous PolyGram representatives, although many of the people in the company's Dutch wing were nice to us.

It was difficult to talk about music and movies with people who had little understanding of our market or our artists. Our culture—the larger American one and the smaller version of it within the walls of 8255 Sunset—was foreign to the PolyGram people. They seemed not to care at all about artists as long as they contributed to the bottom line. This was an attitude with which I was unfamiliar. Buddah had been artist-friendly, we certainly were at Casablanca, and even Warner cared, or seemed to, about artists and their music; if you mentioned an artist, even if he or she was not yet famous, the executives at Warner knew who you were talking about.

Neil and I grew to have so much disdain for PolyGram that we would show up at board meetings in New York tripping on Quaaludes. After one of these meetings, Neil mentioned that he wanted to make me president, and he would become chairman. PolyGram told him they knew I did drugs because I'd been high at the last board meeting (I guess I was slurring more than usual), and they did not want someone who did drugs running the company. But I was already running the company. What did they think I was doing—knitting a sweater? And did they think Neil himself was a squeaky-clean teetotaler? For all intents and purposes, I was already running the day-to-day business of Casablanca; the title bump wasn't going to change anything.

Shortly after this, PolyGram decided that they should have one of their own people looking over our shoulder. They chose David Shein, a young accountant from New York who initially seemed quite conservative and very pro-PolyGram. It took no time at all for us to change that. I'm not sure what he was used to at PolyGram in New York, or what he expected at Casablanca, but he was one of us in about five minutes. Who doesn't like going to the best restaurants, driving the fanciest cars, and traveling first class? David became an integral member of the Casablanca team and a convenient, cooperative mole; in espionage parlance, we'd flipped the spy. But David did more than just keep PolyGram away from us: he also helped out in our bookkeeping and accounting department; and, with Neil's brother-in-law, Joey Ermilio, he helped set up a Wang computer system for us—quite a feat, as it took up a space the size of three or four offices.

Some of the PolyGram distribution people were good at what they did—Rick Blieweis and Emil Patron, to name two—but there were only a few people in the company who understood the record business. They were all in awe of Neil, and they did not dare come close to crossing him. They would do whatever we wanted, no matter how foolish it was. Whenever Neil asked, they would invest more money in Casablanca. Peter Guber was similarly revered. As the golden goose in all of this, Peter was left alone—PolyGram certainly did not want to piss him off and have him head out to the beach again.

A few months after PolyGram became involved with us, Neil and Bruce Bird came into my office. Neil explained to me that I was going to throw a party and spend ten thousand dollars. But not really. He and Bruce would help me get receipts totaling that amount, and I would get PolyGram to reimburse me; I would then give the ten grand to Bruce, who would use it to take care of business. I did as they requested, and it was the closest I ever came to payola. I don't even remember what record they used the money for, but for that amount they could have covered several major-market stations. Of course, they never helped me with the receipts. Just figuring out who I had invited to the party was a pain in the ass—I listed every politician I could think of, plus dead musicians, old war heroes, and Neil and Bruce and their extended families. If anyone was ever questioned about the party, I figured they would just say that they'd been there and it was great.

No matter what corporate umbrella we were under, the sign on the door still said Casablanca, which may as well have been Spanish for "disco boys." Another French import, Leroy Gomez and Santa Esmeralda, came on board in October 1977, bringing their monster hit "Don't Let Me Be Misunderstood" with them. When I heard their record, I couldn't get them signed quickly enough. I almost fell off my chair, and then I got our legal department (then headed by Dick Ettlinger) to take care of the particulars. When all was said and done, it was the best deal we ever made. The entire album cost us thirty-five thousand dollars, with a very low royalty rate of about 6 percent (what they had asked for), as opposed to the new-artist standard of 10 to 12 percent. The record sold millions, almost overnight. "Don't Let Me Be Misunderstood" was one of those once-in-a-lifetime songs that hit with little assistance; we mailed it to the radio stations, and they jumped on it. But, once again, I made the mistake of not seeing a group perform before signing them. Leroy Gomez was not bad looking, but he was a terrible live performer, and Santa Esmeralda, a pair of women, didn't have a clue about performing either. We arranged a small preview of the band, and it was awful. I knew then that this act would fizzle after only a few hits.

Disco and movies were absorbing all of our attention, so it was fortunate for us that the KISS ship was being helmed by Glickman/Marks, and they were doing it well. They kept us informed of the band's touring and promotional plans and consulted us on many matters. KISS's 1977 summer tour had been their biggest success yet, and at a sold-out three-night stand at The Forum in LA, they'd recorded a follow-up to *Alive!* The new live album, a two-record set called *Alive II*, was released on October 24, and it shipped Platinum. KISS had also recently topped Led Zeppelin and the Stones, among others, in a Gallup survey that polled teenagers for their band preferences. KISS had outgrown their next-big-thing status: they were now among rock's premier acts.

George Clinton and Parliament had been busy as well. Two of their 1977 concerts had been recorded and released in May of that year as a two-disc collection we dubbed *P-Funk Earth Tour*. Initial copies of the release included a poster and a catchy iron-on decal that read "Take funk to heaven in '77." The band toured for most of the year (they were major headliners in most markets), and the mothership even made a special landing in Times Square for a documentary, which was eventually scrapped. After Thanksgiving, we released their album *Funkentelechy vs. the Placebo Syndrome* (I had long since stopped asking George what these titles meant), which contained what would turn out to be some of their last sizable hits, including their only No. 1 R&B hit, "Flash Light." We produced an amazing TV spot for the album using some of the animation elements Parliament employed in their live performances.

Donna Summer, meanwhile, had re-signed with Casablanca, and as part of the deal we had acquired the worldwide distribution rights to her current releases and back catalog (thus far, we'd only had North American rights to her current releases). Still riding high on of the success of "I Feel Love," Donna had spent several weeks on tour in Europe. Then, in early November, we rush-released her next album, *Once upon a Time....* Barely five months had passed since her previous LP, but Neil's perpetual sense of urgency tended to dictate our release patterns, and he was desperate to have a new record for Donna's fans to buy before Christmas.

In keeping with the grand, larger-than-life vibe of the disco world, we made the release a gatefold double LP, with each of the four sides representing a different musical genre, including a full side of "I Feel Love"-inspired electronica. The concept album told the story of a girl living in a land where everything real was unreal, a fairytale that in some ways mirrored Donna's own life. One of the album's singles, "I Love You," was a major hit in Europe, while the title track, along with "Now I Need You" and "Working the Midnight Shift," became fan favorites. Though *Once upon a Time…* didn't yield a bona fide US hit, the LP sold very well, and it was certified Gold in December.

By the end of 1977, we were racing ahead faster than I'd ever thought possible. In the last twelve weeks of the year, we had more releases—seventeen—than we'd had in all of 1976. And as the clock struck midnight that New Year's Eve, one of those releases, Donna Summer's *Once upon a Time…*, was sitting atop the disco charts. Casablanca, the disco label, had the top disco act and the top rock act. But the question was: Could we survive life at the top?

16

La-La Land

**Bent over—Gregg Giuffria—*Macho Man*—Love and Kisses—
The future Mrs. Cosby—Bill Tennant—A suicide attempt—
Party for the governor—A spy among us—
Dodger game—Helping Cedars-Sinai—
Slots, belly dancers, and NARM**

January 1978
Casablanca Record & FilmWorks Headquarters
8255 Sunset Boulevard
Los Angeles, California

Gregg Giuffria, Angel's keyboardist, was in my office. He and I had developed a good relationship since we'd signed the group in 1975, and he was my primary contact among the band members. Gregg would stop by the Sunset building frequently, walking from office to office to maintain his presence and remind all the various department heads (there seemed to be more and more of them each day) about Angel. As we sat there bullshitting, he mentioned that as he'd been working his way through the building that day, saying hello to anyone who would give him a minute, he'd wandered into the office of Steve Keator (our director of media relations) and found one of our recording artists, in full costume, bending Steve over the desk and screwing him in the ass. He was about as fazed at the sight as I was at hearing about it—which is to say, not at all. That was Casablanca.

Gregg and I were discussing Angel's latest album, *White Hot*, which was Casablanca's first release of 1978. From the moment we'd signed them, nothing had come easy for Angel. Their looks, talent, and drive all spelled sure thing, but at every turn, some sort of crappy luck or bad karma seemed to be awaiting them—most recently, the eleventh-hour cancellation of their movie *Angel at Midnight*. Gregg was recounting all of the challenges Angel had faced in the past year, including the need to replace bassist Mickie Jones. They'd held secret auditions for the post in LA, and they'd finally found their man in St. Louis native Felix Robinson, whom they knew through another band that Bill Schereck, their tour manager, had been managing.

One of the Casablanca recording acts who also hung around our offices was the Village People. Months after signing the band, Neil and I had finally met that strange cast of characters (which appeared to have evolved since they were assembled for the first LP cover). Jacques and Henri had just finished overseeing the sessions for the second Village People album, *Macho Man*. Their self-titled first release had set 8255 buzzing, and, as usual, the discotheques had jumped on the band-wagon, but the album hadn't produced a breakaway hit. Radio was still keeping its distance. The second album would change all that—we knew it the moment we heard the title track. It had passed the Casablanca test immediately: I don't think I ever had that many people come running into my office at once. The coming months bore out the test's accuracy. "Macho Man," the single, peaked at No. 2 on the charts. Finally, radio and retail had caught on to what the clubs had been saying, and the Village People had their first Gold single and Platinum album.

While their popularity and sales soared, relations within this disco hodgepodge were not so ideal. I heard a rumor that Victor Willis (who portrayed the cop and was the only straight member of the original act) was allegedly bullying the others. Complaints also began to surface that group members were only getting paid one hundred dollars per week, causing some friction within the ranks. It was becoming obvious to us that we couldn't expect them to do everything that was being asked of them (interviews, appearances, concerts) for so little money. Plus, there was their image to consider: music stars don't live on near-poverty wages.

However, any action we should or could have taken was precluded by the fact that we had no say in anything concerning the band members. The Village People were owned and controlled by Morali and Belolo; Casablanca did the manufacturing, distribution, and promotion, and little else. The Village People were becoming so successful that we didn't want to make waves. They were selling as many albums as KISS and Donna Summer, and we just couldn't afford to piss Jacques and Henri off, so we bit our tongues and tried to ignore the problem. Eventually, I had a heart-to-heart with the two about the band members' unhappiness. This led to a slight raise, which seemed to appease the band for the moment.

The Village People were on the superstar launch pad, Angel was going nowhere, and Donna Summer was somewhere in between, in a state of flux. By February 1978, she had hired her third comanager in just three years: Susan Munao, our former publicist. I liked Donna very much, but she was always surrounded by drama. There never seemed to be a state of rest for her—no status quo. Part of that was because she was always in the company of Joyce or Susan, neither of whom was anywhere near low-key; plus, I'm sure she was influenced by any number of the countless people who hovered around her. But Susan, while not always easy to deal with, was at least a known factor.

Donna's itinerary was taking an interesting turn. On January 27, she started a three-night stand at the Sahara Hotel in Lake Tahoe with her new backing band, Brooklyn Dreams. At our request, she had added two new songs to her set (neither of which would be released for several months) so that we could shoot a live promotional film for them. One of these was "MacArthur Park," and the other was a mesmerizing ballad called "Last Dance," which I'd first heard toward the end of the previous summer.

The always chipper Paul Jabara had stopped by my office one day and insisted that I drop what I was doing and listen to a new track he'd written. Most of our artists wouldn't have had this kind of instant access to me (I wasn't living in an ivory tower—I just didn't have the time), but Paul was so disarming that it was hard for me to tell him no. I sat and listened to his demo, and when it was over, without saying a word to him, I got up and opened the adjoining door to Neil's office. Neil was on the phone, so I gave him the look we'd shoot each other when something really important was happening. Saying "I'll get back to you" into the phone, he came into my office. He seemed surprised to see Paul there. As he sat down, I turned up the volume to a deafening level and opened the outer door: the Casablanca test was in progress. Employees started piling in. Paul danced around, singing along with the tape and making grand gestures with the lyrics. It was a great moment, and everyone in the room absolutely knew we had a smash hit. Paul had written it for Donna Summer, and "Last Dance" came to play a key role in her career. It would also become an integral component of our already booming business, to say nothing of what it would do for disco.

One of our other French disco imports, Alec Costandinos, handed over two more releases early in the year: the second LP from Love and Kisses, titled *How Much, How Much I Love You*; and Alec's biggest hit (under his own name), *Romeo and Juliet*. I was able to push the title track of the latter to No. 1 on the disco charts, albeit for only a week. A promo film was even produced, which was a true rarity for a disco producer. It featured Alec on a motorcycle with a blonde riding shotgun. Around the same time, a French record company, Carrere, began placing full-page ads in the US trades seeking distribution for a female singer named Sheila, who supposedly was already No. 1

> • **March 6, 1978: Larry Flynt, publisher of *Hustler*, is shot and paralyzed. Joseph Paul Franklin, a white supremacist serial killer, would later allege that he shot Flynt because of interracial sex photos in the magazine, but this would never be proven.**
> • **April 22, 1978: The Blues Brothers appear for the first time on *Saturday Night Live*.**
> • **June 16, 1978: The movie *Grease* opens, with John Travolta and Olivia Newton-John in the lead roles.**

in France with a disco cover of "Singin' in the Rain." The idea of pitching Neil on a remake of that twenty-five-year-old Gene Kelly number was ridiculous. I thought it through: on the one hand, how many people in the notoriously trendy disco clubs were going to find this song hip? On the other hand, it was French, and it was disco, which in our books was the magic recipe for a hit single. Within an hour of seeing one of the print ads, Neil was on the phone trying to sign a deal to release the LP in the States. The song went nowhere, but Sheila found success later on, most notably with a 1979 album produced by Nile Rodgers and Bernard Edwards of Chic. A similar latter-day success story came from this side of the Atlantic. We bought another go-nowhere record, this one from Jacques Morali and Henri Belolo—a disco concept album of original music about legendary singer and dancer Josephine Baker. The artist was a singer named Phylicia Allen, the wife of Victor Willis of the Village People. By the mid-1980s, Phylicia had become a

household name as Clair Huxtable, Bill Cosby's TV wife on his hit NBC
show.

On January 10, 1978, NBC Television had aired an hour-long special
by revered anchor Edwin Newman called *Land of Hype and Glory*. It pro-
filed the growing successes and excesses of the entertainment industry,
and both KISS and Peter Guber were featured. Hype had long been the
driver of our public persona, but lately—happily—glory had taken the
wheel. In October and November 1977, Casablanca had generated $15.4
million in revenue, a full 107 percent increase over the same period in
1976. Since the October 1 acquisition, PolyGram had posted three consecutive months of record sales, peaking at $27.3 million in December
and keeping pace with old-school giants CBS, Capitol, and Warner
Brothers. For the year, Casablanca had done $55 million, and we were
projecting double that for 1978.

We now had over 160 employees scattered between three buildings
on Sunset and a fifteen-person office in Manhattan headed by Ray
D'Ariano; we also had Robin Taylor, general manager of Pye Records,
ready to help us open the doors to a new London office. PolyGram eventually quashed the idea of the London facility, preferring to control
European operations themselves. In February, we named Marc Paul
Simon vice president of special projects, and soon afterwards we
acquired Simon's company, Provocative Promotions, absorbing his staff
into our ranks. Our subsidiaries were healthy, with hits of their own;
Millennium had Meco's astonishing string of disco soundtrack successes,
and Chocolate City had funk/dance purveyors Cameo.

In mid-March, Cecil, Bruce, and I received title bumps: I became
senior vice president and managing director, Cecil became senior vice
president and special assistant to Neil, and Bruce assumed my old title of
executive vice president. Also in March, David Shein was made vice
president and chief financial officer.

One of the more interesting hires was Bill Tennant, who came over
from Columbia Pictures to be president of the FilmWorks division. Bill
had been a very successful agent, and one of his clients was Academy
Award–winning director Roman Polanski, whose pregnant wife, Sharon
Tate, had been murdered by the Manson clan in 1969. Bill had been
called upon to identify the bodies of Tate and several of the clan's other
victims. His knowledge of the film industry was vast; he'd inked Peter

Fonda's deal for *Easy Rider* and attached Polanski to *Rosemary's Baby*. While he was production VP at Columbia, the studio had produced *Taxi Driver* and *Close Encounters of the Third Kind*, among others. Tennant was brilliant, and Peter Guber knew it. Bill was available because he'd been caught in the crossfire when Columbia studio head David Begelman's check-forging activities came to light. Begelman, whom Bill considered a mentor, had embezzled over forty thousand dollars by forging check endorsements; a scandal had ensued, and Begelman was forced to resign, pulling Tennant down with him. I don't think Tennant spent more than five minutes on the street before Guber approached him with a lucrative job offer. He accepted and thus became the third-highest-paid person in the company, behind only Neil and Peter. I was initially pissed off about this, and I treated Bill somewhat as an adversary, but once we'd had a chance to spend some time together we became friends. After all, we were in similar positions—Bill handled the kind of day-to-day details for Guber that I was handling for the record company.

Another significant hire, at least in terms of its impact on me, was Betty Logan. My former assistant, Terry Barnes, had left to join Scott Shannon at Ariola Records. Shannon had departed in the fall of 1977, and Terry's interest in the promotion field, as well as her interest in Shannon (she had always seemed to have a bit of a crush on him), prompted her to follow. Unknown to me (and as busy as I was, it was easy for me to be oblivious to such things), Terry wasn't the only one in the building with strong feelings for Scott. A tall, blonde female staffer in the legal department, whose name has since escaped me, was so distraught over Scott choosing to take Terry with him that one day she attempted suicide while in the building. We kept the whole thing quiet, and very few people even knew it had happened. Betty Logan came into this mess and didn't miss a beat. She was a bright, beautiful, sweet woman with a dark complexion. She was also brilliant at protecting me from the industry gossip to which record company execs are often subject, and she had no problem putting up with me, my naps, and my drugs, to say nothing of the occasional bouts of flirting with other women that went on. Betty was my ace in the hole.

Neil, meanwhile, who had never been a wallflower, was taking more and more of the company spotlight and branching off into entirely new territory. The first big event that occurred in his life that year was the birth of his and Joyce's son, Evan, on January 23. A month later, on February 22, Neil and Joyce hosted a party for California's Democratic governor, Jerry Brown. The twenty-five-hundred-dollar-a-plate black-tie event, which they hosted at their Holmby Hills estate, was intended to boost the political career of Brown, who was gearing up for a run at the 1980 presidential election. Neil was a staunch Republican and so, politically speaking, the polar opposite of Brown, but the party wasn't about stumping for a presidential candidate. Neil was simply ingratiating himself to someone upon whom he could rely for favors down the line. He was becoming a bit of an elitist. He'd started shopping at the most expensive stores in LA. And he and Joyce had hired Sharon Landa, a famous decorator, to make their house look like a lavish Hollywood estate; they also badgered Candy and me to use Sharon's services. While Neil loved this "fabulous" lifestyle, the idea of hiring a decorator seemed weird to Candy and me—actually, it just felt like more of the superficial LA scene. But Neil was finally in a position where he could entertain the heads of other labels, movie people, and stars in his home. He basked in their attention. He was as much of a groupie in his own way as anyone, in some respects maybe more.

The party was attended by many noteworthy people, among them Warner Brothers exec Joe Smith; A&M Records founder Jerry Moss; Jeff Wald and his wife, Helen Reddy; Linda Ronstadt; actress Marcia Strassman of *Welcome Back, Kotter* fame; William Shatner; Gene Simmons; and Cher. The last two hit it off, and in short order they became something of an item. Gene did a nice sales job on Cher, and we signed her to Casablanca within a month. Jerry Brown did a nice sales job on Richard Trugman, who left the company in March to work on Brown's presidential campaign. Richard felt that he'd made his money with Casablanca, and he didn't think the company's future was as bright as it appeared.

Trugman had not been the most well-liked person in the company. He had a superior attitude and would constantly complain about the volume of the music we played on the floor above. All of us music people upstairs couldn't have cared less. Music was the business we were in; the music came first, and the lawyers could wear earplugs if it got too loud. Bruce Bird was his usual adversary in this ongoing battle; Richard would never complain to me or Neil because he knew how we would react.

Around this time, we began to make some changes to the office. During the renovations, Peter Guber discovered wires running up to Neil's office on the second floor; these wires were connected to a tape recorder in a downstairs office. Neil insisted that he knew nothing about it, and everyone flatly denied any involvement. I was never sure what one of our employees could have gained by eavesdropping on Neil. It bothered me, however, that while everyone claimed that someone else had installed the eavesdropping system, the tape recorder was not well hidden, so it would have been very hard for Neil not to have noticed it.

Due to the discovery of the wires, we met a very strange individual: Arthur Kassel. Art was a self-styled Secret Service man, a staunchly conservative political operative who had a fondness for Quick Tan—he reminded me a bit of G. Gordon Liddy. We hired him to secure the building and our houses, and he made a big production of it. He came to the office, my home, and Neil's home equipped with the latest technology to sweep for bugs. Candy came home one day to find Kassel and his crew of lackeys in suits in our house without permission. She flipped her lid and threw them all out. The most troubling thing was that we had had the alarm on, the gate closed, and the doors locked, but these guys had gotten in without a problem.

Despite the cloak and dagger stuff—or maybe because of it—Neil liked Art, especially after he gave Neil a New York State Narcotics Department badge. Neil kept it in his wallet; he really thought that it would get him a free pass if he ever needed it. It wasn't long before he got the chance to try it out. Bruce Bird and Howie Rosen got loaded at a Dodgers game. When he drank and did coke, Bruce became belligerent, and so did Howie. Someone on the balcony above them started dripping soda or beer on their seats. Grabbing their foot-long souvenir bats, Bruce and Howie ran up to the balcony level to find the culprit. Instead they found themselves confronting a large group of guys. Bruce ended up suspended over the balcony railing, and then both he and Howie were taken away by security personnel. Nancy (by now married to Bruce) rushed off to find Neil, who was elsewhere in the stadium. Neil, stoned on 'ludes and feeling bold, assured her he'd take care of it. He went downstairs to the holding pen where Bruce and Howie were being detained (fortunately, he had the presence of mind to leave his stash of drugs behind). But when he flashed the badge Kassel had given him, the security people burst out laughing and told him to get the fuck out of there. So much for Neil's career in law enforcement.

His philanthropic ventures were a bit more successful. He and Joyce had written a check for one hundred thousand dollars to LA's Cedars-Sinai Medical Center to help fund the construction of a new wing. Their gift was widely covered in the press. Other high-profile events littered Neil's itinerary, including a February 6 appearance with Donna Summer and Joyce on *The Merv Griffin Show*, the first of several appearances for Neil on this show. In April, we produced a thirty-second TV spot to promote KISS's *Double Platinum*, a greatest hits collection. Neil was growing so comfortable with being the face of Casablanca that Howard Marks was able to talk him into being the pitch man in the ad. I am sure Howard did not have to twist his arm very much, as Neil always wanted to be in the limelight, and this was just another opportunity. It was one of the cheesiest commercials I have ever seen. It wasn't even quality cheese—more like Cheez Whiz. If you were a fourteen-year-old KISS fan, would you be motivated by a guy in his late thirties trying to sell you on their record? It just did not work, but who was going to tell Neil that?

If there was limelight to be had, we would fall all over ourselves to get into it. At the twentieth annual NARM (National Association of Recording Merchandisers) convention, we broke the bank—and we also defied common sense, but when didn't we do that? The big, three-day industry get-together was held on the fourth floor of the New Orleans Hyatt Regency, beginning on March 18. Our booth, for lack of a better word, was huge. It was designed as a miniature Moroccan-motif (of course) casino, featuring blackjack, roulette, and other gambling games, all of which had label tie-ins. In one game, guests could win prizes by throwing beanbags at a life-size Dick Sherman prop. We hired veiled belly dancers to mingle with the conventioneers and hand out Casablanca exhibit passes and free gambling chips. We scattered cocktail napkins bearing the names or artwork of Donna Summer, the Village People, Love and Kisses, and Roberta Kelly; and we distributed a nice promotional sampler album, *Return to Casablanca*, specially created for NARM attendees. The capper was a stunning sixty-minute live performance by Donna Summer. The Casablanca experience was the hit of the convention, and talk of it circulated through the gossip columns of industry publications for the next several weeks.

Because *Return to Casablanca* had been such a hit at the NARM convention, we decided to press an additional twenty-one thousand units and send them out to retailers in a specially made carton containing not only the double LP but also cassette and 8-track versions of the same release. And we continued this excess with several key releases throughout 1978. We always loved producing these promotional materials, but the main reason we did them was to make radio people feel special. Most were excited to own a limited edition sampler with a unique cover, and that made them more inclined to give us airplay.

We were moving at warp speed. Somewhere in the back of my mind I knew this couldn't be sustained. I knew the piper would have to be paid. But when? And how much? I was far too intoxicated with this life to care.

17

Writing the *Billboard* Charts

**The land of the beautiful people—Playing the
charts—Studio 54 and the disco label—Osko's—*Thank
God It's Friday*—The battle with *Saturday Night
Fever*—The battle with Wardlow—*Midnight Express*—
KISS meets the Phantom—Accident on Sepulveda—
The solo album catastrophe**

April 26, 1978
254 West Fifty-fourth Street
Manhattan, New York

There was blow everywhere. It was like some sort of condiment that had
to be brushed away by the waitstaff before the next party was seated.
Cocaine dusted everything. It was on fingertips, tabletops, upper lips,
and the floor. How many people were doing blow and how many were
being blown? The race was too close to call.

I was seated at a table with Bill Wardlow to my left and Neil Bogart to
my right. Wardlow was one of the most important and influential men
in the business. As the charts editor for *Billboard*, he held the entire
music industry in his hands. The bottom line of every record company,
from some backroom independent in Detroit to Capitol in LA, could be
changed with a flick of Wardlow's pen.

Over the course of the evening, we watched a succession of legends—
who could have collectively accounted for the cover shots of a year's
worth of *People* and *Rolling Stone*—parade past. Celebrities and syco-
phants were everywhere. And then there was me, Larry Harris, a kid
from Queens. The scene was surreal. It was like witnessing a great empire
grown fat on its own arrogance and hedonism, soon to crumble and fall.
It was a Hieronymus Bosch painting come to life.

Welcome to Studio 54.

Bill, Neil, and I weren't just in Studio 54—that was for the public, or at least whatever beautiful part of it could worm its way past the red velvet ropes. We were in the catacombs, a series of very exclusive and somewhat private areas in the basement of the renowned disco oasis. And we were here for a reason: to perpetuate our carefully cultivated myth of Casablanca. We were regarded as the gold standard of the record world. With our stable of hot artists, we'd skyrocketed to heights that no young record company had ever (before or since) attained. Disco was the hottest music around, and we owned the niche. We *were* disco. We had a trophy case bursting with so many Gold and Platinum awards that even Atlantic and Warner Brothers couldn't compete, and we had a grip on the charts that was the bitter envy of the industry. We had earned some of that. The rest of it was hype, and Bill Wardlow had helped us to create it out of whole cloth.

I liked Bill. He was in his mid-fifties, tall, relatively thin, not unattractive, with a full head of gray hair. He always dressed smartly and was fond of long-sleeved, crisply ironed button-down shirts. He tended to talk as if he thought he was smarter than most, though I was never really put off by his vaguely snide demeanor. I found him to be a personable and tractable man, and I enjoyed his company on the many occasions we met. Truth be told, if Bill hadn't been in charge of the charts for *Billboard*, we probably wouldn't have had any sort of relationship, and I certainly wouldn't have been at Studio 54 with him. The ability to manipulate the *Billboard* charts was a major advantage to Casablanca.

To comprehend how Casablanca influenced the charts, it's helpful to know the players involved and the position each held in the industry hierarchy. In the 1970s, there were eight major music trade papers: *Billboard*, *Cashbox*, *Record World*, *Radio & Records*, Kal Rudman's *FMQB*, *The Gavin Report*, *The Bob Hamilton Radio Report*, and *Bobby Poe's Pop Music Survey*.

Billboard was the oldest and most influential of them all. Large distributors such as the Handleman Company sold to major retailers like Kmart and Walmart, and they would only buy product if it was on the *Billboard* charts. The initial orders placed by these distributors could be in excess of one hundred thousand units, so it's easy to see how *Billboard* was vital to sales. In addition, numerous radio stations consulted *Billboard* before deciding whether to add a record to their playlists. *Record World* was regarded as having the most honest and relevant charts, although it lacked the widespread influence of *Billboard*. *Cashbox*, another old-line magazine, was owned by Mr. George Albert, who would not hesitate to make deals on chart positions in exchange for advertising.

The other trade charts were based on airplay. They manipulated record companies using advertising as a threat, and they had little or no influence on retail. They did, however, have some marginal influence on radio play. *Radio & Records*, *The Gavin Report*, *The Bob Hamilton Radio Report*, *Bobby Poe's Pop Music Survey*, and *FMQB* had this kind of influence, as did a few other regional or format-oriented sheets around the country.

Radio & Records (R&R) appeared on the scene at about the same time Casablanca did. It dealt with radio airplay exclusively, and it was (and still is) the sheet around which much of the pay-for-play and payola revolved. About the time *R&R* was being launched, its owner, Bob Wilson, met with Neil to try to secure an advertising commitment. Neil, of course, leaped at the chance. He was a big believer in helping those who were starting out, because then he could call in the favor when he needed it. And, although he was a big gambler, he would never risk being seen as uncooperative by industry-oriented publications.

In a short time, *R&R* became very influential in the music industry. Its charts were done in such a way that they actually quantified the importance of each radio station—something that opened the door to abuse. It grouped stations into three categories: parallel I markets (more than a million people), parallel II markets (more than half a million), and parallel III markets (more than a quarter million). The publicity ran upstream: if it acquired airplay on enough parallel III stations, your record would begin to look good to parallel II stations. Once it had substantial airplay on parallel II and III stations, then the important parallel I stations would begin to consider playing it, and so forth. A record's movements on the *R&R* charts directly affected its level of national airplay and thus determined its success or failure. National promotion people who did not understand how to manipulate the *R&R* system would find themselves out of a gig.

Independent promoters benefited handsomely from this process, as it allowed them to approach the big record companies with concrete figures in hand and get compensated accordingly. The charts took the guesswork out of determining how valuable it would be to have an artist added to a radio station, and the independent promotions market grew exponentially as a result. Also, radio program directors found that by relying on the *R&R* charts, they could protect themselves from being fired for choosing the wrong records to play. If a PD's boss asked him why he'd added a particular record, he could always just point to the *R&R* charts.

At the time, *Billboard* did not have the most scientific method for compiling charts; none of the publications did. The *Billboard* Broadcast Data System (BDS), which made the charts much more scientific, was not invented until 1992. When it came to album sales, a record company would tell the *Billboard* chart department, headed by Bill Wardlow, how many copies of an album it had sold and what level of airplay the album was getting; it would also inform *Billboard* about any special support initiatives, such as tours or advertising blitzes. Bill would somehow rate this information—I still firmly believe

> - **September 7, 1978: Keith Moon of The Who dies of a drug overdose.**
> - **October 25, 1978: John Carpenter's *Halloween* premieres in Kansas City, Missouri.**
> - **October 27, 1978: Egyptian president Anwar Sadat and Israeli prime minister Menachem Begin win the Nobel Peace Prize for completing a peace treaty between their two nations.**

he used a Ouija board—and decide where to place the album. Airplay was not considered in compiling the album charts; sales was the only criterion. The singles charts were based on a combination of Top 40 airplay and sales, weighted more heavily toward airplay.

When I first moved to Los Angeles, at the end of 1973, I started visiting *Billboard* weekly to present our product information. I soon curtailed these visits. I didn't have much to discuss with Bill; our product was not selling very well, and, anyway, Warner already had someone whose job it was to visit *Billboard* and inform them about our product. After we left Warner, in the summer of 1974, I resumed my weekly visits to the trades, determined to find a way to make a substantial impact on the charts. One day, as I spoke with Bill, I noticed that his attitude toward me had changed. He was trying to ingratiate himself to me. It didn't take me long to figure out why: Bill Wardlow loved disco.

The math was easy. Bill loved disco. Casablanca *was* disco. I was in like Flynn. Bill wanted very much to be a part of our scene, even going so far as to create a separate disco chart called National Disco Action Top 40. If you look at the album charts from that era, you will notice that disco product appears much more influential than it should have been. Bill's love for disco was the human element of this inexact science. He enjoyed talking to me about disco artists such as Donna Summer, Pattie Brooks, and Paul Jabara, and when the Village People arrived, he was absolutely beside himself. Bill especially loved the attention he'd get when Neil invited him to some disco event we were throwing.

We leveraged the relationship as much as we could. Eventually, I could walk into Bill's office, tell him the position on the charts I felt a given album should have, and, lo and behold, there it would be. If we needed a bullet on an album or single to show upward momentum, I would just tell Bill that I needed a bullet. In 1977, I was able to get four KISS albums (*Alive!*, *Destroyer*, *Rock and Roll Over*, and *Love Gun*) on *Billboard*'s Top 100 at the same time. Of those four albums, only two deserved anywhere near the numbers they were allegedly achieving. This, of course, led us to mount a major retail and industry advertising campaign. Having four albums on the charts at once was something that no one else had ever accomplished: this was a coup.

The volume of trade advertising we were doing was still far greater than it should have been. Early on, Neil had asked me to ensure that everyone was getting the message that we were hot and successful, so I made contractual arrangements with *Billboard*, *Cashbox*, and *Record World*. We would take their front inside covers every week for a year; if we didn't have new product to advertise, then we'd run the same ads over and over. We also tried to secure the front cover of *Billboard*, which had three available advertising spaces. Our spending on ads in the trades was obscene, but it did serve to plant our name in front of everyone on a weekly basis. Our ads extolled not just our artists but also the company in general.

We were shaping Casablanca's reality out of a faux public perception. It didn't make our bottom line any less real, but it was a grand bit of illusion making. Even we were tempted to believe our own carefully crafted press—and that was dangerous. In the disco era, we had as many as eight albums on the *Billboard* disco chart; for a company less than five years old, it was an amazing position to be in. We even knew the chart positions hours before they were released to the industry. The numbers were not generally available until 3:00 p.m. on Wednesdays, but I would have them by noon.

Neil was very close to Studio 54's owners, Steve Rubell and Ian Schrager. They were partners, but, through the sheer force of his personality, Rubell was the de facto leader. He was a relatively short guy in his mid-thirties with thinning brown hair and an aggressive look in his eye—a blend of wild enthusiasm, anxiety, and annoyance. He was endlessly energetic and would just as soon bully you as charm you. He could, and did, work a crowd to a degree to which P.T. Barnum might aspire, but he was prone to childish tantrums. If he was in a bad mood or a coke-induced rage, he was uncontrollable—even Ian would steer clear of him. I once saw him dress down an employee over some perceived infraction; for three solid minutes, he screamed himself hoarse as the poor kid cowered from the onslaught. Schrager was about the same age, slightly taller, with more polished good looks. He was by no means quiet and could be very engaging when he wanted to be, despite a speech impediment, but he was far more relaxed than Rubell. I worked with the two occasionally, but I didn't hang with them as much Neil did.

Although Rubell's arrogance put many people off, Neil got along well with him; when any of us went to Studio 54, we were treated as major personalities and brought straight into the club's restricted areas. We never waited outside with the crush of people desperate to be allowed into the cultural nirvana Rubell and Schrager had crafted in midtown Manhattan. We always called ahead, and either Steve or Ian would usher us into his private office to discuss business; in Rubell's filtered world of beautiful people, we were top-flight celebrities. Studio 54 was a disco club, and Casablanca, especially to Rubell, was the very essence of disco. For us, Studio 54 was flash money—a name and a place we could use to impress anyone, from members of the press to potential artists.

We included Bill Wardlow in the events and parties at the infamous club to make it even easier for us to exert influence over the charts. Wardlow began to visit our offices just to feel more involved in the disco phenomenon. Neil might have been in his company only half a dozen times, but he always made those times count by lavishing attention on Bill. I felt that Bill had been on my side from the start, but a movie called *Thank God It's Friday* put him in my back pocket for good. In early 1977, Neil had the idea to do a disco movie featuring Donna Summer, Paul Jabara, and a few of our other artists. If that sounds like an expensive and lengthy commercial for Casablanca, that's exactly what it was. Neil and Peter Guber had a meeting about the project with the powers at Columbia Pictures, and after some prodding they agreed to the movie, pending their approval of the script. Neil enlisted Ellen Wolf and Walter Wanger, our two brightest publicists, to begin work on the screenplay, with input from our disco people and Paul Jabara. Neil kept a tight rein on the script, adding his own ideas and corrections as it moved along. When it was almost finished, Columbia called to say there was a problem: they had promised Motown that they could make a disco movie, too.

This led to all kinds of bickering, but finally it was agreed that the movie would be a coproduction, with Neil representing us and Rob Klann representing Motown. Casablanca would release the soundtrack, but it would contain songs by both labels' acts. The budget, as I remember, was pretty skimpy, even for those days—under a million dollars. This would not have presented such a big hurdle if we had been able to find a discotheque willing to serve as our movie set. But no discotheque in the LA area wanted to shut its doors for two months and forgo thousands of dollars in income while we shot our crappy little movie. Eventually, however, we did find one: Osko's. The odd-shaped, thirty-thousand-square-foot property, located on La Cienega Boulevard, had just been overhauled to the tune of one hundred thousand dollars, and it had been transformed into a veritable Studio 54 West. This gargantuan, multilevel, multiroom club had everything from an arcade to an ice cave to a series of hidden enclaves, all of which ringed the dance floor; an egg-shaped DJ booth was suspended above the stage. My favorite feature was an elevator operated by a guy in a gorilla suit.

Throughout the 1977 holiday season, Neil was always on the set at Osko's. Whenever I needed to see him, I had to go there. I took Bill Wardlow to these on-set visits as often as I could, knowing that in return I could write next week's charts. *Thank God It's Friday* not only kept Bill Wardlow under our influence, but it also gave a significant boost to the careers of Donna Summer, who starred in the movie, and Paul Jabara, who also appeared in the movie and who wrote the award-winning song "Last Dance" for its soundtrack.

This was Neil's baby, and it was our first real venture into the world of film (*The Deep* was mostly completed by the time we'd merged with Guber). We now kicked everything else to the curb. Everyone at Casablanca had to be focused on *Thank God It's Friday*. The marketing campaign had to be nothing less than spectacular. The title song, performed by Love and Kisses, had to be huge. Cost was no barrier. The song had to be a hit before the movie was released; it needed to be big enough to get people interested in the movie. We spent two million dollars promoting the movie and the soundtrack—almost double what it cost to produce the film itself. Premieres, each attended by a large portion of the cast and followed by a massive party, were held at Studio 54 and at Osko's; there was a third gala in San Francisco. A thirty-minute making-of documentary was produced for syndication by FilmWorks, as was a fifty-minute promotional film, which was taped on the Osko's set. The latter featured Donna hosting a disco fantasy party at which she, Love and Kisses, Paul Jabara, and others performed songs from the soundtrack for an audience of paid extras; it was aired as an episode of *The Midnight Special*. We purchased billboards all over the country, and we sponsored *Thank God It's Friday* dance contests, which were heavily advertised in high school newspapers. Five promotional 12-inch singles were issued to radio, and we even had a deal with Real cigarettes to print ads on the backs of cigarette packages (try doing that today.) Promoting this movie with a straight face wasn't easy. The script suffered through several rewrites and conflicting input from the Casablanca and Motown camps. But the movie's obvious shortcomings didn't really matter. What finally sank us was the one thing we could not control: the competition.

That competition was one of the biggest movies and soundtracks of the decade, if not of all time: *Saturday Night Fever*. There was only room for one picture centered on dancing, and RSO's Robert Stigwood (famous primarily for managing Cream and the Bee Gees) had the better one. Yes, we did have a hit album, with sales approaching one million, which should have inspired more people to see the movie than eventually did, but *Saturday Night Fever* left us in the dust. The motion picture was overwhelmingly successful, and the accompanying two-disc soundtrack album spawned five No. 1 singles.

The biggest *Thank God It's Friday* promotion of them all came during the last week of May, when two ninety-minute *TGIF*-themed episodes of

The Merv Griffin Show were broadcast. Neil and Bill Wardlow were featured on both episodes as celebrity judges of a disco dance-off. Neil was
an easy sell to the show's producers, but convincing them of Wardlow's
value took more effort. Failure was not an option here: I had to get Bill
on the show. After months of enticing him with various carrots—allowing
him onto the Osko's set while Donna performed "Last Dance"; getting
him into Studio 54's first anniversary party—I was finally poised to push
TGIF to the top. Our LP (which also included a bonus 12-inch single)
had debuted in the May 13 issue of *Billboard* at No. 74 and had been
quickly moving up the Top 200 LPs and Tapes chart. The chance to put
the fifty-eight-year-old Wardlow on national TV—for three hours, no
less—would come once in a lifetime, and it would be a real dream come
true for Bill, who loved the spotlight maybe even more than Neil did. A
few weeks after the Merv episodes aired, Bill promised me our soundtrack would be No. 1 for the week ending July 1. I was over the moon.
This was the first time we'd ever had a No. 1 album, and, best of all, we'd
go down in the history books as the LP that pushed *Saturday Night Fever*
from the No. 1 spot after a twenty-plus-week ride. I told Neil, and everyone
was ecstatic.

But, as it turned out, even pulling Wardlow's strings couldn't elevate
us to the top spot. This triggered a huge blowup between us. I screamed
at Wardlow over the phone for reneging on his promise. It was a good
demonstration of how much ego and a sense of entitlement had grown
at 8255. We had so gorged ourselves on our own press that we had completely lost our perspective. We thought we owned the charts, and to be
shafted out of the No. 1 slot when it had been promised to us made me
absolutely livid. How *dare* he! After shredding Bill for fifteen minutes, I
slammed down the phone and gradually calmed myself. Fortunately, Bill
was forgiving, and the incident was pretty much forgotten after a couple
of weeks had passed. I'm sure that Neil was torn between thinking I was
insane to go off on someone as powerful as Wardlow and impressed that
I had it in me to stand up to him.

This will give you an idea of what I was up against. I read somewhere
that RSO top man Al Coury had flown to Venice in early May for the
1978 IMIC (International Music Industry Conference). I remember wondering why. I later discovered that it wasn't the conference he'd been
interested in; what he wanted was the chance to sit beside Bill Warlow

Above: The full-sized Mothership is set up for Parliament's headlining performance at the Los Angeles Memorial Coliseum on June 4, 1977. (Michael Ochs Archives/Getty Images)

Previous page: Donna Summer in 1979, during her *Bad Girls* era. (Harry Langdon/ Getty Images)

Below: Donna Summer and producer Giorgio Moroder sit on a couch, circa 1978. (Echoes/Redferns)

Above: 1977, Angel's dramatic finale: the band members would climb into the box, which would then rise above the stage and explode. Goodnight! (Barry Levine)

Below: Angel in 1979, during their *Sinful* era. *Left to right:* Felix Robinson, Gregg Giuffria, Frank DiMino, Punky Meadows, and Barry Brandt. (Barry Levine)

KISS Manager Bill Aucoin, NARM President Joe Cohen, Meatloaf, Gene Simmons, Cher, and Larry Harris at the March 1979 NARM banquet in Hollywood, Florida. (Collection of Larry Harris)

Casablanca VP of Promotion, Bruce Bird, looks on as Bogart leads Dick Sherman, Pete Jones, Irv Biegel, and Larry in "In the Navy" at the March 1979 NARM Convention. (Collection of Larry Harris)

At the NARM banquet in Hollywood, Florida, March 1979. *Back row:* Village People members Victor Willis and Glenn Hughes flanking their managers Henri Belolo and Jacques Morali; *front row:* Larry Harris (in sailor suit) and NARM President Joe Cohen. (Collection of Larry Harris)

Above: The Village People perform "In the Navy" onstage during their 1979 Go West tour. (Richard E. Aaron/Redferns)

Below: The Village People get sleazy in their first photo session with new "Hot Cop" lead singer in 1979. *Left to right:* Ray Simpson, David Hodo, Randy Jones, Glenn Hughes, Alexander Briley, Felipe Rose. (GAB Archive/Redferns)

Above: KISS visiting the locals outside Mann's Chinese Theatre in Hollywood, California, on February 20, 1976, as their head of security "Big John" Harte and DJ Rodney Bingenheimer look on. (Michael Ochs Archives/Getty Images)

Below: Gene Simmons pumps up the crowd on the tail end of KISS's Alive! tour in 1976. (Fin Costello/Redferns)

on the plane. Why? Because he wanted to ensure that Yvonne Elliman's "If I Can't Have You" (the fifth and final single from *Saturday Night Fever*) hit No. 1. Sure enough, if you look at the May 13, 1978 issue of *Billboard*, you'll see the single sitting pretty atop that week's Hot 100 chart. If Al would travel halfway around the world for a single, what would he do to get Bill to keep the LP at No. 1 for another week?

PolyGram couldn't have been happier that we were tussling with RSO over the top spot on the charts: they distributed *both* albums. From the careful-what-you-wish-for file, they soon became so swamped by the success of the *SNF* soundtrack that all they did for months was scramble to keep up with the orders. This indicates just how huge the album was—for a short time, the entire industry suffered a manufacturing logjam due to its enormous volume of sales.

With most of 8255 Sunset hip-deep in disco, Peter Guber and the FilmWorks division had begun work on their next project. Guber had acquired the movie rights to a 1977 book by Billy Hayes entitled *Midnight Express*. The book, which had topped the best-seller lists, was the true account of Hayes's 1970 arrest and imprisonment in Turkey for attempting to smuggle hashish back to the United States. The first I heard of the movie was when I was invited, along with Giorgio Moroder, to attend a screening of it. Neil had done a sales job on Peter and convinced him to get Giorgio to compose the film's score. Giorgio's initial reaction to the offer was cool, but he eventually capitulated, and for his efforts he won the Academy Award for best original score. The book was adapted for the screen by a young ex-military man by the name of Oliver Stone, who won an Academy Award for his work on the film.

Christy, my sister-in-law, became good friends with one of the film's producers, David Puttnam (she'd befriend just about anyone with a British accent), who for months sat downstairs at FilmWorks and edited the movie. During production, I often visited his editing space—a trailer parked in the employee parking lot—to check on his progress. I never had anything to say to him, but I was intrigued by the editing process, and when I needed to get away from the chaos of Casablanca I found Puttnam's trailer to be a great hiding place. I've no idea how closely it paralleled actual events, but the story depicted in the film was harrowing. This was a far, far better product than *The Deep*, and there was zero comparison between it and the throwaway disco movie that Neil was making across town. Stone and director Alan Parker took *Midnight Express* to the 1978 Cannes Film Festival, where it was nominated for the Palme d'Or, the festival's highest honor. Guber's first two FilmWorks films were a summer blockbuster followed by a critical darling. *Midnight Express* opened the door for David Puttnam, who would to go on to make *Chariots of Fire* and later run Columbia Pictures.

There had been so many new people added to the company, so many new acts, a merger, and a buyout—all in the space of a year. We were very fortunate that throughout it all, KISS, our premier act, had sailed on so smoothly with comparatively little attention from us. But by May of 1978, there were growing divisions between the band members. One of the advantages of KISS's signature makeup was that onstage it gave all four band members more or less equal importance, and that helped keep egos at bay. However, KISS had always been (and always would be) the vehicle of Paul Stanley and Gene Simmons: they wrote and sang almost all of the songs, and they were the dominant personalities. But now Ace Frehley and Peter Criss had begun to rebel. Their behavior was becoming more erratic, although most of it was of the drug-and-alcohol-related kind, which was still the acceptable standard in the rock and roll world. In May, the band began shooting a TV movie of the week called *KISS Meets the Phantom of the Park*; we started hearing reports that Ace and, in particular, Peter were showing up late for shoots and were generally moody and difficult.

Most of these headaches fell under the purview of Bill Aucoin or Glickman/Marks, and we were more than happy to let them wage the war for us. Then, on the morning of May 27, 1978, Neil received an urgent a phone call from Aucoin, who explained that Peter Criss had been involved in a car crash. The circumstances surrounding the accident weren't yet fully known, but what we did hear wasn't good. Peter and one of KISS's roadies, Fritz Postlethwaite, had totaled a Porsche on Sepulveda Boulevard. Fritz had been found in the burning wreckage; Peter had been thrown through the windshield onto the pavement. Both had been rushed by ambulance to a hospital in Marina del Rey.

The movie had wrapped that day, and the two had been up all night at a high-stakes poker game. As the sun rose, they had jumped into their rented Porsche and taken off, destination unknown. At around 6:00 a.m., they'd hit a tree at a very high speed. September 18 was the target release date for four new KISS albums, and the KISS movie was slated for an October premiere on NBC. Any negative news about the band at this point would be pure kryptonite. Again, I was not told what strings Neil pulled to keep the story quiet, but the lack of press coverage was impressive.

The specter of four new KISS albums was very troubling to me. They weren't KISS albums per se, but solo records by each of the band's four members. As far back as mid-1976, when Glickman/Marks had arrived on the KISS scene, solo albums had been mentioned in their contract. Under the terms of their agreement, one such solo effort would count as half an album; this meant that by releasing four solos at once, they would eliminate two full albums from their contractual obligations. For a long while, very little had been said about doing solo records, and the idea was largely forgotten, at least around our offices. Then, probably in the summer of 1977, the idea began to heat up and take shape, and by the beginning of 1978, Aucoin was pressing it hard. This may have been an attempt on his part to appease Peter and Ace, to soothe egos and repair the band mates' relationships.

We hated the idea and did our best to stonewall Aucoin. Solo albums were a lose-lose proposition for a record company. They rarely did well, so financially they made little sense, but by saying no to your artists you ran the risk of fracturing the always-fragile act-label relationship. KISS wanted to do four at once? No thanks. It wasn't until Bill implied that the band would break up if we refused that we finally agreed to it, but we were still skeptical about their motives. We thought that they might be attempting to fulfill their contract with us quickly so they could find a new record company or that they were trying to force us into offering them a sweeter deal.

Faced with no other alternative, we began to look for ways to make it work. Neil initially thought that we could release a total of two million albums (which was by now standard for KISS, anyway)—half a million units for each guy. It had been over a year since KISS's previous studio album, an eternity for them, and the opportunity to offer their huge fan base four new albums at once certainly held some appeal. A half million each; sure, we can do that. But Howard Marks balked. Sticking the contract in our faces, he pointed out that in order to abide by its terms, we'd have to press one million copies of each solo album. This would amount to a minimum of four million dollars in recording and advertising costs, to say nothing of manufacturing and promotion costs. At that point, albums still sold for less than ten dollars each, so we needed to ship a large number in order to cover costs and maintain the KISS hype machine. PolyGram was not happy about this. Wow, big surprise. We didn't like it much either. We had to beg, plead, and cajole them into it.

Considering that all of KISS's previous albums had gone Gold, Platinum, or better, shipping a million of each album didn't seem *too* ridiculous, or so we told ourselves. Neil, gambler that he was, eventually embraced the idea. We not only came out with the four solo albums, but we also issued a limited edition of each album as a picture disc for collectors. The picture discs did very well, so, true to the Casablanca "damn the torpedoes" attitude, we quickly printed more of these not-quite-so-limited editions.

On September 18, we shipped over 5.3 million albums. It was the biggest release in industry history to that point. We had to make sure that PolyGram saw that this four-million-dollar investment was going to succeed, so we created an equally enormous marketing campaign. We supplied retailers with half a million white plastic bags printed with the four solo album covers, along with an assortment of point-of-purchase displays and foam-board signs. Hundreds upon hundreds of lavish press kits went out. We spent $1.2 million on ad buys in various forms of media. We bought sixty-second radio spots on over one hundred stations nationwide. We placed expensive thirty-second spots on youth-oriented prime-time TV shows like *Happy Days* and *Laverne and Shirley*. There were bus and subway ads in Manhattan, as well as billboards there and in LA. We did four digital ads—one for each album—on the nineteen-month-old JumboTron in Times Square. We shipped out looped videocassettes of a two-minute presentation on the pressing of the solo albums to over four hundred retailers, as well as promotional calendars for 1979. The campaign seemed endless.

It wasn't just PolyGram that was pissed at us—it was the entire industry. Neil's aggressiveness had always been the subject of water-cooler gossip in the various record companies. At first, we'd seemed like ambitious underdogs. Our naïveté was probably endearing: "Oh, look at those Casablanca guys going a million miles an hour." But then raised eyebrows became contempt because we started to promote to ridiculous extremes—and, worse, we even promoted ourselves, as record company execs. This unquestionably made life difficult for our counterparts at other record companies. Now Warner execs, for instance, had to field calls from artists asking, "Why can't you promote us like Casablanca promotes their acts?" Our rampant spending was forcing other labels to keep up with the Joneses, whether they wanted to or not. The new KISS albums were the worst example of this, because not only had we spent more on a single campaign than any other record company had ever spent before, but we'd also done it for solo albums, the bane of the record exec's existence. You could just imagine the top guy at MCA grumbling, "God, if Townshend and Daltrey come in here screaming for three million each for solo albums, we're fucked."

Not long after the KISS albums hit the stores, it became apparent that we were royally screwed. The Gene and Paul solos, the ones we thought would do the best, were miserable failures, as was Peter's effort. The best seller of the lot was Ace's, which scored with a relatively strong single, "New York Groove," but that wasn't enough to save us, nor was having four Platinum albums (only because we'd shipped a million each). Our projected sales figures were frighteningly off, although I'd bragged in an interview that they would be at six to eight million by Christmas. We had another Carson album on our hands—times four. The albums actually sold about half a million units each: Gold status. Had we fought Howard Marks and shipped them Gold to begin with, everyone would've survived. But given our cash outlay for recording, pressing, and advertising, we needed to sell the entire run just to approach the breakeven point. To eat two million returns was a crippling blow.

PolyGram, unbeknownst to us or to KISS, sold the lion's share of the returns to discount retailers and flea markets, contravening the terms of our contract with KISS. If your albums landed in the cutout bin, it usually meant that you were finished. This certainly didn't help KISS's career, which by 1979 would begin to decline in the US. Years later, KISS would sue PolyGram for this infraction and win. For Casablanca, there would be no such salvation.

18

Cracks in the Casbah

Prestige—Foxes—Rejected cover—The worst year ever—
Ambition undimmed—Merv Griffin—Dance Fever—President
Ford—Cher—The shotgun approach—A meeting with Bob
Dylan—Another Wardlow soiree—Village People—NARM
again—Lip-synching?!—Robin Williams and the TV
connection—Business with the golden arches

October 28, 1978
Hilton Hotel
Manhattan, New York

If you're Jewish, one of the highest honors you can receive is having a dinner thrown for you by the United Jewish Appeal (UJA). In the fall of 1978, Neil was chosen. This was the major honor of his life to that point, and he was beaming when the announcement was made.

It is understood that UJA honorees will use the event to raise funds for the appeal. All my life, I'd heard plenty about the monetary and political sides of religion, so this was no surprise to me. The UJA dinner would highlight Neil's entire career in the business, and so he wanted it to be the organization's most successful fund drive ever. He had Ellen Wolf, Walter Wanger, and Chris Whorf plan a multimedia presentation based on his childhood and his career, and he assigned Casablanca's press department the task of laying out an industry campaign to make everyone aware of the event. He also instructed Dick Sherman and his sales staff to sell an ad in the *UJA Journal* to everyone we dealt with—every manufacturer, every printer, every major chain store. These ads were the primary vehicle for raising money for the organization. Casablanca's art department, its finance department, and everyone who spent a nickel of the company's money were ordered to get an ad from all of their vendors, no matter how small. Millennium, Chocolate City, and the rest of our subsidiary labels took ads, even though we actually put up the money for many of them. Finally, we made sure that every one of our artists took ads.

As the dinner drew near, Neil followed up on stragglers who had committed to a donation but hadn't yet paid up. He was tireless in his drive to ensure that everyone he knew contributed to the effort. At least half of our employees would be attending the dinner, and the per-plate ticket prices weren't cheap. Many of the companies we dealt with were expected to buy an entire table plus take out an ad in praise of Neil in the *UJA Journal*, which included an extended professional bio of Neil Bogart.

In New York on the big night, Candy and I were seated on the dais next to Walter Yetnikoff, president of CBS Records. Warner executive Joe Smith was the emcee. Joe had been master of ceremonies at so many of these events that it was practically his second career. Launching into his introduction, he spoke with great gusto about Neil. He went on and on, and finally Yetnikoff leaned over to Candy and me and said, "He's making such a fuss—Neil this, Neil that—I thought he was talking about Neil Diamond." Candy and I giggled quietly. The evening was wonderful. It was announced that seven hundred and fifty thousand dollars had been raised—a record amount. It crossed my mind that the next guy the UJA honored was not going to have an easy time following in Neil's footsteps.

A week or so after we'd returned home, our chief financial officer, David Shein, along with a few accounting people, came into my office and showed me the bills for limos from the night of the UJA dinner. It seemed that each person who had attended the event, including those who lived in New York, had taken a limo (over thirty in all), and many had kept them until the wee hours of the morning. Limo, hotel, air fare, and other expenses associated with the dinner totaled in excess of seventy-five thousand dollars. It would have made more sense for us to have stayed home and donated the money to the UJA. Seeing those expense reports, I lost it. I couldn't keep up the who-cares-it's-only-money pretense any longer. I just could not stomach any more of this whistling past the graveyard, this willful ignorance. We were hemorrhaging money. "David! What the fuck is this?! I don't care if people used the limos to go to and from the event, but to have them standing by overnight outside their hotel?" I was livid. "Look at this shit!" I pointed to several of the invoices. "At least half of these limos only had one or two people in them. We were all staying at the same hotel, for God's sake! How much common sense does it take to coordinate trips to an event?"

I finally took a breath. "David, I don't get it. We treat our people well—better than any company in the business. Even if they don't outwardly appreciate that, these assholes don't get to abuse the privilege!" Everything we did for our employees was first class. Remember, even the mailroom guys got birthday parties with, literally, crates of expensive champagne. When some idiot hit-and-run driver severely damaged several employee cars in the company parking lot, Neil had rentals delivered for each affected employee within the hour. We never pitted one executive against another when it came to expenses. Everyone who had to travel went first class and enjoyed the trip. After all, if you happened to run into industry colleagues en route, your first-class accommodation would reinforce their perception that Casablanca was doing well, and that perception was very important to us.

Of course, that policy led to some iffy decisions. For instance, for the sheer spectacle of it, Neil and I were among the first to have cell phones. These were the early models—enormous, clumsy, non-user-friendly contraptions that we had to cart around in briefcases. We'd call each other from our cars, just because we could. Did we need them? No, of course we didn't. No one else had them. Hardly anyone was aware that we had them, so only a select few knew that we could be reached in the car. It was prestige. It was boys and their toys. But that was Casablanca.

Yes, we permitted our people to spend more money than any other company did, but they would never leave us because we treated them like royalty. On occasion, we would jump in to help with an employee's family or health emergency, covering deductibles or fronting money for medical treatment; this generosity and family feeling extended down through the ranks from the executive level to the mailroom. Neil was even known to call in a favor at Cedars-Sinai Hospital to get specialist treatment for an employee's family member. He would sometimes pay medical bills for someone's kid out of his own pocket. He was very compassionate, and such actions go a long way toward explaining why he remains so revered by so many people.

Not long after the UJA event, I attempted to walk into my office one morning. I wasn't entirely successful. I was impeded because every teenage actress in Hollywood seemed to have taken up residence in the hallway. Our FilmWorks division was producing our next theatrical project for our new film distributor, United Artists—a coming-of-age drama called *Foxes*. The movie, which was about the mistreatment of 1970s youth, would have four female leads, so an army of pert, flirtatious minions had come to hang out at 8255 for days on end, vying with each other for a lead role. Former Runaways lead singer Cherie Currie landed one of the parts, and she did such an incredible job portraying a zoinked-out teenager that I'm convinced the only reason she didn't go on to have a major film career was that no one thought she was acting. Academy Award–winner Jodie Foster, whose dad, coincidently, had sold Neil our Sunset Boulevard headquarters in 1975, scored another lead role. Also included in the cast were Randy Quaid (fresh from *Midnight Express*) and Scott Baio (who was then starring in the ABC Television hit *Happy Days*). Laura Dern would make her screen debut in *Foxes*, as would a tween-aged girl named Jill Bogart, who was surprisingly convincing in her role as an annoying younger sister. (One of the actresses—or, more accurately, future actresses—running up and down the Casablanca halls during this time was a precocious six-year-old named Christina. She was a charming little kid whom everyone immediately liked. We had hired her father, Bobby Applegate, to work in our promotions department, and from the day he arrived he would tell anyone who would listen how his little girl was going to grow up to be a star. He was right.)

Also included in *Foxes* were the members of Angel, finally making it to the big screen in a small but key performance role. Angel's next release was imminent, and, being as frustrated as we were that we hadn't broken them yet, they decided to call the LP *Bad Publicity*. The title was a self-deprecating shot at their failure to generate or sustain any sort of visibility. It's possible that Neil missed the point and took it as an attack on Casablanca for failing to break the band, but, for whatever reason, he balked at the cover art, which depicted the band partying it up at the Riot House (the Continental Hyatt House in LA). Despite the fact that the pressing plant in New Jersey had already printed ten thousand copies of the jacket, Neil called one of the reps and gave the order to destroy the album covers. Retitled *Sinful*, the LP was released in January 1979. Angel was effectively a lost cause in our minds, and any enthusiasm we'd had to promote them was long gone. We scaled back our Angel advertising, which had previously included full-page ads in the trades, and we shelved a promotional film (shot during the Riot House photo session) for the LP's first single "Don't Take You Love," which we didn't bother to work or even send to the trades. Angel probably suffered from being in the wrong place at the wrong time. I would bet the house that had they first come onto the scene in 1985 instead of 1975, they would've been as big as latter-day peers like Poison or Bon Jovi. I took that gamble in the mid-1980s, when I became comanager of Giuffria, Gregg's post-Angel band, which had been signed by MCA Records.

As 1978 drew to a close, our press department continued to grow, and we assigned most of the new people to work on Neil's endeavors or on Donna Summer. We also concentrated our energies to establish other artists, movies, and projects. After Susan Munao left to become Donna's comanager,

- November 18, 1978: Jim Jones leads 912 of his People's Temple followers to mass suicide in Jonestown, Guyana.
- December 15, 1978: *Superman: The Movie*, starring Christopher Reeve, opens in the United States.
- December 31, 1978: Gas hits 63 cents per gallon.

Neil called Bobbi Cowan, another Gibson and Stromberg alum, and offered her the job of vice president of publicity. Not realizing what she was getting into, she accepted. Bobbi thought she would be working for Neil, and she wasn't happy to find herself more under my direction than his. I did not demand very much from her, as I immediately saw that she was in way over her head. She was a good publicist, but at that stage in her career she was not equipped to handle a sixty-person department that had about one hundred artists depending on it. The demands of the job overwhelmed her, and she soon left the company. She rebounded quickly and ended up being the inspiration for Bobbi Flekman, the nasal-voiced publicist portrayed so famously by Fran Drescher in *This Is Spinal Tap*.

For Casablanca and PolyGram, 1978 was a banner year, the embarrassing KISS solo album debacle notwithstanding. Casablanca logged $102 million in sales, while PolyGram posted $470 million domestically and over a billion worldwide. We had ten Platinum and thirteen Gold albums that year, second only to Columbia. However, 1979 would be the worst year in the history of the music business.

We didn't know it at the time (our only indication might have been slower-than-forecasted sales during the 1978 holiday shopping season), but a number of factors had combined to pull the rug out from under the entire industry. Due to flagging confidence in the economy and the escalating Cold War with the Soviet Union, consumer goods prices rose dramatically, while economic growth slowed at an equally alarming rate. This left consumers with considerably less disposable income. Music, of course, isn't bread, it's a luxury, and the entire industry suffered as the record-buying public went into hiding.

Due, to some degree, to the KISS solo LPs disaster, we were ahead of the pack when it came to cutting back on spending. We only released four albums (about one a month) to fill out 1978, and by the new year, we'd already made considerable cutbacks in our trade advertising. Albums that would have received a full-page ad six months earlier now got to be part of a two-page collage featuring six to ten releases. But all of this wasn't happening because we at Casablanca had suddenly decided to be sensible; it was in response to a decree that was handed down to Neil, Dick, and me during PolyGram's national sales meeting in New Orleans just a few days into 1979. Overshipping was another sore spot with the PolyGram brass, which meant that our days of shipping out a million plus units of every major release were over. And although these messages were probably intended for all the subsidiary labels, the speaker looked directly at Neil from the podium as he addressed the issue of unnecessary expenditures. Neil sat there displaying his best poker face. He didn't bat an eye. The era of true independence was over for us: we now had to answer to Mom and Dad.

Neil's ambition remained undimmed, however. I'm still not sure whether I found that inspiring or alarming, but, in any case, his sense of opportunism ran strong. The publicity department at Casablanca was the biggest in the company. Neil required an entire contingent just to work on his own publicity. We were sitting in his office one day discussing his growing public presence, and he came right out and told me, "If I'm seen with famous people, I will be famous." This declaration perfectly captured what he was becoming, and it made me cringe. Neil had fully succumbed to the Hollywood mentality. It struck me hard that we were fucked. If he was signing artists simply because they were famous, then the company was in more trouble than I realized. The line became a running joke around the office. Maybe all of this had begun in the fall of 1977, when Susan Munao had secured Neil a cover story in *New West* magazine (a *People*-like West Coast publication). Or maybe it had come out of Neil's *Merv Griffin Show* appearances, which had been set up for him by Steve Keator, a relative of Merv's who worked for us ostensibly in the publicity department, but who was really there because of his connection to Merv.

The Merv Griffin Show helped us to showcase Donna Summer, the Village People, and the movie *Thank God It's Friday*. Merv bent over backwards for us, devoting entire shows to stuff we wanted to promote and market. Despite Neil's ease with people and his natural confidence within the music industry, he was always uncomfortable delivering a major speech, and he was truly scared to appear before millions on TV. But, regardless of his stage fright, he knew that Merv's show, which drew solid ratings, was an important means to expose our artists and projects. So Neil and Merv became friends, to a degree (with Merv, it was always to a degree). Although Merv appeared warm and caring on television, in person I didn't find him quite so friendly. He had a tough-guy shark for a business manager and would always blame him for any difficulty that arose in negotiations—as if Merv himself wasn't the real shark. The Merv Griffin–Casablanca love fest came to an abrupt end when we realized that Merv had taken an idea we'd developed and paid for and turned it into a TV show himself, cutting us out completely.

It began in May 1978, when we had the idea of doing two ninety-minute *Thank God It's Friday*-themed episodes of Merv's show featuring several of our acts and a big dance contest. To do this, we would need a custom-built set with a state-of-the-art lighted dance floor and other discotheque touches. We would have to pay for it ourselves, since Merv was very—oh, let's say—thrifty (in fact, every time we had an artist on his show we would later get a bill from his company for union fees). But we had no problem spending thousands of dollars for the set, because we planned to use it later for a TV pilot centered on a dance contest. And the episodes were a huge success, scoring for Merv the highest ratings of his career to that point.

Four or five months later, Merv's people contacted us about doing a new show of his called *Dance Fever*. We arranged for several of our acts, including the Village People and Pattie Brooks, to appear. Then Steve

Keator told us that Merv had stolen the idea for *Dance Fever* from us—it was our TV pilot concept, and he was shooting it on the set we'd paid for in May. Neil hit the roof; he was probably angrier than I had ever seen him. He called Merv to work it out, but either Merv would not take his call or he just blew him off. This only compounded the problem. Neil started screaming about suing and going to the press to expose Merv as the slime he was. He finally calmed down when he spoke to one of our lawyers about legal remedies. The lawyer told him that if we didn't drop the whole thing and pretend it had never happened, then we'd never get another act on Merv's show. Furthermore, certain old-line Hollywood types would not want to see Merv's dirty laundry exposed for their own reasons, and if Neil decided to pursue this, he could kiss many of his TV and film aspirations goodbye.

Neil took the legal advice and never brought it up again. As it happened, we never did have another act on *The Merv Griffin Show*. In retrospect, I can see that it would have been better to go to court and get the rights for the show, as *Dance Fever* was an instant hit and stayed on the air in syndication for over eight years. Merv made very good money on it. Years later, I read a piece about *Dance Fever* and learned that Denny Terrio, the show's host, had been mistreated by Merv and had threatened Merv with a workplace harassment suit. What a surprise. I often wondered whether the little old ladies who loved Merv so much would have been such fans of his show if they'd known that Merv had used his friendship with Eva Gabor as a cover for his alternative lifestyle. Before Steve Keator fell victim to AIDS, he told me about Merv's bisexuality, and about his preference for younger men; he also said that the Eva Gabor relationship was completely transparent to those who knew Merv well.

Merv was a rich guy and a legit TV industry player, but he was small potatoes compared to some of the people who ran in the circles Neil was now a part of. On February 21, 1979, Neil and Joyce hosted a dinner party for former president Gerald Ford at their home. I asked myself why they would want to do this for the only man ever to hold the office of president without having been elected to it. Ford had ascended to the presidency after Richard Nixon resigned, in August 1974; he had become vice president when Nixon's original VP, Spiro Agnew, resigned over a tax fraud scandal in 1973. I could have understood wanting to throw a party for Nixon, despite his damaged reputation, but Ford? At least this

time (unlike the time he'd hosted Jerry Brown) Neil shared the political
views of his guest of honor, but we all knew that the party had nothing
to do with politics. Art Kassel had helped organize the affair, which was
a see-and-be-seen event, nothing more. These political gatherings, as
well as the one-hundred-thousand-dollar contribution to Cedars-Sinai
Hospital, were strategic attempts on Neil's part to become a major force
in Hollywood. He believed that if he had name recognition in Hollywood as a player in philanthropic and political circles it would help
Casablanca get artists, TV shows, and motion picture deals. He really
wanted to become a major power broker in the entertainment industry,
and he almost made it.

Neil insisted that any Casablanca employees at the Ford party be on
their best parochial school behavior: no one should even think about
getting high; those who showed up with fun substances would find
themselves polishing their résumés. With an army of Secret Service guys
running around, Neil was intent on ensuring that he didn't become publicly associated with a bunch of glazed-over employees (I don't know
what he did with those bags of Quaaludes he normally kept in the
pocket of his suit jacket). All of the guests donned masks just prior to
Ford's arrival, and though I forget the purpose of the stunt, I do recall
that Ford did not like it. Candy and I were uncomfortable with the vibe
of the event, and we both started looking for an excuse to leave as soon
as we got there. Later on, I beat Frankie Crocker in a series of Pong
games that we played in the pool house—in fact, the highlight of my
night was taking hundreds off Peter Guber and Richard Trugman, who
had bet against me.

Neil's foray into the spotlight was mostly a source of amusement for
me. I'd watch him squirm and sweat in front of the cameras, figuring
that at least he was getting the Casablanca name out there. Unfortunately, as his public persona grew, his business acumen, which had been
so keen, began to waver. Neil had always bravely risked failure to achieve
great rewards, and I'd never questioned his judgment when it came to
artists, but I was beginning to have my doubts. Seeing something in
KISS, a band that none of the major labels would touch, and helping
them reach the rock stratosphere, or giving the madcap George Clinton
free rein, or predicting Donna Summer's future, or damned near single-
handedly creating disco—this was the Neil Bogart I knew. He was the

man who discovered and created tomorrow's stars. But the person in the office next to mine was now signing yesterday's sensations: acts like the Captain and Tennille, Tony Orlando, Don McLean, the Sylvers, and Mac Davis. They all had name recognition, but almost all of them had peaked before Neil walked them in the door. This star-signing rampage was disconcerting to me, even when the star was someone like Cher, who would have a Top 10 hit for us with the song "Take Me Home" (the single that caused Neil to set Howie Rosen's desk on fire to show how hot we were). After she had signed with us, Cher told me what a great guy Neil was. "How gracious of her," I thought, "to pay a compliment to Neil and share her enthusiasm at being on the Casablanca roster." Then she added that she found it especially nice of Neil to pay her more per album than she had asked for. I was dumbfounded. Neil always threw money at things, so that was nothing new. But he wasn't stupid, either. When you have someone sold at ten dollars, you don't insist that they take fifteen. I nearly choked trying to keep myself from saying "What the fuck?!"

Cher's manager, Sandy Gallen, was a pretty well-connected person in the Hollywood film, television, and music arenas, which was another advantage of signing Cher. Sandy put Bill Sammeth in charge of Cher. We knew Bill from his work with David Joseph and the Hudson Brothers, and we liked him a lot. Cher was good to work with, too. She was an artist who knew what she wanted, and she made sure that she got it.

She played a big role in pushing "Take Me Home" into the Top 10. It debuted fairly well, but then it stalled at around No. 30. We sent Don Wasley out on the road with her to do a promo tour—it was just the two of them. They went from market to market working whatever they could, wherever they were. When they landed in Atlanta, Wasley called WQXI and told them he was coming in with Cher and wanted to see what he could do to get the record added. Much to the surprise of both Cher and Don, the station was hosting a parade. In short order, Cher was tooling down the street on a float shaped like a giant shoe (which, I was told, looked like something right out of Mother Goose). I'm sure she was thinking "What the hell have I gotten myself into?" As the tour progressed up the East Coast, they stopped in Washington DC, where a local station invited Cher to a roller-skating party. At the rink, it turned out that the regular patrons were more gang members than disco fans, which created an interesting dichotomy: Cher skated along surrounded by thug-like rockers. She did everything we asked, never complaining, and the record did make it into the Top 10.

Neil became so smitten with Cher that he had the company buy her a Jeep for Christmas in 1978. But his grand gestures always seemed to have fallout: when Donna Summer heard about it, the shit began to fly, so Neil had to get Donna an even fancier Jeep. Donna deserved it, as she was selling tons of records, but why he would spend that kind of money on a present for Cher was beyond me. It got worse. He presented Cher with a Gold LP on *The Tonight Show*. That was the type of publicity we'd always done: celebrate your successes in public, as loudly as possible. But the thing was, the album wasn't Gold, so we went into a mad scramble to ship extra copies of the LP out to keep Neil from looking like a fool, or a liar. The PolyGram distribution guys were none too pleased to be pushing out albums when the demand wasn't there.

Neil's excitement was growing beyond my ability to manage its effects. He began to chase all sorts of grand ideas. I didn't like the role I was playing—I was constantly having to temper his increasingly erratic behavior. Had it always been this way? Had I just failed to notice it in my state of starstruck naïveté? We were working on a line of live concert releases for home video; VHS was not yet a household standard, and the retail market for music video product was nonexistent. A demonstration by Philips (PolyGram's parent) and a subsequent keynote convention speech from Warner exec Stan Cornyn on an emerging technology called the compact disc had us all excited about its enormous possibilities (and left Bruce looking for new speakers when the Philips sample disc blew out the cones in his enormous Altec Lansing cabinets). Neil was also working on a deal with ABC Television to produce five specials— a variety show, two documentaries, and two movies of the week—all with heavy music spinoffs. An opportunity to dispense cassette tapes from vending machines was being investigated. Neil wanted to develop new divisions for classical music and country and western. Mounting Broadway shows in Las Vegas and New York was on the agenda, as was a plan to open offices in London, France, and Holland. Our New York office, still headed by Irv Biegel, was now located in a posh townhouse at 137 West Fifty-fifth Street, and Neil was committed to spending a good third of the year in Manhattan. All of this was in addition to the

January opening of our BookWorks division, which had already acquired its initial offering: a hardcover novel by Jackson Rice, called *Flash Point*, about a fire that sweeps through Los Angeles. It was an absolutely dizzying display of ambition. Neil was starting to seem totally manic rather than just enthusiastic.

In the midst of Neil's constant epiphanies, other things would pop up. We received a call out of the blue from Bob Dylan. He wanted a meeting, and Neil, of course, accepted. A day or two later, Dylan and his manager met with Neil and me at our offices on Sunset. Dylan wanted to arrange a production deal. He was signed to Columbia, but he was interested in producing other bands on the side. The discussions were going along well—they liked us and we liked them—until I decided to open my mouth. The moment stands as a shining example of what bad judgment and an inflated sense of self-importance can lead to; it's also a good demonstration of why you should never hold a business meeting when you're stoned (I had a pretty good buzz going). I asked Dylan, "Bob, do you produce your own albums?" "No, I don't." "Then why the hell do you think we'd pay you to produce ours?!" End of meeting.

A couple of days after the Ford party, I flew to New York to attend the *Billboard* Disco Forum V at the Hilton. These three- or four-day conventions were Bill Wardlow's personal parties. There were daytime meetings and panel sessions, followed at night by a live performance and party at a nearby venue, usually the Roseland Ballroom. On the final evening of the forum, there would be an awards ceremony. To lend the event an aura of importance, Bill would arrange to have famous artists in attendance, and no one had more famous disco artists than we did. Bill also needed the record companies to pay for the awards dinner and presentation ceremonies, and we were more than happy to help bankroll the event. The night prior to the forum, Casablanca threw a huge party in Brooklyn at a skating rink called the Empire Rollerdome. Cher hosted the event, but even if she hadn't, the see-through top she wore would still have made her the center of attention. Wardlow would usually corral me into moderating a forum panel discussion, and this year he'd asked me to moderate one with the wordy title "Disco TV Shows and Their Importance to the Future Growth of Disco." Most years, we'd turn the awards banquet into our own personal press conference. This year, we did it big-time: Casablanca was named the best disco label for the third time; Donna Summer won six awards; and thirteen awards in all went to the company or our artists.

At some point during those thirteen trips to the podium, a problem arose. Jacques Morali was in attendance to supervise his band, the Village People. Prior to the awards ceremony, Jacques, Bill Wardlow, and I had agreed that the group would win three awards. In return, Morali had arranged for the Village People to do a forty-five-minute performance after the awards presentation. Everything was going smoothly, the Village People had snared two awards, then Wardlow goofed: he gave the third award to the Bee Gees. Morali went nuts, pulled me off of the dais, and began screaming at me that the Village People would not be performing. He ranted and raved for a good ten minutes. I eventually calmed him down and explained that the award was not the important thing in the long run—selling product was. If he backed out of performing, Wardlow would be embarrassed and take it out on the group by lowering their chart position, thereby hurting their sales. I actually think Morali believed that if he seemed out of control then he would win his point, but I was not going to fall for that. I berated Bill in front of Morali to make Morali think I really cared, but I was beyond giving a shit about him or his act. I was concerned with protecting Casablanca's interests, not the Village People's. If the Village People had backed out of performing, then all of our products and chart positions could have been compromised. Then I remembered that Wardlow had a close relationship with Al Coury, who ran RSO, the Bee Gees's label. It's likely we weren't the only ones playing backroom dealer—we were just better at it than most.

Three weeks later, we were back at the NARM convention in Miami. Again, the Village People were slated to perform. Their single "YMCA" had sold over three million copies, and it was not only the best-selling single in Casablanca history but also in PolyGram history. On the heels of the single's huge success, we'd released another, "In the Navy," which was selling almost as quickly. It had been licensed to the US Navy to use in their recruiting program. The Village People had been permitted on board the navy frigate *USS Reasoner* to shoot a video for the song, and the navy had made them honorable mates for the day. (The "don't' ask, don't tell" irony here is far too amusing to ignore.) Then, in response to some grumbling about tax dollars being used to promote a band, especially one comprised mainly of gay men singing about gay issues, the navy washed their hands of the whole thing. By that point, however, so much attention had been drawn to the group and the song that we didn't care.

The song was selling so well that we decided to get all the Casablanca employees at NARM to perform Village People songs dressed as sailors. We had custom-designed navy whites made for about a dozen of us, including Neil, me, Dick Sherman, Pete Jones, Bruce Bird, Al DiNoble, and Joyce. We walked around NARM wearing them and caused quite a stir in the halls, meeting rooms, and restaurants; everyone got a big kick out of our shenanigans. PolyGram had created a forty-minute Casablanca multimedia production for NARM, narrated by Orson Welles and titled "Sounds of Success," which heavily promoted a forthcoming disco-tinged KISS album called *Dynasty*. Even our lone real rock act was turning disco, and this shows the genre's growing influence and commercial potency. Though they'd been influenced heavily by the likes of The Beatles, the Stones, The Who, and Led Zeppelin, KISS's artistic sensibilities had been easily overwhelmed by the money-generating power of disco. Paul and Gene had always been clever songwriters and excellent mimics, so it wasn't difficult for them to crack the formula for a disco song. They wrote an excellent one, "I Was Made for Lovin' You," which would become their second biggest single up to that point.

The NARM convention coincided with a promotion Bruce Bird had arranged with Miami Top 40 station Y100. The Village People were set to perform for the station at a big outdoor event. The promotion was the back end of a quid pro quo arrangement: Y100 had earlier agreed to help us break certain records in the Miami market if we gave them a major headliner for their show. We left the hotel for the Village People/Y100 show in a procession of limos. We hit some traffic and arrived a little late. The group had already begun performing. As we were ushered behind the curtains that served as the band's backdrop, we passed a reel-to-reel tape recorder set on a chair with a microphone in front of it. It suddenly dawned on us that all of the band members—except Victor Willis, the lead singer—were lip-synching. It was tacky enough to have used studio singers and musicians on the recording, but to perform to a tape in front of a live audience was beyond the pale. Most if not all of us had seen the group perform before, but no one had ever noticed that they were lip-synching. We thought that they were a *real* band who danced and sang their own stuff. But, ultimately, our embarrassment and our outrage meant zilch. We couldn't vent at Morali, who would have blown us off—or, worse, lost his cool. Morali was volatile enough without our help. He controlled the Village People from top to bottom; for all intents and purposes, he *was* the Village People, and we were just a tool to get that product to the marketplace.

We were distracted from all of this on the evening of April 9, 1979, during the annual Academy Awards ceremony at Hollywood's Dorothy Chandler Pavilion. It was Johnny Carson's first time as emcee. Paul Jabara, Donna Summer, Giorgio Moroder, and Oliver Stone walked off with Oscars for *Thank God It's Friday* and *Midnight Express*. It sounds a bit arrogant, but although we were elated, we weren't all that surprised. Paul and Donna's combined efforts on "Last Dance" had already received Grammy and Golden Globe Awards; Giorgio had garnered a Golden Globe, too; and Oliver had won both a Golden Globe and a Writer's Guild Award. Still, this was a huge coup for the FilmWorks division, and Peter Guber and Neil were ecstatic. Jabara's win was especially sweet for Neil, as "Last Dance" had beaten out RSO's "Hopelessly Devoted to You." In light of all these awards, the summer-blockbuster status of *The Deep*, the success of *Thank God It's Friday*, and the FilmWorks merger, we were feeling pretty triumphant.

- February 2, 1979: Sid Vicious, bassist for the Sex Pistols, dies of a drug overdose.
- March 28, 1979: America's worst commercial nuclear accident occurs inside the Three Mile Island plant near Middletown, Pennsylvania.
- June 11, 1979: John Wayne succumbs to cancer at age 72.

Our attention was refocused on the Village People not long after this, when Morali tried to get us to make him a multiyear offer. Neil, who was always afraid of losing a band that would be successful for someone else, was about to do it. I was concerned and very frustrated. I never liked disagreeing with Neil, but he was beginning to make a lot of amateurish mistakes. I'd revered the guy for years for his ability to find hot new artists, an ability that was so keen it practically amounted to clairvoyance. Now I felt like I was holding his hand and walking him through decisions. "Look, Jacques's pitch isn't ridiculous. I'll grant you that. He wants to sweeten his current contract by offering us a longer term for more upfront money. The Village People are arguably the biggest act in all of disco, and they're doing a million units with every album they release. But their longevity is limited. Face it—they're little more than a very successful novelty act, and you want to sign a five-year multimillion dollar deal with them?" I finally won the argument, and we did not extend the original contract. We saved millions of dollars by not renegotiating, as each of the group's subsequent albums sold fewer and fewer units.

Between her sustained success with 1978's *Live and More* (singles "MacArthur Park" and "Heaven Knows" had been huge hits for us) and her sweep of the 1979 award circuit, Donna had unquestionably reached superstar status. By April 14, she was on tour again with her backup band, Brooklyn Dreams, who were also signed to Casablanca. One of the band's founding members, Bruce Sudano, had begun dating the disco diva, and we couldn't have been happier. Unlike Donna's previous boyfriend, Peter Mühldorfer, who had given her (and us) so much trouble, Bruce was great for Donna's head. The two got along wonderfully, and they married in July. We were thrilled for them. The marriage seemed to relax Donna, who was becoming increasingly frustrated with Neil, Joyce, and Casablanca in general, because she found that the touring-recording-promotion schedule that had been set for her was far too demanding. Looking back, I'm sure she was exhausted and needed a vacation. We rush-released "Hot Stuff," the first single from her 1979 album *Bad Girls*, in early spring, and it took off, eventually reaching No. 1 on the *Billboard* chart; it held that spot for three weeks. The follow-up single, "Bad Girls," also held the No. 1 spot (for five consecutive weeks), and this propelled the album to the top of the charts. Donna became the only artist to twice have a No. 1 single and album at the same time (*Live and More* and "MacArthur Park" had done it the previous year). *Bad Girls* became the best-selling LP of her career, moving over three millions units. As an aside, the other "bad girls" on the album cover were comanagers Joyce Bogart and Susan Munao.

Despite the overall doom and gloom that characterized the industry for most of 1979, we did have some interesting signings. Producer Tom Moulton was one of the biggest names in the disco world. Neil is often credited with inventing the 12-inch, but it was Tom who invented the format; he also helped pioneer the genre with his very influential "Disco Mix" column in *Billboard*. We signed a deal to distribute his Tom n' Jerry label through Casablanca, though I don't recall much coming of it.

I was responsible for signing a few artists who proved unsuccessful, but the deals were inexpensive, so we didn't take a bath on any of them. One was an icon of my childhood, Meadowlark Lemon of Harlem Globetrotters fame. Meadowlark, now a singer, was a pleasure to deal with, and signing him put me in contact with his manager, Randy Phillips. This was Randy's first foray into the music business, and it was a learning experience. (He would go on to help guide the careers of Lionel Richie and Rod Stewart, among others.) Randy drove the promo guys a little crazy, but they put up with him because they really loved Meadowlark and considered him a childhood hero. We made a particularly cheesy video for one of Meadowlark's songs, "My Kids"; it was shot in a park and featured Meadowlark surrounded by a group of children.

Even comedians were a target. Back on September 14, 1978, I had been lounging around at home—we now lived in a gated one-acre estate in Sherman Oaks, and Stan Cornyn of Warner and actor Stacy Keach were among our neighbors. Finishing up a joint, I turned on the TV to watch the pilot episode of a program called *Mork & Mindy*. I'm sure the pot played a role in my reaction, but I laughed my ass off at the show's manic lead, a comedian named Robin Williams. As the credits rolled, I saw that some old friends of mine were involved in the production. I immediately called Neil to tell him about it, barely able to contain my enthusiasm. He told me to go sign the guy and said I could go as high as one hundred thousand dollars to make it happen. I then contacted Larry Brezner, who comanaged Robin with Buddy Morra, and I told him we wanted to sign Robin. In a matter of moments it was done. It was another example of just how fast the industry moves: the *Mork & Mindy* broadcast had scarcely concluded, and we already had a verbal agreement with Robin. I was certainly not the only one to have noticed Williams's tremendous talent—the next day Larry was inundated with calls from other record companies, many offering considerably more money than we had.

Larry was a man of his word, and he stuck by the deal he and I had agreed upon. He also liked the fact that the four of us—Neil, Buddy, he, and I—got along very well, plus I was close friends with Robert Klein, another of his clients; Robert would still stay at my house when he had a gig in LA.

Neil was equally impressed with Robin after watching the next few episodes of *Mork & Mindy*, and, as usually happened, he was soon bursting with enthusiasm. He decided that he would produce the album himself (a big plus for both Larry and Buddy, as they held him in such high regard), and from that point on, the budget flew out the window. Neil quickly made plans to record the album live over a period of four nights at Manhattan's Copacabana, which had been closed for a while. We staged the show and made sure that the audience was comprised mostly of fans, plus as many national media heavies as we could fly in on short notice. We all piled into the first-class cabin of a 747 and had a Casablanca party at thirty thousand feet. I spent most of the flight losing money to Neil in an endless game of gin (I couldn't beat him to save my soul).

Neil and Robin spent considerable time together sorting out what Robin needed in the way of sound, lighting, and backstage accoutrements; nonetheless, at the first show, held on April 11, the Copa was the madhouse I'd expected it to be. Cocaine flowed like water backstage. So when Robin blew the doors off the place, we were all on a high, both literally and figuratively. He was the most brilliant comic any of us had ever seen. We were left speechless at the way he could destroy an audience. Offstage, however, he was a completely different person; he was shy and didn't make eye contact unless he knew and trusted you. Later, when the stories about him and John Belushi doing drugs together came out, I realized that the shyness may have been a side effect of his cocaine habit—coke can certainly induce paranoia. Plus, his fame was burgeoning and he was little prepared to handle it.

Several weeks later, Neil told me that he was going into the studio with Robin to edit the live performance for the album. He emphasized that he did not want to be disturbed, which meant that I would be temporarily presiding over everything, including stuff he'd probably forgotten to tell me about. After a week of neither seeing Neil nor hearing from him, I began to wonder how a live comedy album could take so long to edit. I stopped by the studio to check on their progress, only to find them in the middle of a weeklong cocaine bender. This, naturally, was making the editing task a lot more difficult than it needed to be. Eventually, they muddled their way through the process, and the album was released, quickly earning Gold status.

Robin was hardly the only comedian with a drug habit—the lifestyle of a stand-up comic is as brutal as that of a rock star. As vice president of artist development, Don Wasley would spend a lot of time on the road with our artists, and he told me that the wildest guy he ever traveled with wasn't a rock star at all: it was Rodney Dangerfield. Rodney always kept a Noxema jar filled with cocaine in a pocket of his leisure suit. One day, they were both at Chicago's O'Hare Airport waiting for their bags when Don noticed Rodney partaking. Don said, "Rodney, you can't do that here." Rodney just replied, "What are they going to do, arrest me? I'm Rodney Dangerfield!"

After that successful incursion into TV, Neil thought it would be a good idea to sign the Lenny and Squiggy characters from ABC's *Laverne & Shirley* (both *Laverne & Shirley* and *Mork & Mindy* were spinoffs of *Happy Days*). *Laverne & Shirley* was one of the most popular programs on TV, and Lenny and Squiggy were a major part of it. I loved the characters, so I was all for signing them, and we did. I never became close to Michael McKean (who portrayed Lenny), and, as far I know, he never did drugs; however, David Lander (Squiggy) was always happy to indulge with me.

We planned a show at the Roxy featuring the duo performing as Lenny and The Squigtones and arranged to tape it for a live comedy album. We loaded the Roxy with TV insiders and Hollywood people for the taping. The place was so crowded that it was hard for the band to get to the stage. Finally, when Lenny and The Squigtones began to play, we experienced a big letdown. The music was terrible. It was meant to be funny, but it was just bad. I left way before the show was over. The next day at the office, I found out that everyone had had the same reaction: this was a bad idea, and we should stop pursuing TV acts. We did issue the record, but we didn't put much effort into marketing or promoting it.

Lewis Merenstein, a producer who had worked with Van Morrison, was a good friend of Neil's, and he'd worked with us at Buddah for a time. He knew some McDonald's Corporation executives, and he brought Neil an idea for a project involving the restaurant chain. They would produce kid-oriented record albums that would be marketed by McDonald's and sold in their restaurants. The guy who had coined the term "bubblegum" was again thinking about the younger audience. These albums would be both entertaining and educational. The market was there, too: kid's music was a growing niche; a recent *Sesame Street* album had even hit Gold status. It was an idea that would have given Casablanca the financial success it so desperately needed. If it had worked, it would have catapulted us into the stratosphere.

Once the idea was hatched, Neil had to come up with the actual product before McDonald's would even consider becoming involved with us. The corporation was famous for testing new ideas; they tested their television commercials for months before running them. This was a very conservative outfit, and they would take no chances when it came to their brand. Who could blame them?

As he'd done with *Thank God It's Friday*, Neil brought in Ellen Wolf and Walter Wanger from our creative services division and put them to work. We conjured up a division name for the product, to boot: Casablanca KidWorks. No one at PolyGram knew what we were doing, and we kept it that way on purpose. In fact, most of the people in the company had no idea what was happening; news was communicated on a need-to-know basis only. We knew that PolyGram would not have wanted us to make the expenditures necessary to realize the project.

The project began slowly. Ellen and Walter consulted some well-known child psychologists and researched what would work for children, as well as for McDonald's. They hired songwriters known for their understanding of children's music. They met with Neil often to report on their progress and to get his input. I saw and heard their reports after the fact, and I was very impressed with the quality of their work. I liked that the concept behind the project was uplifting at a time when what was happening in the world seemed so dire. Ellen and Walter did a magnificent job creating the albums, which were titled *Rainy Day Fun Starring Ronald McDonald*, *Ronald McDonald Visits America*, and *Birthday Party Starring Ronald McDonald Dee-Jay*. They all had interactive (long before the term started to be applied to everything) elements—puzzles, books, or maps that kids could work with and learn from. The songs were geared to the appropriate age group, and they had a seal of approval from every child educator we spoke with. We tried them out on our own kids and our friend's kids, and they worked. The artwork was also first class, as we had spared no expense in developing it.

The biggest hurdle was McDonald's. Walter, Ellen, and Lewis went to Chicago and presented the project to McDonald's numerous times, and finally McDonald's came to LA to view the commercials, which had been created in the McDonald's mold. After listening to our masterful sales pitch, McDonald's agreed to all of it, including the marketing plan that Neil had presented.

Having McDonald's, with their impressive advertising capability and massive customer base, market the albums in their restaurants would have ensured their success. But, like many huge corporations, McDonald's did everything very slowly and very cautiously. The three albums were manufactured in very, very small quantities just to test the project, and they were eventually released to some critical acclaim. However, coordinating in-store sales in McDonald's restaurants would prove to be a lengthy endeavor, and we were already on borrowed time.

19

Last Dance

**Cooking the books—The jig is up—Creating the
list—Execution day—Summer and Somers sue—
Disco at the precipice—Demolition in Chicago—Another
Wardlow forum—Stiffed at Studio 54—
A change in the wind—Exit**

June 29, 1979
Casablanca Record & FilmWorks Headquarters
8255 Sunset Boulevard
Los Angeles, California

In the middle of 1978, about nine months after PolyGram had acquired a majority stake in Casablanca, I drafted the quarterly sales forecast. I was responsible for generating Casablanca's sales projections, and although much of it was guesswork, I based the projections on the previous period's sales and the level of commitment we were planning to give our projects. I ran the numbers and showed them to Neil. He told me that we had to show PolyGram a rosier picture and I should add millions of records to the sales column. I did as I was told and added enough sales to the projections to make PolyGram comfortable, even though I knew we would never hit such lofty heights.

PolyGram never questioned the figures. Whether they weren't familiar enough with Casablanca to be suspicious or simply weren't paying close enough attention, I cannot say. In retrospect, the fact that they had no clue that we were unprofitable speaks volumes about their lack of due diligence prior to the buyout and/or our ability to shape reality out of thin air and good PR. I think PolyGram's ignorance stemmed from the fact that we had painted the building so well they never realized that they'd bought twelve coats of paint without a building underneath. It was just a question of when they would finally poke a finger through the layers and figure out it was an empty shell.

After the four KISS solo albums had emphatically bombed, we knew that PolyGram would at last realize that we were losing a fortune. They were handling all distribution for us, and it was impossible that they would fail to notice two million returns. No amount of cooking the books was going to hide truckloads of unwanted records, especially since those trucks were backing up to their doorstep, not ours. When at last the ruse was up, PolyGram insisted on dramatic changes. Our marketing and advertising budgets were slashed and then watched closely with very wary eyes. Loss of freedom was the trade-off for big-bother corporate protection. By June 1979, PolyGram wanted more, and they demanded that we start cutting staff. Our employee roster was in excess of 175, and PolyGram expected us to cut big. Neil called Bruce and me into his office and informed us that he needed a list of expendable people. Bruce and I both knew that this had been coming, but that made the task no easier. Even though the company had long since grown so large that I couldn't know everyone intimately, axing over a third of our workforce felt like sawing off my left leg.

So we sat down to create a death row roster. One person Bruce and I agreed should be let go was Irv Biegel, the former cohead of Millennium, who had been running our New York office for some time. I'd had little interaction with Irv, as I rarely visited New York, and, frankly, I hadn't trusted the man from the moment I met him. At our first meeting he'd made grand claims like, "Larry, I'm just here to look out for your welfare." After knowing me for five minutes, *that* was his primary motivation? No way. He registered high on my bullshit meter. Irv was near the top of the Casablanca pay scale, too, and he did nothing that we felt had produced results, so his name went to the head of the list.

We tried to be as fair as we could, consulting with all the department heads and asking them who should be kept on. This was hard on them, of course, as they were friends with many of the people they would have to fire. When the list was finished, it contained the names of dozens and dozens of people. Bruce and I brought it to Neil. He crossed off Irv's name: we were not allowed to fire Irv. This stunned me. Neil hadn't even asked us why Irv was on the list—he'd just vetoed the cut immediately. Bruce recovered quickly and asked why Irv was protected, since he was clearly overpaid and did nothing to generate dollars. Neil claimed that Irv had a contract. I was completely astounded by this response. Of all the reasons Neil could have offered, it was the last I would ever have expected to hear. In fact, it was an out-and-out lie. I felt insulted and incredibly pissed off. I knew that Irv didn't have a contract. The only people with contracts were those who owned company stock: Neil, Peter, Cecil, and me. Even Bruce did not have a contract.

What was worse was that Neil knew that I knew, but he still lied. Bruce and I strongly suspected that Neil was sheltering Irv because Irv had close ties to Jeff Franklin, and Neil was afraid of upsetting Franklin. Neil read through the rest of the list and approved it, looking like he wanted to crawl under his desk and hide. Bruce and I met again with the department heads and gave them their final cut lists. They handled the firings themselves. The bloodletting took place on June 29, 1979.

To make this ugly situation worse, when a few of the people who had been fired went to say goodbye to Neil, he feigned ignorance. "What? You were fired? I had no idea!" He had the damned list on his desk and he'd had no qualms about cutting anyone loose—except Irv, of course. He was making Bruce and me out to be the bad guys, and probably me most of all. I would ultimately be perceived as the executioner. People lose their jobs every day, and when Neil had told us that Poly-Gram was demanding the cuts and then asked us to get it done, I wasn't angry.

- **August 10, 1979: Michael Jackson releases his debut album, *Off the Wall*. It goes on to sell over seven million copies domestically.**
- **December 3, 1979: Outside Cincinnati's Riverfront Coliseum, eleven people are killed in a crush of fans waiting for the doors to open for a performance by The Who.**
- **December 7, 1979: *Star Trek: The Motion Picture* opens in US theaters.**

It's never a fun scenario, but it's part of doing business, and I accepted it. But his acting surprised at the firings when he had approved them himself was to me a betrayal.

To add to the turmoil, Bruce Bird came in one day with some shocking news. He and Nancy had had dinner with Donna Summer's lawyer and his wife the night before, and the lawyer had told them that Donna was going to hire the famed and feared music attorney Abe Somers to represent her in her bid to break her contract with Joyce and Casablanca. Neil might have been skittish about pissing off Jeff Franklin, but at the mention of Abe Somers's name, he cowered under the table. He called Joyce right away and told her to retain Abe before Donna could, which would force Donna to find another attorney. We'd actually been expecting Donna to try to get out of her contract for months, but Neil never expected that we'd be going up against Abe Somers. Back in the Sherbourne days, someone represented by Somers had threatened to sue Neil. Neil had agreed to an immediate settlement. So, either Abe was an incredible attorney or he had done something in the past that had made Neil extremely wary of him—I was never certain which.

One of the legal arguments that Donna's lawyer would make was that Joyce was in conflict of interest, since she was both Donna's manager and the wife of the president of Donna's record company, and this was detrimental to Donna's career. I believe that Joyce was also making as much as 25 percent of Donna's adjusted revenue stream—a very sizable take for a manager. Another point was that Joyce sometimes placed Casablanca's interests above Donna's interests. It was a legitimate argument. From my perspective, Neil and Joyce were perfect for one another. He used her as a sounding board for every business idea that came into his head. Joyce had a keen sense of business herself, but she was loyal to Neil to a fault, and she almost always agreed with him, at least publicly; whether she could privately sway him to her way of thinking, I'm not sure.

Neil believed that with Joyce as Donna's manager, he could control Donna's career much more effectively, but he also thought that in helping the company in that way he would benefit Donna herself. He was probably right. Through Joyce, he heard all about Donna, and based on what he learned, he came up with some great marketing and sales schemes for her. He always had Donna on his mind. Joyce's relationship with Neil also helped loosen the company's purse strings when it came to her client. This situation is not quite parallel, but it's instructive: when Mariah Carey and Sony head Tommy Mottola became an item, there was no way a record of Mariah's was not going to become a hit, no matter what it cost or what Sony employees had to do to make it happen; but the first record Carey released after divorcing Mottola sank like a rock in quicksand. The pressure that comes with this kind of relationship is enormous. Are you going to let your wife, girlfriend, or sister fail? No. Not if you have the power to prevent it.

I was now in a quandary. I liked Donna and her comanager Susan Munao, and I thought that they were being screwed by their lawyer and by Neil. The lawyer, who also represented Casablanca in numerous deals, had a definite conflict of interest. After much soul-searching, I decided that the only honest thing for me to do was to betray Neil and tell Susan that Joyce was planning to hire Abe Somers. This was a hard decision to make, especially because I knew that Donna would go to Geffen Records if she got out of her contract with us, and this would really irk me, as I didn't like the company president, Eddie Rosenblatt. I didn't know David Geffen, but I knew that there was no love lost between him and Neil. I still loved Neil and respected what we'd tried to build together, but our relationship and everything around it had changed. I had begun to dread going into the office.

My outlook was dimmed even further by what I saw happening around us in the industry: disco was about to crash. All the telltale signs were there—the too-rapid expansion, the market saturation, the growing contempt among the music-buying public. Despite our penetration of various areas of the entertainment industry (much of it via cheap signings that held little hope of long-term profit), the Casablanca ship was afloat on disco waters, and disco waters alone. Without disco, we had almost nothing to sustain us. Remember that even our lone rock act of any value, KISS, had edged into disco territory. Our fortunes were pinned to disco, and no amount of spin doctoring was going to change that.

The crash came on July 12, 1979. A popular Chicago DJ named Steve Dahl had lost his job when his station changed its format to disco. When he landed at another local station, he wasn't shy about publicly sharing his white-hot hatred of the music. To vent his feelings, Dahl staged an event he dubbed the Disco Demolition between games of a doubleheader with the Chicago White Sox and the Cleveland Indians. He invited anyone wishing to destroy their disco albums to bring them to Comiskey Park on Chicago's south side. He would stack the albums in the outfield and blow them to smithereens with a stick of dynamite, or some such explosive. The White Sox helped out by announcing that anyone with a disco album could gain admission to the park for only ninety-eight cents (Dahl's station was at 97.9 on the FM dial). This drew a beyond-capacity crowd of over fifty thousand. The demographic was atypical—read: pot-smoking rock music lovers—and the crowd had no sense of baseball etiquette. Dahl gathered a huge pile of disco albums and, as promised, blew them sky-high. A small-scale riot ensued. Thousand of spectators rushed onto the field and refused to leave, wandering around in a pot-induced daze. Due to this, the White Sox had to forfeit the second game.

In a moment of great irony, that very night I was in New York for yet another of Bill Wardlow's Disco Forums. It hadn't even been five months since his previous soiree. These gatherings had been a cash cow for Wardlow, and he thought that disco was still popular enough for him to now hold two forums a year. These events were normally a pleasure to attend; we won awards by the truckload and were always the belle of the ball. Who wouldn't enjoy all that glad-handing? None of the other Casablanca execs attended this forum. It was just me, Christy Hill (Candy's sister, who was still working publicity for us), and three or four of the disco department people; I felt lonely and not at all in my element.

The forum was decidedly humdrum, and the fact that I remember so little of it shows how disengaged I was. The most noteworthy moment occurred before the event even got underway. We had arranged with Studio 54's Steve Rubell to hold a forum-opening promotion party at the club on July 12. In each forum attendee's welcome package we included special passes for the event, which was to begin at midnight. Once the forum's opening night concerts at Roseland had concluded, pass holders walked the two blocks to Studio 54 to continue partying. But they were stopped at the door by Rubell, who refused to honor their passes to our party. This was a real slap in the face, particularly since just two weeks earlier we had released a special two-disc album for the club called *A Night at Studio 54*. Bill Wardlow was furious with Rubell, and there was a loud confrontation. Wardlow was so enraged that he vowed (quite publicly, too; it was in the newspaper the next day) to do everything in his power to cripple Rubell's operation, including his plans to roll out Studio 54 locations in London and Tokyo. I doubt Studio 54 suffered much because of Wardlow, but he was not someone you wanted as an enemy.

I had missed the entire dustup, but it was the talk of the forum the next morning, and I was not looking forward to mediating between Wardlow and Rubell in the days to come. On the evening of July 15, after the convention-closing awards banquet, I went back to my hotel room with an armful of trophies and laid them out on the bed. From a certain perspective, it was amazing to see them all spread out like that, but still I knew that they were arbitrary awards bestowed upon the products of a quickly fading genre—one that we had leveraged to the hilt for years. I sat there looking at them, gleaming and boastful. We'd had so many successes, we'd won more awards than I could possibly recall, we'd expanded more rapidly and with greater fanfare than any record company in history, and we'd been granted more opportunities than I could catalog. Gold, Platinum, Grammys, People's Choices, Oscars, one hundred artists, and one hundred million fucking dollars—it all raced through my mind, and all I felt was a crushing emptiness.

I was depressed. I was deeply affected by the changes I saw in Neil and by what I was discovering about the character he was becoming. He believed his own publicity, the publicity we had created, and that was the most dangerous thing you could do. The stunning, bold-faced lie he had told Bruce and me had crippled our relationship, and I no longer saw a future for myself at Casablanca—at least, I no longer saw any kind of future I wanted. Staring at a shining chorus line of trophies on a Manhattan hotel bedspread, I decided it was time to leave.

The receiver weighed fifty pounds when I picked it up to call Neil and tell him of my decision. He asked me to take some time off before I made it final. I don't believe he saw it coming; we had always been so close, and we had gone through the bad times as well as the good together. In my heart, I did not really want to leave, but I saw no other choice. Casablanca had been my life for many years, but I wanted to be able to look at myself in the mirror, and going to work frustrated every day was not my style—never was, never will be.

Neil told me to take a few weeks off, probably figuring that if I had time to reflect, I would change my mind. I returned to work almost immediately and for a few days conducted business as usual. On maybe my third day back, Paul Schaefer, one of the attorneys who had worked on the contract details for the PolyGram buyout, stopped by my office. We were chatting about various things when I mentioned that I was thinking of leaving. Paul let slip that if I left, according to the contract, Neil and Peter would have to buy out my stock, which would amount to half of what I'd received from the initial PolyGram payout. And they would also have to pay out the remainder of my contract. I knew that Casablanca would never make a profit, and I strongly suspected that

PolyGram would never promote me to president, even if Neil vacated the position for a more hands-off chairman of the board role. I could leave this situation and get paid nearly half a million dollars to do it. There wasn't even a decision to be made here.

On Monday, July 23, 1979, I packed a few personal items, said one or two goodbyes, and quietly walked out the door onto Sunset.

20

Now and for the Rest of Your Life

**Who knew?—A golden parachute—A job with Ray Stark—
Profitless prosperity—Shown the door—Meet the
new boss—Casablanca gutted—The remaining shell—
Flashdance—Neil starts anew—Life on the Boardwalk—
It's not the flu—Departure—Elegy from the
industry—The image still remains**

July 1981
Nate 'n Al Delicatessen
Beverly Hills, California

Nate 'n Al is a delicatessen on Beverly Drive, just south of Santa Monica Boulevard in Beverly Hills. It's an unassuming little place, but Hollywood cognoscenti have flocked there for breakfast and lunch meetings since the late 1940s. In the summer of 1981, two years after I had left Casablanca, I was at Nate 'n Al finishing a lunch meeting over a salad of some sort. I don't remember who was dining with me, or why we were there. As the meeting wrapped, I happened to look up and see the unmistakable form of Peter Guber walking toward the door. We made eye contact, and he walked over to say hello. I hadn't seen him since I'd left the company, and it was good to meet up with him again. Guber said to me, "How did you know?"

~ ~ ~

When I left Casablanca, in July 1979, I did not take any time off. After years of working at Neil's side, I knew that you did not leave him and stay on good terms. My immediate task was to find an attorney who could extract me from our messy contract situation. Attorneys are a dime a dozen in LA—the trick was to find someone experienced in entertainment law who had no ties to either Casablanca or PolyGram. After some fretful searching, I hired David Braun. David, an Ivy Leaguer, was a tall, solid-looking guy in his mid-forties who had represented some high-profile clients (such as George Harrison and Bob Dylan) and who came highly recommended. He knew the biz, but he'd spent most of his time practicing in New York and had no links to Casablanca or PolyGram that we could discern. David quickly dug into the contract and did an exemplary job of helping me navigate the legal obstacle course in front of me. Per the terms of my deal, Neil and Peter were required to buy the remaining portion of my stock in Casablanca for 50 percent of what had originally been paid to me, and PolyGram had to pay me my salary for the duration of the contract, which translated into a severance package of a little more than a quarter of a million dollars. On top of that, David managed to land me two Mercedes: Candy and I could keep our Casablanca vehicles.

This left me free and clear from a contractual standpoint, but I still needed to put a public face on it. One of my last projects at Casablanca was to craft my exit announcement for *Billboard*, *Cashbox*, and *Record World*. To avoid making either party look bad, we announced that "Larry Harris is on an extended vacation, and talks about his own label or a production deal with Casablanca are underway." This was complete crap. No such talks ever took place, and we never intended them to. It was simply a way to get me smoothly out the door. We'd spent years filling as much column space as possible and making mountains out of the tiniest Casablanca molehills, but my departure went almost entirely unmentioned in the trades. *Billboard* ran a very low-profile blurb, as did *Record World*, and that was it. The cherry on top of it all was that Donna Summer's "Bad Girls" was No. 1 on the *Billboard* charts the day I resigned.

Leaving Casablanca was bittersweet. My feelings of doubt in the company, my disappointment over Neil, and my growing frustration with my own inability to pull away from the mess had combined to make me dread going to work. Assessing the situation months later, after I had some perspective on it, I could see that it had been worse than I'd realized at the time. Neil had begun to drive a wedge between Bruce Bird and me, telling Bruce negative things I had supposedly said about him, and then telling me negative things that Bruce had supposedly said about me. This was Neil's Machiavellian way of holding on to power, though the motivation was pure paranoia: neither Bruce nor I had any designs on his position.

I was sad that by leaving Casablanca I would lose my relationship with Neil. But I should have given him more credit than that. Neil wasn't angry with me at all. In fact, he almost seemed to envy my ability to leave it all behind, and he was surprisingly sympathetic to my circumstances. A few months after I'd gone, he happily recommended me to Ray Stark (Peter Guber's old mentor) for a position at a record company Stark wanted to launch. I had a meeting with Stark, but due to some bad advice, I brought Jeff Franklin along as my negotiator. Had I gone in alone, which was my first inclination, I would have jumped at Ray's initial offer and that would have been that. Jeff, a notorious hardballer, kicked Ray's offer back and made some overly aggressive demands. Stark balked, and the opportunity vanished almost instantly.

I soldiered on, and so did Casablanca. Neil immediately promoted Bruce Bird to fill my spot, and Bruce assumed the duty of running the company's day-to-day operations. Howie Rosen, whose enthusiasm had waned as mine had, left two weeks after me, and Danny Davis replaced him as VP of promotions.

It was the fall of 1979, and global economic conditions were still tenuous, so Neil, perhaps biding his time until the other shoe dropped, maintained a noticeably low company profile (low for Casablanca, at least). He particularly kept things low-key in the trades, as reports of any extravagant expenditure on Casablanca's part would certainly be seen by PolyGram execs, who were watching him with increasing skepticism. The entire industry had seemed to notice that we'd been moving suicidally close to the brink for the better part of a decade. In fact, all of the big boys—like Warner and Capitol—were in trouble, and industry-wide changes were being instituted to stem the bleeding. Return policies were made much stricter, and PolyGram eliminated free goods entirely and instead began offering cash discounts. This would have been unthinkable just two years earlier. Neil did, however, make a couple of high-profile TV appearances during this time—on *Dinah! and Friends*; and, with Peter Guber, on *Tomorrow with Tom Snyder*. He also branched out into the field of education (briefly), teaching a course on the music business at UCLA in the fall semester.

Casablanca kept issuing product, so much of it bad, at full bore. It had become a throw-it-at-the-wall-and-see-if-it-sticks operation. In the six months between August 1979 and February 1980, the company released thirty-six albums, most of which were just filler. The artists (ever heard of Platypus, Mike Heron, Bad News Travels Fast, or Loose Change?) should never have been signed in the first place.

As 1979 wound down, Neil continued to expand the Casablanca portfolio by pushing ahead with projects related to Broadway and country music that he'd been developing for the better part of a year. He started a new division called StageWorks to mount the Robert Klein–Lucie Arnaz vehicle *They're Playing Our Song*. He also partnered with Snuff Garrett (famous for his work with Sonny and Cher, as well as with the young Phil Spector) to create a Nashville-based country imprint label called Casablanca West. Though this agreement folded after a single release, it did produce a hilarious piece of label art featuring a team of cowboys, apparently extras from a western movie, taking five outside the Casablanca Record & FilmWorks casbah. Neil's KidWorks project with Lew Merenstein and McDonald's was still moving forward. They debuted the three albums at a McDonald's national sales meeting that fall and hoped to sell them in the chain's five thousand restaurants and through a special record club.

In an interview with *Billboard* that fall, Neil remarked on the increasingly dire music landscape: "I have learned the good stores, good racks, good retailers, good record companies will survive. The people who have lived off of each other and worked in the business that for the last four to five years has mostly been profitless prosperity will not survive." If I had a hundred years to think about it, I don't think I could come up with two words that described Casablanca better than "profitless prosperity." It had been that way since *Alive!* had broken, at the end of 1975. We'd had many, many successes, but our excesses always outweighed them. Neil had orchestrated a marvelous juggling act and sustained it for years, to the company's apparent benefit. But, in the final tally, you can paint the building as much as you like, but no matter how many times you do it, or how pretty the colors are, in the end it's just paint. Casablanca always looked good. But I'm not sure it ever *was* good.

Neil's demise was a long time coming. Rumors that he was going to be bought out by PolyGram began to surface upon my departure in July

1979, though Neil strongly denied them. But, between the flood of returns of the KISS solo albums, the unforeseen downturn in the US economy, the looming death of disco, and the loss of his second in command, Neil had to have sensed a change in the wind. His personal and business lives were both suffering. In the fall of 1979, a fire severely damaged part of his and Joyce's Holmby Hills estate, forcing them to take up temporary residence in Diana Ross's mansion. And then, in February 1980—more than eight months after I had given them the inside information about Joyce and Abe Somers—Donna Summer's attorneys finally filed her multimillion-dollar lawsuit. Donna sought termination of her contract and ten million in punitive damages. Casablanca, Neil, and Joyce were all named in the suit.

This was finally enough for PolyGram. On Friday, February 8, 1980, Neil Bogart's reign as president of Casablanca Record & FilmWorks ended. Depending upon whom you believe, and people I trust have told me both stories, he was either forced out by PolyGram or he engineered his own way out because he had again grown tired of big-corporation bureaucracy. He did not receive any payout from PolyGram whatsoever. A few miles away, at the Century Plaza Hotel (the site of the Casablanca launch party nearly six years to the day earlier), yet another *Billboard* Disco Forum was getting underway. Casablanca won its usual glut of hardware from Bill Wardlow, but word spread quickly through the crowd that Neil had been ousted. During the forum, several panel discussions turned into unplanned tributes to the man. Neil walked out on top, with Captain and Tennille's "Do That to Me One More Time" at No. 1 on *Billboard*'s Hot 100.

I was surprised by none of this. I'd seen it coming for months, if not years. I knew that despite all the awards, the glad-handing, the industry spotlight—despite all the public successes—we were just kidding ourselves. When Peter Guber and I ran into each other at Nate 'n Al that summer day in 1981, what Peter was asking me was *how* I knew. The answer was simple. Since before the PolyGram merger, I had been responsible for drafting pro forma sales projections. I knew what the real sales figures were, and I at least had an idea of what the future numbers might be. Nearly from the moment PolyGram merged with Casablanca, Neil had me create rosy sales forecasts for our Dutch and German bosses—much rosier than the facts could support. There at the deli, contemplating Peter's question, my first thought was, "How could anyone *not* know?" If PolyGram (or anyone else, for that matter—Peter included) had paid any attention to the music side of the company, then they would have seen that the sales projections were fiction.

PolyGram named Bruce Bird as Neil's successor, but without Neil, the Casablanca that I had known ceased to exist. Neil was to remain on as a minority shareholder and consultant. I doubt that anyone believed that this meant anything. Neil's firing was the first domino to fall in a tremendous run of changes implemented by PolyGram. Within weeks of Neil's departure, they terminated sixty-five of Casablanca's remaining one hundred and fifty employees—including Irv Biegel, which meant that the largely useless New York office would be closed. PolyGram then divided their domestic music company into PolyGram East and Poly-Gram West, with Casablanca remaining part of the PolyGram West division, along with Mercury Records. Additional cutbacks occurred when PolyGram reduced the number of affiliated pressing plants from twenty to four. By the end of March 1980, another thirty to forty people were trimmed from the Casablanca staff, and the company name reverted to Casablanca Records. The FilmWorks division became PolyGram Pictures; Peter Guber remained on to chair the company.

Although they finally realized what a liability Casablanca was and made the necessary cutbacks to fix it, PolyGram again didn't do their homework very well. The McDonald's concept had the potential to help Casablanca regain its footing in a spectacular way, but I don't think Bruce bought into the idea, and the albums made no impact. I wish now that I'd discussed the project with Bruce; I might have been able to sell him on the idea.

PolyGram's lack of due diligence was far worse with regard to KISS and Donna Summer, who had top-man clauses in their contracts stipulating that they could terminate their agreements if Neil left the company. Now that Neil was gone, both acts gave PolyGram their sixty days' notice. Angel was a never-was, Parliament was more or less over, the Village People were in decline, and now the label's two biggest acts were walking. I'm sure PolyGram tried to prevent it, but Donna was moving to David Geffen's upstart label, and there was nothing they could do to change that. So they set their sights on keeping their only remaining viable commodity: KISS. KISS's co-business manager Howard Marks was of course aware of the leverage the situation gave him. He put together a six-album deal with PolyGram in late April 1980. This included a jaw-dropping two-million-dollar advance per album. Weeks after the signing, the band announced the departure of drummer Peter Criss; Peter's long-deteriorating relationship with his band mates was finally over.

Following the dismal reception of their 1981 concept album *Music from "The Elder,"* KISS saw their already waning popularity plummet, and Glickman/Marks made enough of a case against Bill Aucoin that KISS finally edged him out of the picture in the spring of 1982, ending a very successful nine-year relationship. Ace Frehley followed Aucoin out the door in 1983, creating a multimillion-dollar problem for KISS. The band's April 1980 contract with PolyGram defined KISS as Gene Simmons, Paul Stanley, and Ace Frehley (Peter Criss was not included, because his departure had been decided upon weeks prior to the signing). When Ace left, this effectively voided the contract. The band was now worth far less than the two-million-per-album advance provided by the 1980 contract, and PolyGram insisted on a renegotiation.

As for Casablanca, in November 1980, its final founding partner, Cecil Holmes, left. In December, PolyGram terminated an additional twenty-five employees. The four big employee cutbacks demanded by PolyGram in 1979 and 1980, compounded by the usual rats-fleeing-the-sinking-ship attrition, had left a skeleton crew of twenty-five piloting whatever remained at 8255 Sunset. The December 1980 purge included Bruce Bird, Al DiNoble, Bobby Applegate, and Don Wasley. Surprisingly, my attorney, David Braun, was hired to succeed Bruce and to oversee all US record operations for PolyGram.

Once the undisputed champion of new record companies, Casablanca was now nothing more than a vanity label. From 1981 to 1985, Poly-Gram used Casablanca as a dumping ground for artists and sound-tracks—they even threw rereleases from their newly acquired 20th Century Fox Records catalog onto the label. At some point in 1981, the company shifted headquarters to New York (to 810 Seventh Avenue, the very same building where Buddah was located), and 8255 Sunset was vacated. While virtually all product issued during this time was forgettable, one release did stand out. In the summer of 1983, the soundtrack of *Flashdance*—with its megahits "Maniac," by Michael Sembello, and "(What a Feeling) Flashdance," by Irene Cara—sold over six million copies. I thought of all the lifeblood we had pumped into Casablanca through the lean years; all the bragging and boasting; all the deal making, risk taking, swindling, and finagling. Now the biggest-selling album in Casablanca history had arrived, and the label wasn't much more than a name on a door, two phones, and a couple of Kelly Girl staffers. Those fuckers!

On November 18, 1985, the soundtrack of *A Chorus Line* was released. It was the final album issued on the original Casablanca Records label. Eleven years and 289 albums by over 140 artists. It was a hell of a ride.

As for Neil, he rebounded as quickly as I would have expected—or, at least, he attempted to. He took out a full-page ad in the February 23, 1980 issue of *Billboard* that read, "To my Casablanca family and friends—here's looking at you, kids. See you in the sequel . . . coming soon. With love, appreciation and wishes for good fortune, Neil." The ad featured a drawing of Humphrey Bogart walking away from the camera. Neil also sent a letter to the remaining Casablanca employees in which he quipped, "I'm still your landlord," referring to the fact that he retained co-ownership of the buildings in which Casablanca was located.

By the end of February, Neil had designs for his new label laid out. Initially, he planned to call it BogArts, but he changed it to Boardwalk Entertainment. Neil, Jon Peters (Barbra Streisand's former hairdresser and producer of *Caddyshack* and *A Star Is Born*), and Peter Guber were on the board of directors, and by August many former Casablanca employees had made the leap to Boardwalk—among them Irv Biegel, Ellen Wolf, David Shein, and Ruben Rodriguez. A young executive named Gary LeMel (who would eventually helm Warner's worldwide music division) became Neil's new right-hand man. Boardwalk's first release was the Harry Chapin LP *Sequel*, in October 1980; and among the more notable names on its roster were Ringo Starr, the Ohio Players, Night Ranger (managed by Bruce Bird), and Joan Jett, who would deliver the label's only No. 1 hit: "I Love Rock 'n Roll." The roster represented the worst and the best of Neil's Casablanca approach: he was signing past-their-prime stars (Starr) and finding new artists for a new generation (Night Ranger and Joan Jett). A few Casablanca acts showed up on Boardwalk, as well, including—tangentially, at least—Robin Williams; Robin had starred in the movie *Popeye*, and the label released the soundtrack. Boardwalk meandered along, scoring some decent hits, but nothing they did could compete with the fireworks we'd ignited at Casablanca.

Free of the Casablanca yoke, Neil was able to spend more time with his family, and he could pursue other interests, such as coaching Little League baseball. I rarely saw or spoke to him during this time. One day, probably in late 1980, I happened to be picking someone up at LAX when I ran into Neil near the baggage retrieval area. There was nothing awkward about the encounter. He seemed genuinely happy to see me, and I was happy to see him. We chatted briefly about our families and about business, and then we went our separate ways.

A year later, near the end of 1981, Neil went on tour with Carole Bayer Sager and Marvin Hamlisch. Carole was one of Neil's Boardwalk acts, and he wanted to join her on the road for a short time. When he returned home, he complained to Joyce that he wasn't feeling well, but because both Carole and Marvin had been suffering from the flu, they didn't think much of it. Joyce had already booked a doctor's appointment for herself, so Neil tagged along. The doctor told him that he didn't have the flu, ordered a battery of tests, and finally diagnosed Neil with lymphoma. The disease was at an advanced stage. It had already consumed one of his kidneys.

News of his illness did not spread quickly. Neil had always been very guarded about his health. Once, in 1979, he didn't show up at the office for several days. There were no phone calls, no messages, nothing—he was completely MIA. Fearing that something was terribly wrong, I went to his house and knocked on the door. When Joyce answered, I said to her, "I haven't been able to reach Neil on the phone, and he hasn't been in the office, and no one seems to know what's going on." She assured me that everything was fine, that Neil simply had a respiratory virus. This just shows that when it came to his health, Neil could be quite secretive. By the time he was diagnosed with cancer, I was no longer close to him, or Joyce, or Bruce. He received treatment, and his cancer went into remission briefly, but by early 1982, I had begun to hear rumors that he was very ill again.

I went to see Neil at home. The housekeeper answered the doorbell. I told her who I was, and she disappeared inside. A few moments later, Neil shuffled to the door. His eyebrows had fallen out and he was shockingly pale. The endlessly energetic man I'd known for decades was now a fragile husk; the infectious, madcap light in his eyes had gone out. He smiled and said he was glad to see me, and we walked out under the long portico to chat. I don't remember much about our conversation, except that it was short. The effort of standing and talking for more than a few seconds was clearly exhausting him. He seemed so tired, and I didn't want to impose. After only a few minutes, I made my excuses and left. That was the last time I saw him alive. Shortly after that, Neil was admitted to Cedars-Sinai for more intensive treatment. He would never leave. On May 8, 1982, Neil Bogart died at the age of thirty-nine.

I can see the memorial service as clearly as if I were there right now. It was held on May 11, a warm, sunny day, and the large funeral home was filled with Neil's family and friends. I sat next to his mother and father, with whom I still had a warm relationship. The saddest of sights was his children and Joyce. I had been so close to them for a time, and the thought of his kids growing up without him overwhelmed me. I couldn't stop crying. I had never before lost someone with whom I'd been so close. I thought about all those years, the thousands of days we'd spent in our adjoining offices. Every day we had fought battles together, not always knowing exactly what we were doing, but sure that we'd win in the end. Neil had given me my shot, taught me everything, and then set me loose.

As grief-stricken as I was, I was inspired to see the crowd that had turned out to honor Neil. The funeral home, which was huge, couldn't come close to containing the turnout. There were as many people left standing outside as there were inside. I walked so many mourners up to the casket that I lost count. There were a lot of industry heavyweights. Mo Ostin and Joe Smith were among the Warner representatives; Art Kass, Jerry Sharell, Arnold Feldman, and Ron Weisner from Buddah were there, as was Morris Levy from Roulette. Executives from almost every record company in southern California were in attendance. So was nearly everyone who had ever worked at or with Casablanca: including me and Candy, Christy Hill, Cecil Holmes, Bruce Bird and his entire family, Peter and Lynda Guber, as well as Jeff Franklin and others from ATI. Bill Wardlow came, along with the publishers of *Billboard* and many of their staffers; there were also representatives from *Record World*, *Cashbox*, and the other trade papers. There were radio people from around the country. Dozens of artists and their managers from the Casablanca, Boardwalk, and Buddah days were there: Donna Summer, Paul Stanley, Gene Simmons, Joan Jett, Paul Jabara, Giorgio Moroder, Jacques Morali, Henri Belolo, Bill Aucoin, Frankie Crocker, and Roy Silver. Other stars and industry giants were also present—such as Dick Clark, Burt Bacharach, Marvin Hamlisch, Bill Withers, Bob Dylan, the Isley Brothers, Neil Diamond, and Gladys Knight and the Pips—many of whom gathered to sing "Gonna Keep an Eye on Us," a song from *The First*, a Broadway musical about Neil's boyhood idol Jackie Robinson.

So many images flashed through my head—our first meeting at my parents' house in 1961, the job interview at Buddah and those awful purple walls. I thought about the guy who hired all his relatives and gave them Mercedeses. The office showman with his flash paper, lighter-fluid bonfires, gongs, and five-hundred-pound speakers. The guy who found KISS. The guy who beat Elvis. The guy who made disco. Who survived the Carson album fiasco. Who divorced Warner Brothers. Who sent boxes of Casablanca LPs to orphanages. Who dined with presidents. Who drove a Rolls Royce Corniche with a vanity plate that read "PS 203"—his Brooklyn elementary school. The guy with the big hair, the camel in his office, that smile, and that gleam in his eye. That inextinguishable gleam.

Afterword:
The Casablanca Legacy

The image of Casablanca that most people are familiar with was painted by Frederic Dannen in his 1990 book *Hit Men: Power Brokers and Fast Money inside the Music Business*. While I don't mean to unduly disparage the book or its author, *Hit Men*'s portrait of Casablanca is deeply flawed. Dannen contacted Joyce Bogart-Trabulus and given her the false impression that he would write positively about Neil, and Joyce then asked me to contribute to the book. Somewhat reluctantly, I made some minor contributions. In the end, however, Dannen got most of his first-hand information from a single source: Danny Davis, VP of promotions. Danny hadn't joined the company until late summer 1979—after I'd left, a good six years after the company had been founded, and long after most of the Casablanca story had been written. When the book came out, I compiled a laundry list of the falsehoods it contains.

Dannen's chapter on Casablanca begins: "If you were cruising along Sunset Boulevard in the late seventies and saw what appeared to be an enormous Mercedes dealership, chances were good that you'd just stumbled upon the parking lot of Casablanca Records." The "Mercedes dealership" was not at the Sunset location but at the Sherbourne building, which we used in 1974 and 1975. The staff parking lot on Sunset was behind the building and not visible from the street. Dannen also claims that 8255 Sunset was razed at some point. In fact, it's still standing; as of this writing, it's home to CineTel Films.

He also maintains that the Casablanca offices closed at 3:00 p.m. every day. While I can appreciate overstatement for humor's sake, the comment is very misleading. We had a ton of fun at Casablanca, and we indulged in all the vices you'd expect, but that never kept us from working hard and putting in long hours. If people were regularly checking out in the middle of the afternoon it would not have escaped our notice. Neil and I (and many others) were typically in the office by seven or eight in the morning and often wouldn't depart until seven at night, sometimes later.

Hit Men also contains a story about a "drug girl" who dropped by Casablanca almost every day, like a deli waitress. To be sure, there was never a shortage of drugs—all varieties—on the premises. I had a stash in my desk drawer, Neil regularly indulged, and I'm also certain that many Casablanca people had their own connections, but there was no Casablanca drug girl. Several people (all of whom were at Casablanca after I left) have mentioned to me that a young relative of one of the newer Casablanca execs provided a lot of the drugs consumed during the late stages of the company's existence; it seems to me that this drug girl anecdote is just a way to protect the true identity of the culprit—who was not female. Many of financial particulars in the book are wrong as well. And Dannen ends his Casablanca chapter by saying that Neil didn't have a good ear for music. By every possible measure, Neil had one of the best ears in the business. Of course, he swung and missed a few times, but he certainly signed many more monster records and artists than he passed on. To complete the baseball metaphor, his batting average was way over the magic .300 mark—I would guess it was somewhere in the .750 range.

Dannen means to sound dramatic, to spin a good story, but a lot of what he describes just never happened. Others have written about Casablanca and hit closer to the mark, such as Elmore Leonard in his 1999 novel *Be Cool*. Yet it's Dannen's take that has, for many people, defined Casablanca.

Timing is everything, and *Hit Men* struck gold in that regard. In the early 1990s, an unexpected thing happened: the 1970s returned. Everything from fashion to movies to music was suddenly in retro mode. Perhaps it was inevitable, but I certainly never saw it coming. Then one day, in the early 1990s, I was killing some time in a retro clothing store, and I was taken aback to find several Casablanca T-shirts. The teenage girl working behind the counter saw me looking at the shirts and asked, "What is it about this Casablanca Records? Everyone stops and looks at these shirts with awe." Next thing I knew, a home video called *Inside the Casbah: A Visual History of Casablanca Records* was released, and PolyGram issued a four-CD set entitled *The Casablanca Records Story*. We now seemed so popular it made me wonder if we'd missed an opportunity to brand our own line of clothing, as Coca-Cola had in the 1980s.

Casablanca Records was eventually absorbed by PolyGram, and, in 1998, Philips, PolyGram's parent company, sold PolyGram to Seagram's, which was then part of the Universal Music Group. In 2000, Tommy Mottola, Mariah Carey's former manager and husband and past CEO of Sony Music, revived the Casablanca Records name. Lindsay Lohan was his premier act. Even though the only connection between Mottola and us was the logo art and the name, I was rooting for him, but for the life of me I could never figure out why he'd done it. If he had signed Donna Summer or Cher or anyone else who had been involved in the original company I might have understood, but unless he just took the name because he was a fan of the original Casablanca Records I don't get it— there was no synergy there at all. Sadly, by the time Mottola came along, the music industry had changed dramatically and was facing a whole new set of challenges, so the revived Casablanca didn't do much. As this is written, Casablanca is again dormant.

These days, when someone who knew Neil speaks about him, they often conclude by saying, ". . . and how amazing it would have been to see what he'd do in the next twenty years." People often ask me what I think would have become of Neil Bogart had he lived. While he did see the dawn of the CD and MTV age, he effectively missed the MTV generation, and he never dreamed of such things as downloading, iPods, and YouTube. What would he have made of all this? How would he have adapted his record company to today's music landscape? It all depends upon which Neil you mean: the Neil of the Buddah days and the early years of Casablanca, who took chances when others ran and hid; or the Neil who had begun to believe his own press and no longer had to fight and scratch his way to each success. I don't have a definitive answer. I can tell you that Neil would likely have jumped right on the rap and hip-hop bandwagon. It sounds a little counterintuitive to say that a solidly Jewish guy would have synched with a largely African American cultural movement so quickly, but cultural differences posed no challenge for Neil—they were virtually invisible to him. He had an affinity for anything that was natural and not contrived. Parliament, for example, was as out-there as you could get, but despite the weird window dressing, George and his crew were doing what they wanted to do, not what they thought others wanted them to do. That's exactly why Neil (and the rest of us) liked them. I think Neil would have seen the same thing in many rap or hip-hop artists. He also had a special feel for R&B music and street music, so he would have certainly been ahead of the curve on that.

As for MTV, Neil would have had an entire division devoted to ensuring that his product was always prominently featured. He would have handled the MTV powers the same way he handled the radio powers, and he would have hired the best video directors for his projects, maybe even securing them under exclusive contracts. Keep in mind that Casablanca was way ahead of most other labels when it came to using video and film for artist marketing and promotion.

I can also say with some certainty that Neil would have figured out how to thrive in the world of downloading. The initial industry reaction to downloading was to panic that product was being stolen and then to fight those who were stealing it tooth and nail. I think Neil would have been quick to acknowledge the inevitable growth and permanence of the downloading phenomenon, and he would have adapted to it much faster than others. I can clearly see him, being the promotion guy he was, gravitating toward things like Facebook and Twitter, making early overtures to the originator of Napster, and investing heavily in new media applications, from YouTube to Microsoft. The business model that most record companies follow today is outdated, and it has been for years. I think it's likely that Neil would have shed that albatross to become a pioneer of the big 360 deals now being offered by companies like Live Nation to proven artists within the industry. He would have seen the Internet and downloading for what they are, just two new vehicles for getting music to the people, like vinyl, tape, and the CD were before them. As much as the landscape changes, people remain constant. Neil always believed that, and he would have believed it no matter when he lived.

Acknowledgments

First, let me thank my cowriters, Curt Gooch and Jeff Suhs, for all their help in researching various aspects of this book and keeping the story accurate. They found me by accident while they were consulting on another book. I told them about the manuscript, which I had written years ago, and they were immediately interested in working with me and finding a publisher. Thanks also to Mike Edison at Backbeat Books, who realized the potential of my story about one of the most fabled record companies in history.

My thanks for help in jogging my memory about stories I had completely forgotten or did not know at the time to: Karmen Beck (a fountain of knowledge), Dick Sherman, Sherrie Levy, Nancy Lewis, Cecil Holmes, Dick Clark, Robert Klein, Gregg Giuffria, Brett Hudson, Joyce Bogart-Trabulus, Bill Aucoin, Peter Lake, Felix Robinson, Don Wasley, Ruben Rodriguez, T.J. Lambert, Barb Amesbury, Soozin Kazick, and Bill Schereck.

Thanks to Paula Manzanero for coming up with a title for this tale.

Most of all, I want to thank my partner and true soul mate for thirty-five years: Mary Candice Hill Harris (the unidentified woman). You lived through my Casablanca years, which was not always the smoothest of rides, stood by me, and believed in me and my crazy ideas. You've made my life richer and certainly more interesting than it would have been without you.

~ ~ ~

Curt Gooch and Jeff Suhs would like to thank Steve Clark of Superior Graphix for his time and effort, Ken Sharp, and Jeff Falk. They would also like to thank Marc Scallatino for photo editing, Mary Williams for copyediting, and Joe Fields for timeline research.

Where Are They Now?

Name	What's Going On Now
Bill (Barb) Amesbury	Following sexual reassignment surgery, Bill is now named Barb and is a documentary filmmaker.
Bill Aucoin	Living in Florida and still dabbling in the music industry.
Long John Baldry	Died July 21, 2005 of a chest infection.
Lester Bangs	Died April 30, 1982 of an accidental drug interaction.
Chris Bearde	Resides in Las Vegas; runs Chris Bearde's International Comedy Hall of Fame.
Karmen Beck	Worked with Bruce Bird until his death in 1994, then became president of The Album Network; now an indie producer of various functions.
Henri Belolo	Still working in France as a producer.
Irv Biegel	President of Sumthing Distribution; cofounder of Boardwalk with Neil Bogart.
Bruce Bird	Died in 1994.
Nancy Bird	Remarried and found religion.
Ira Blacker	Owns and operates a commercial printing company, Printing Source; owns valuableclocks.com
Beth Bogart	Married to Peter Guber's older brother, Charlie.
Joyce Bogart-Trabulus	Married to Neil's doctor; has stewarded the Neil Bogart Foundation since Neil's death.
Jheryl Busby	Became president of Motown and made a fortune on the sale; found dead in his hot tub in Malibu in November 2008 at age fifty-nine.
Phyllis Chotin	Does indie design work.

Name	What's Going On Now
Dick Clark	Suffered a stroke in late 2004; continues to host *Dick Clark's New Year's Rockin' Eve* annually.
George Clinton	Still funkifying the world.
Alec Costandinos	Produced Tina Turner's debut solo LP; lives in Europe and reportedly writes jingles for TV spots.
Al Coury	Retired and living in Oxnard, California.
Peter Criss	Retired from KISS; married and living in New Jersey; pursuing a solo career.
Frankie Crocker	Died October 21, 2000.
Ray D'Ariano	Doing radio in Rhode Island.
Clive Davis	Chief creative officer at Sony BMG; now seventy-eight years old.
Ron Delsener	Sold Ron Delsener Presents to Clear Channel Communications.
Al DiNoble	Doing various indie projects.
Jeff Franklin	Still out there making deals.
Ace Frehley	Left KISS in 2002; once again pursuing a solo career.
Ken Friedman	Died of AIDS.
Gregg Giuffria	Megarich, though no longer in the music business; works with gambling casinos.
Carl Glickman	Philanthropist and a member of the board of directors for The Bear Stearns Companies; still resides in Cleveland.
Randee Goldman	Currently works in the animal rescue field.
Merv Griffin	Died of prostate cancer August 12, 2007.
Allen Grubman	Became the most powerful attorney in the music business.
Peter Guber	Owner of a movie production company; very, very rich from the sale of the Guber-Peters Entertainment Company to Sony.
Morgan Harris	Works out of Chicago, creating marketing and PR campaigns for the film and television industries.
Christy Hill	Retired and living in LA.
Cecil Holmes	Worked at Columbia Records for 10 years; currently driving a limo in LA.

Name	What's Going On Now
Jimmy Ienner	Rich from some great investments.
Brian Interland	Working various deals in the music industry; VP of label relations with Bus Radio.
Paul Jabara	Died of complications from AIDS, September 29, 1992.
Arthur Kassel	Cofounded the Beverly Hills Gun Club; married Tichi Wilkerson, who owned the *Hollywood Reporter*.
Soozin Kazick	Retired and living in LA.
Steve Keator	Died of AIDS.
Allen Klein	Passed away July 4, 2009, from complications of Alzheimer's.
Robert Klein	Starred with Adam Sandler in *Reign over Me* in 2007; recently released a DVD titled *Robert Klein: The HBO Specials 1975–2005*.
Mike Klenfner	Died July 14, 2009, of congestive heart failure.
Peter Lake	Went on to his true love, writing; during the 1980s, testified in a murder trial against white supremacists while working undercover for a short-lived Larry Flynt news publication.
T.J. Lambert	Spent sixteen years at ABC and ESPN; now chief operating officer of Radiolicious.
Mauri Lathower	Retired.
Howard Marks	Died in June 1990.
Curtis Mayfield	Died December 26, 1999 from complications of diabetes.
Wally Meyrowitz	Died in 1984, reportedly of drug-alcohol complications.
Buddy Miles	Died February 26, 2008 of congestive heart failure.
Meco (Domenico) Monardo	Still recording movie-based music.
Jacques Morali	Died of AIDS November 15, 1991.
Giorgio Moroder	Involved in musical stage productions; one of his songs was used during the closing ceremonies of the 2008 Olympic Games in Beijing.
Susan Munao	Owns a management firm in California that handles Debby Boone.
Scott Muni	Died at age seventy-four on September 28, 2004.

Name	What's Going On Now
Mo Ostin	Retired in 2004, when DreamWorks Records was sold.
David Puttnam	Ran Columbia Pictures from 1986 to 1988; currently chairman of a London-based digital marketing agency.
Patti Quatro	Living in Austin, Texas; with her husband, runs a tour business for musicians.
Russ Regan	Sold his record company in 2007 to Clearvision Entertainment; became CEO as part of the acquisition.
Bob Regehr	Died of cancer, September 16, 1984.
Buck Reingold	At last report, living in a trailer park in Florida.
Artie Ripp	Living in California.
Ruben Rodriguez	The hottest R&B indie promoter in the country.
Renny Roker	Founder and CEO of Teens on the Green.
Howie Rosen	Owns a successful indie promotion company in California.
Steve Rubell	Died of hepatitis on July 25, 1989.
Kal Rudman	Still running *FMQB*.
Kenny Ryback	In LA doing indie AAA radio.
Larry Santos	Made his money singing and writing commercial jingles; retired to Las Vegas.
Ian Schrager	Owns several unique upscale hotels; recently partnered with the Marriott hotel chain.
Scott Shannon	Program director and morning man at WPLJ-FM in New York.
Dick Sherman	Died of cancer, July 2, 2008.
Gene Simmons	Still in KISS; currently executive producing the successful A&E show *Gene Simmons Family Jewels*.
Marc Paul Simon	Died in 1989.
J. R. Smalling	Founder and president of Elite Music Tours.
David Sonenberg	Manages Fergie, the Black Eyed Peas, and others.
Paul Stanley	Continues to front KISS; avidly pursuing a career in painting.

Name	What's Going On Now
Ray Stark	Died January 17, 2004 leaving an estate valued at two billion dollars.
Alison Steele	Died of stomach cancer on September 27, 1995.
Bruce Sudano	Married Donna Summer; acts as her manager.
Donna Summer	In 2008 released *Crayons*, her first CD since 1991, to much critical acclaim.
Richard Trugman	Still practicing law in California.
Bill Wardlow	Fired from *Billboard* in 1983; died December 29, 2001.
Don Wasley	Helped to launch L.A. Gear; working on various projects.
Chris Whorf	Retired and believed to be living in Mexico.
Norm Winer	VP adult rock programming for CBS Radio and still PD at WXRT-FM after some thirty years.

Casablanca Discography

What follows is a complete list of audio recordings
released under the original Casablanca Records
label, with nearly 300 albums by more than 140
artists between 1974 and 1985.

Catalog #	Album	Artist
NB 9001	*KISS*	KISS
NB 9002	*What Am I Gonna Do*	Gloria Scott
NB 9003	*Up for the Down Stroke*	Parliament
NB 9004	*Feel So Good*	Danny Cox
NB 9005	*Jus' a Taste of the Kid*	Bill Amesbury
NB 9006	*Light of Love*	T.Rex
NB 9007	*Rock and Roll Survivors*	Fanny
NB 9008	*Hollywood Situation*	Hudson Brothers
NBLP7001	*KISS*	KISS
NBLP7002	*Up for the Down Stroke*	Parliament
NBLP7003	*Jus' a Taste of the Kid*	Bill Amesbury
NBLP7004	*Hollywood Situation*	Hudson Brothers
NBLP7005	*Light of Love*	T.Rex
NBLP7006	*Hotter Than Hell*	KISS
NBLP7007	*Rock and Roll Survivors*	Fanny
NBLP7008	*Feel So Good*	Danny Cox
NBLP7009	*One for the Road*	Greg Perry
NBLP7010	*Harry and Tonto-OST*	Bill Conti
SPNB1296	*Here's Johnny: Magic Moments from "The Tonight Show"*	various artists
NBLP7011	*You and Me Together Forever*	James and Bobby Purify
NBLP7012	*Good to Be Alive*	Long John Baldry
NBLP7013	*What I Was Arrested For*	Lenny Bruce
NBLP7014	*Chocolate City*	Parliament
NBLP7015	*Einzelgänger*	Einzelgänger
NBLP7016	*Dressed to Kill*	KISS
NBLP7017	*The Boy's Doin' It*	Hugh Masekela
NBLP7018	*Larry Santos*	Larry Santos
NBLP7019	*More Miles per Gallon*	Buddy Miles
NBLP7020	*Alive!*	Kiss
NBLP7021	*Angel*	Angel
NBLP7022	*Mothership Connection*	Parliament

Release date	RIAA status	Notes
2/8/1974	Gold	Pressings from June 1974 onward contain the single "Kissin' Time"
3/11/1974		
7/10/1974		First Casablanca album to be promoted with a TV spot
3/12/1974		
7/10/1974		
N/A		
N/A		
N/A		
8/13/1974		
N/A	Gold	
N/A		
N/A		
N/A		
10/22/1974	Gold	
N/A		
N/A		
3/11/1975		
10/2/1974		
11/15/1974	Gold	Issued with a large fold-out poster
2/4/1975		
3/5/1975		
3/5/1975		
3/12/1975		
March 1975		
3/19/1975	Gold	
6/12/1975		
6/11/1975		
7/18/1975		
9/10/1975	Platinum	Originally issued with an eight-page booklet
10/27/1975		
12/15/1975	Platinum	

Catalog #	Album	Artist
NBLP7023	*Colonial Man*	Hugh Masekela
NBLP7024	*Bicentennial Gathering of the Tribes*	Buddy Miles
NBLP7025	*Destroyer*	KISS
NBLP7026	*Where Is the Love*	Margaret Singana
NBLP7027	*Thanks for the Music*	Giants
NBLP7028	*Helluva Band*	Angel
NBLP7029	*Cherries, Bananas and Other Fine Things*	Jeannie Reynolds
NBLP7030	*You Are Everything I Need*	Larry Santos
NBLP7031	*Presents the Disco Suite Symphony No. 1 in Rhythm and Excellence*	Frankie Crocker's Heart and Soul Orchestra
NBLP7032	*The Originals*	KISS
NBLP7033	*Moon over Brooklyn*	Group With No Name
NBLP7034	*The Clones of Dr. Funkenstein*	Parliament
NBLP7035	*Welcome to Club Casablanca*	Long John Baldry
NBLP7036	*Melody Maker*	Hugh Masekela
NBLP7037	*Rock and Roll Over*	KISS
NBLP7038	*Four Seasons of Love*	Donna Summer
NBLP7039	*Just Like a Recurring Dream*	Meisburg and Walters
NBLP7040	*Stallion*	Stallion
NBLP7041	*Love to Love You Baby*	Donna Summer
NBLP7042	*Get Down and Boogie*	various artists
NBLP7043	*On Earth as It Is in Heaven*	Angel
NBLP7044	*Cinnamon Flower*	Charlie Rouse Band
NBLP7045	*Wildflowers 1: The New York Loft Jazz Sessions*	various artists
NBLP7046	*Wildflowers 2: The New York Loft Jazz Sessions*	various artists
NBLP7047	*Wildflowers 3: The New York Loft Jazz Sessions*	various artists
NBLP7048	*Wildflowers 4: The New York Loft Jazz Sessions*	various artists
NBLP7049	*Wildflowers 5: The New York Loft Jazz Sessions*	various artists

Release date	RIAA status	Notes
1/30/1976		
2/24/1976		
3/15/1976	Platinum	
2/24/1976		
4/21/1976		Final album issued with original blue label artwork
5/18/1976		First album issued with new tan label artwork
6/1/1976		
10/1/1976		
N/A		
7/21/1976		Reissue of Casablanca NBLP7001, 7006, and 7016 in a combined limited edition release
9/3/1976		
7/20/1976	Gold	
10/1/1976		
11/1/1976		
11/1/1976	Platinum	Originally issued with two copies of a multicut sticker
10/11/1976		Initial pressings included a 1977 calendar
12/29/1976		
1/20/1977		
January 1977		
1/12/1977		
1/24/1977		Originally issued with a poster
February 1977		
March 1977		
March 1977		
March 1977		
March 1977		
March 1977		

Catalog #	Album	Artist
NBLP7050	Frankie Crocker & The Heart and Soul Orchestra	Frankie Crocker & The Heart and Soul Orchestra
NBLP7051	Delights of the Garden	Last Poets with Bernard Purdie
NBLP7052	The Washington Hillbillies	Washington Hillbillies
NBLP7053	Parliament Live: P. Funk Earth Tour	Parliament
NBLP7054	Life	Jimmy James
NBLP7055	Shut Out	Paul Jabara
NBLP7056	I Remember Yesterday	Donna Summer
NBLP7057	Love Gun	KISS
NBLP7058	Munich Machine	Munich Machine
NBLP7059	Disco Calypso	Beckett
NBLP7060	The Deep-OST	John Barry
NBLP7061	Don't Let the Music Stop	Larry Santos
NBLP7062	Would You Dance to My Music	Eddie Drennon and the B.B.S. Unlimited
NBLP7063	Love and Kisses	Love and Kisses
NBLP7064	Village People	Village People
NBLP7065	From Here to Eternity	Giorgio Moroder
NBLP7066	Love Shook	Pattie Brooks and the Simon Orchestra
NBLP7067	Love's an Easy Song	Meisburg and Walters
NBLP7068	A Year at the Top	Greg and Paul
NBLP7069	Zodiac Lady	Roberta Kelly
NBLP7070	Another Island	Arthur Wayne
NBLP7071	Bobby Deerfield-OST	various artists
NBLP7072	Rare Gems Odyssey	Rare Gems Odyssey
NBLP7073	Daydreamer	Pat Hollis
NBLP7074	Flame Thrower	Wildfire
NBLP7075	One Wish	Jeannie Reynolds
NBLP7076	Alive II	KISS
NBLP7077	Sphinx	Sphinx

Release date	RIAA status	Notes
7/2/1976		
4/20/1977		Douglas reissue
4/27/1977		Last of the tan label issues
5/5/1977	Gold	First album to be issued with the FilmWorks artwork; originally issued in a gatefold sleeve with a poster and iron-on transfer
1977		
5/25/1977		Issued exclusively on red vinyl
6/1/1977	Gold	
6/17/1977	Platinum	Originally issued with a paper toy gun
5/17/1977		
6/15/1977		
6/2/1977		Issued on blue vinyl with a poster of Jacqueline Bissett
4/4/1977		
6/22/1977		
July 1977		
7/18/1977		Issued as a picture disc NBPIX7064
7/22/1977		
10/3/1977		
10/3/1977		
8/12/1977		
10/3/1977		
10/3/1977		
10/3/1977		
10/13/1977		
10/3/1977		
10/3/1977		
10/3/1977		
10/24/1977	Platinum 2X	Originally issued with KISS rub-off tattoos and an eight-page booklet
2/24/1978		

Catalog #	Album	Artist
NBLP7078	*Once Upon a Time . . .*	Donna Summer
NBLP7079	*You Told Your Mama Not to Worry*	Hugh Masekela
NBLP7080	*Don't Let Me Be Misunderstood*	Santa Esmeralda Starring Leroy Gomez
NBLP7081	*At Last. . . the Pips*	Pips
NBLP7082	*Tribal Fence*	Margaret Singana
NBLP7083	*Hey Everybody*	Stallion 2
NBLP7084	*Funkentelechy vs. the Placebo Syndrome*	Parliament
NBLP7085	*White Hot*	Angel
NBLP7086	*Romeo and Juliet*	Alec R. Costandinos and the Syncophonic Orchestra
NBLP7087	*Golden Tears*	Sumeria
NBLP7088	*The House of the Rising Sun*	Santa Esmeralda 2
NBLP7089	*Gettin' the Spirit*	Roberta Kelly
NBLP7090	*A Whiter Shade of Pale*	Munich Machine Introducing Chris Bennett
NBLP7091	*How Much, How Much I Love You*	Love and Kisses
NBLP7092	*Trigger*	Trigger
NBLP7093	*Singin' in the Rain*	Sheila and B. Devotion
NBLP7094	*Pleasure Principle*	Parlet
NBLP7095	*It Don't Mean a Thing*	Eddie Drennon
NBLP7096	*Macho Man*	Village People
NBLP7097	*Night and Day*	Eclipse
NBLP7098	*Confessions*	D.C. LaRue
NBLP7099	*Thank God It's Friday—OST*	various artists
NBLP7100	*Double Platinum*	KISS
NBLP7101	*Got a Feeling*	Patrick Juvet
NBLP7102	*Keeping Time*	Paul Jabara
NBLP7103	*Forever Yours*	Sylvers
NBLP7104	*Love's in You, Love's in Me*	Giorgio and Chris
NBLP7105	*Confidential Affair*	Harvey Scales
NBLP7106	*Our Ms. Brooks*	Pattie Brooks
NBLP7107	*I Wanna Make It on My Own*	Evelyn Thomas

Release date	RIAA status	Notes
10/31/1977	Gold	
11/9/1977		
10/3/1977	Gold	
12/28/1977		
11/9/1977		
12/29/1977		
11/28/1977	Platinum	Originally issued with a poster and an eight-page booklet
1/1/1978		
1/16/1978		
1/20/1978		
1/27/1978		
3/13/1978		
5/24/1978		
4/10/1978		
3/27/1978		
3/13/1978		
2/24/1978		
6/12/1978		
2/24/1978	Platinum	
3/27/1978		
4/24/1978		
4/22/1978	Platinum	
4/24/1978	Platinum	
5/15/1978		
7/24/1978		
7/10/1978		
7/24/1978		
8/28/1978		
9/25/1978		
7/10/1978		

Catalog #	Album	Artist
NBLP7108	*Josephine Superstar*	Phylicia Allen
NBLP7109	*Beauty*	Santa Esmeralda
NBLP7110	*Gypsy Woman*	Leroy Gomez
NBLP7111	*Deliverance*	Space
NBLP7112	*Wright Brothers Flying Machine*	Wright Brothers Flying Machine
NBLP7113	*Callin'*	Pips
NBLP7114	*Midnight Express—OST*	Giorgio Moroder
NBLP7115	*Pleasure Train*	Teri DeSario
NBLP7116	*Paris Connection*	Paris Connection
NBLP7117	*Trocadéro Bleu Citron—OST*	Alec R. Costandinos
NBLP7118	*Cruisin'*	Village People
NBLP7119	*Live and More*	Donna Summer
NBLP7120	*Gene Simmons*	KISS: Gene Simmons
NBLP7121	*Peter Criss*	KISS: Peter Criss
NBLP7122	*Ace Frehley*	KISS: Ace Frehley
NBLP7123	*Paul Stanley*	KISS: Paul Stanley
NBLP7124	*Hunchback of Notre Dame—OST*	Alec R. Costandinos and His Syncophonic Orchestra
NBLP7125	*Motor-Booty Affair*	Parliament
NBLP7126	*Theme from "Battlestar Galactica" and Other Original Compositions from Giorgio Moroder*	Giorgio Moroder
NBLP7127	*Sinful*	Angel
NBLP7128	*Ultimate*	Ultimate
NBLP7129	*Hoodoo Voodoo*	C.D. Band
NBLP7130	*Highway*	Sean Delaney
NBLP7131	*Just Blue*	Space
NBLP7132	*My Kids*	Meadowlark Lemon
NBLP7133	*Take Me Home*	Cher
NBLP7134	*Nothing Is Sacred*	Godz

Release date	RIAA status	Notes
6/12/1978		
7/24/1978		
7/8/1978		
11/28/1978		
8/14/1978		
8/14/1978		
9/11/1978		
9/25/1978		
9/25/1978		
8/1/1978		
10/23/1978	Platinum	Issued as picture disc NBPIX7118
8/31/1978	Platinum	Issued as a single picture disc under *The Best of Live and More* NBPIX7119
9/18/1978	Platinum	Issued with an interlocking poster, and later as picture disc NBPIX 7120
9/18/1978	Platinum	Issued with an interlocking poster, and later as picture disc NBPIX 7121
9/18/1978	Platinum	Issued with an interlocking poster, and later as picture disc NBPIX 7122
9/18/1978	Platinum	Issued with an interlocking poster, and later as picture disc NBPIX 7123
10/16/1978		
11/22/1978	Gold	Issued as picture disc NBPIX7119 on 2/13/79
12/11/1978		
1/15/1979		Initially pressed as *Bad Publicity* with different cover art
1/15/1979		
2/13/1979		
1/8/1979		
1/15/1979		
2/21/1979		
1/25/1979	Gold	Also issued as a picture disc NBPIX7133 on 2/13/79
1/15/1979		Reissue of Millennium MNLP8010

Catalog #	Album	Artist
NBLP7135	Sleepless Nights	Brooklyn Dreams
NBLP7136	Superman and Other Galactic Heroes	Meco
NBLP7137	Body Shine	Munich Machine
NBLP7138	Look Out	Bad News Travels Fast
NBLP7139	Nightlife Unlimited	Nightlife Unlimited
NBLP7140	Like an Eagle	Dennis Parker
NBLP7141	They're Playing Our Song—OCR	various artists
NBLP7142	Agatha—OST	various artists
NBLP7143	Doin' It	Alma Faye Brooks
NBLP7144	Go West	Village People
NBLP7145	Standup Comic	Woody Allen
NBLP7146	Invasion of the Booty Snatchers	Parlet
NBLP7147	Beckmeier Brothers	Beckmeier Brothers
NBLP7148	Lady Night	Patrick Juvet
NBLP7149	Lenny and Squiggy Present Lenny and The Squigtones	Lenny and Squiggy
NBLP7150	Bad Girls	Donna Summer
NBLP7151	Disco Fever	Sylvers
NBLP7152	Dynasty	KISS
NBLP7153	I Got Rhythm	Tony Orlando
NBLP7154	I Got It Bad	Leroy Gomez
NBLP7155	Moondancer	Meco
NBLP7156	Play It Again Sam	Sam the Band
NBLP7157	You Must Be Love	Love & Kisses
NBLP7158	Party Girl	Pattie Brooks
NBLP7159	Feel It	Cindy and Roy
NBLP7160	Forces of the Night	D.C. LaRue
NBLP7161	A Night at Studio 54	various artists
NBLP7162	Reality. . . What a Concept	Robin Williams
NBLP7163	The Third Album	Paul Jabara
NBLP7164	Hot Foot: A Funque Dizco Opera	Harvey Scales
NBLP7165	Joy Ride	Brooklyn Dreams

Release date	RIAA status	Notes
1/25/1979		Reissue of Millennium MNLP 8011
1/25/1979		Reissue of Millennium MNLP 8012
4/26/1979		
4/27/1979		
5/29/1979		
3/1/1979		
2/14/1979		
2/26/1979		
2/26/1979		
3/23/1979	Platinum	Originally issued with a poster
September 1979		
4/16/1979		
5/14/1979		
4/16/1979		
4/26/1979		Originally issued with a poster
4/25/1979	Platinum 2X	
4/26/1979		
5/29/1979	Platinum	Originally issued with a poster
5/24/1979		
5/24/1979		
6/25/1979		
6/11/1979		
5/29/1979		
7/27/1979		
6/25/1979		
6/25/1979		
6/25/1979	Gold	
6/25/1979	Gold	
7/16/1979		
7/16/1979		
7/6/1979		

Catalog #	Album	Artist
NBLP7166	*Bad Reputation*	Ritchie Family
NBLP7167	*Winds of Change: A Musical Fantasy—OST*	Alec R. Costandinos
NBLP7168	*Experience*	Joel Diamond Experience
NBLP7169	$E=MC^2$	Giorgio Moroder
NBLP7170	*Lightning*	Lightning
NBLP7171	*Street Babies*	Platypus
NBLP7172	*TJM*	TJM
NBLP7173	*Chain Lightning*	Don McLean
NBLP7174	*Ronald McDonald Visits America: A Child's Tour of the 50 States*	K.I.D.S. Radio
NBLP7175	*Another Cha-Cha*	Santa Esmeralda
NBLP7176	*I Can't Forget You*	Joey Travolta
NBLP7177	*J. Michael Reed*	J. Michael Reed
NBLP7178	*Moonlight Madness*	Teri DeSario
NBLP7179	*Night Miracles*	Kenny Nolan
NBLP7180	*4 on the Floor*	4 on the Floor
NBLP7181	*Ordinary Man*	Bad News Travels Fast
NBLP7182	*Alec R. Costandino's the Synchophonic Orchestra Featuring Alirol and Jacquet*	Alec R. Costandino's the Synchophonic Orchestra Featuring Alirol and Jacquet
NBLP7183	*Live and Sleazy*	Village People
NBLP7184	*Prisoner*	Cher
NBLP7185	*Steal the Night*	Cindy Bullens
NBLP7186	*Mike Heron*	Mike Heron
NBLP7187	*Burnin' Alive*	Tony Rallo and the Midnite Band
NBLP7188	*Make Your Move*	Captain and Tennille
NBLP7189	*Loose Change*	Loose Change
NBLP7190	*Persia*	Persia
NBLP7191	*On the Radio: Greatest Hits Volumes I and II*	Donna Summer
NBLP7192	*Strange Spirits*	Skatt Brothers
NBLP7193	*Tears*	C.O.D.
NBLP7194	*Roller Boogie—OST*	various artists

Release date	RIAA status	Notes
7/16/1979		
7/24/1979		
7/16/1979		
8/27/1979		
8/13/1979		
8/13/1979		
8/27/1979		
7/26/1979		Unreleased; later issued on Millennium
N/A		
8/13/1979		
8/13/1979		
8/27/1979		
10/22/1979		
9/17/1979		
9/17/1979		
9/17/1979		
late September 1979		
9/24/1979	Gold	
10/22/1979		
10/15/1979		
10/15/1979		
10/15/1979		
10/15/1979	Gold	
10/15/1979		
10/15/1979		
10/15/1979	Platinum 2X	Originally issued with a poster
11/19/1979		
11/19/1979		
mid-November	1979	

Catalog #	Album	Artist
NBLP7195	*Gloryhallastoopid or Pin the Tale on the Funky*	Parliament
NBLP7196	*Music from "Star Trek," Music from "The Black Hole"*	Meco
NBLP7197	*Mouth to Mouth*	Lipps, Inc.
NBLP7198	*All That Jazz—OST*	various artists
NBLP7199	*Bugs Tomorrow*	Bugs Tomorrow
NBLP7200	*Thelma Camacho*	Thelma Camacho
NBLP7201	*Greatest Hits Volume One*	Donna Summer
NBLP7202	*Greatest Hits Volume Two*	Donna Summer
NBLP7203	*Live without a Net*	Angel
NBLP7204	*Mizz*	Mizz
NBLP7205	*Suzanne Fellini*	Suzanne Fellini
NBLP7206	*Foxes—OST*	various artists
NBLP7207	*It's Hard to Be Humble*	Mac Davis
NBLP7208	*Ultimate*	Ultimate
NBLP7209	*Livin' for the Music*	Tony Orlando
NBLP7210	*Danielle*	Danielle
NBLP7211	*Jeff Kutash and the Dancin' Machine*	Jeff Kutash and the Dancin' Machine
NBLP7212	*Firin' Up*	Pure Prairie League
NBLP7213	*707*	707
NBLP7214	*Edge*	Edge
NBLP7215	*John and Arthur Simms*	John and Arthur Simms
NBLP7216	*Don't Be Shy Tonight*	Santa Esmerelda featuring Jimmy Goings
NBLP7217	*Room with a View*	Player
NBLP7218	*The Hollywood Knights—OST*	various artists
NBLP7219	*Pattie Brooks*	Pattie Brooks
NBLP7220	*Can't Stop the Music—OST*	Village People

Release date	RIAA status	Notes
11/28/1979	Gold	
1/7/1980		
1/7/1980	Gold	
early February 1980		
2/19/1980		
2/19/1980		
late January 1980		
late January 1980		
late January 1980		
2/19/1980		
2/19/1980		
late February 1980		
3/11/1980	Gold	
3/11/1980		
3/21/1980		
3/11/1980		
3/21/1980		
4/21/1980		
3/21/1980		
3/21/1980		
3/21/1980		
4/21/1980		
4/24/1980		
5/16/1980		
5/23/1980		
5/20/1980		

Catalog #	Album	Artist
NBLP7221	*Cherry*	Platypus
NBLP7222	*Have You Heard*	Edmund Sylvers
NBLP7223	*Give Me a Break*	Ritchie Family
NBLP7224	*Play Me or Trade Me*	Parlet
NBLP7225	*Unmasked*	KISS
NBLP7226	*Won't Let Go*	Brooklyn Dreams
NBLP7227	*Diamond in the Rough*	Bobbi Walker
NBLP7228	*Barry Mann*	Barry Mann
NBLP7229	*No Respect*	Rodney Dangerfield
NBLP7230	*Bob McGilpin*	Bob McGilpin
NBLP7231	*Caught*	Teri DeSario
NBLP7232	*The Final Countdown—OST*	various artists
NBLP7233	*The Real Thang*	Tony Joe White
NBLP7234	*Black Rose*	Black Rose
NBLP7235	*California Son*	Paul Waroff
NBLP7236	*Rainy Day Fun: Starring Ronald McDonald*	K.I.D.S. Radio
KDLP 1003	*Birthday Party: Starring Ronald McDonald Dee-Jay*	K.I.D.S. Radio
NBLP7237	*The Chase Is On*	Carol Chase
NBLP7238	*Freddie Beckmeier*	Freddie Beckmeier
NBLP7239	*Texas in My Rear View Mirror*	Mac Davis
NBLP7240	*Out of Control*	Peter Criss
NBLP7241	*Movin' On*	Gloria Covington
NBLP7242	*Pucker Up*	Lipps, Inc.
NBLP7243	*Rock America*	Nick Gilder
NBLP7244	*Walk Away: Collector's Edition (the Best of 1977–1980)*	Donna Summer
NBLP7245	*Excuse Me*	Devin Payne
NBLP7246	*People's Choice*	People's Choice
NBLP7247	*Star, Baby*	D.C. LaRue
NBLP7248	*The Second Album*	707
NBLP7249	*Trombipulation*	Parliament

Release date	RIAA status	Notes
6/20/1980		
7/21/1980		
5/23/1980		
7/20/1980		
5/29/1980	Gold	Originally issued with a poster
7/21/1980		
6/26/1980		
8/18/1980		
6/26/1980		
7/21/1980		
8/18/1980		
7/21/1980		
8/18/1980		
8/21/1980		
9/8/1980		
early August 1980		
early August 1980		
9/8/1980		
N/A		
9/8/1980		
9/8/1980		
9/8/1980		
9/8/1980		
9/8/1980		
9/8/1980		
10/16/1980		
10/6/1980		
10/24/1980		
1981		
12/5/1980		

Catalog #	Album	Artist
NBLP7250	*Keeping Our Love Warm*	Captain and Tennille
NBLP7251	*Rising*	Dr. Hook
NBLP7252	unknown	unknown
NBLP7253	unknown	unknown
NBLP7254	*Eugene*	Crazy Joe and the Variable Speed Band
NBLP7255	*Something in the Night*	Pure Prairie League
NBLP7256	*Mantra*	Mantra
NBLP7257	*Midnight Crazy*	Mac Davis
NBLP7258	*Tonight!*	Four Tops
NBLP7259	*Body Talk Muzik*	Nick Gilder
NBLP7260	*Meco's Impressions of "An American Werewolf in London"*	Meco
NBLP7261	*Music from "The Elder"*	KISS
NBLP7262	*Designer Music*	Lipps, Inc.
NBLP7263	*Aerobic Dance Hits Volume One*	Carla Capuano
NBLP7264	*Players in the Dark*	Dr. Hook
NBLP7265	*Tantalizingly Hot*	Stephanie Mills
NBLP7266	*One More Mountain*	Four Tops
NBLP7267	*Funky Fitness*	various artists
NBLP7268	unknown	unknown
NBLP7269	*Tempest—OST*	various artists
NBLP7270	*Creatures of the Night*	KISS
NBLP7271	*White Heat*	Dusty Springfield
NBLP7272	unknown	unknown
NBLP7273	*Interplay*	Larry Santos
NBLP7274	*Forty 82*	Mac Davis
NBLP7275	*L-O-V-E*	Robert Winters and Fall
NBLP7276	*Heavyhands the Ultimate Exercise*	Heavyhands Band and the T.M. Orchestra and Chorus
NBLP7277	*Monsignor—OST*	John Williams
NBLP7278	*Flashdance–OST*	various artists

Release date	RIAA status	Notes
10/6/1980		
11/28/1980		
N/A		
N/A		
2/9/1981		
4/13/1981		
3/13/1981		
9/14/1981		
8/17/1981		
10/31/1981		
8/17/1981		
11/16/1981		
10/19/1981		
2/8/1982		
3/8/1982		
7/17/1982		
8/9/1982		
N/A		
N/A		
September 1982		
10/22/1982	Gold	
11/8/1982		
N/A		
N/A		
11/8/1982		
N/A		
12/6/1982		
October 1982		Last album to be pressed with NBLP on the jacket
4/11/1983	Platinum 6x	Released as 422 811 492-1; all of the remaining albums were given an NBLP designation, but none were issued with it; all were released with a PolyGram catalog number

Catalog #	Album	Artist
NBLP7279	*Throbbing Python of Love*	Robin Williams
NBLP7280	*4*	Lipps, Inc.
NBLP7281	*Soft Talk*	Mac Davis
NBLP7282	*The Karate Kid—OST*	various artists
NBLP7283	*Take Your Passion*	Helen St. John
NBLP7284	*Very Best and More*	Mac Davis
NBLP7285	*I've Got the Cure*	Stephanie Mills
NBLP7286	*A Chorus Line—OST*	various artists

Release date	RIAA status	Notes
3/7/1983		Released as 422-811 150-1 M-1
6/29/1983		Released as 422-811 022-1 M-1
1/16/1984		Released as 422-818 131-1 M-1
6/15/1984		Released as 422-822 213-1 M-1
N/A		
9/10/1984		Released as 422-822 638-1 M-1
9/10/1984		Released as 422-822 421-1 M-1
11/18/1985		Released as 422-826 306-1

Casablanca Promotional Films and Music Videos

Six years before the term "music video" came into popular use with the advent of MTV, Casablanca was making what were then known as promotional films. Most of these haven't been broadcast in North America since their original release, and they remain buried in the warehouses of Universal Music Group. This list most likely isn't complete, but I thought it was important to include in the book.

KISS, "Rock and Roll All Nite" (1975)

KISS, "C'mon and Love Me" (1975)

Donna Summer, "Love to Love You Baby" (1975)

Parliament, "Do That Stuff" (1976)

Angel, "Tower" (1976)

Angel, "That Magic Touch" (1976)

Angel, "You're Not Fooling Me" (1976)

Angel, "Feelin' Right" (1976)

KISS, "I Want You" (1977)

KISS, "Hard Luck Woman" (1977)

KISS, "Love 'em and Leave 'em" (1977)

Donna Summer, "Winter Melody" (1977)

Giorgio Moroder, "From Here to Eternity" (1977)

Donna Summer, "I Remember Yesterday" (1977)

Village People, "San Francisco (You've Got Me)" (1977)

Village People, "Fire Island" (1977)

Santa Esmeralda, "Don't Let Me Be Misunderstood" (1977)

Angel, "Ain't Gonna Eat Out My Heart Anymore" (1977)

Angel, "The Winter Song" (1977)

Alec R. Costandinos and the Syncophonic Orchestra, "Romeo and Juliet" (1978)

Village People, "Macho Man" (1978)

Village People, "Medley: Just a Gigolo/I Ain't Got Nobody" (1978)

Love and Kisses, "Thank God It's Friday" (1978)

Paul Jabara, "Disco Queen" (1978)

Village People, "YMCA" (1978)

Donna Summer, "MacArthur Park" (live) (1978)

Donna Summer, "Heaven Knows" (live) (1978)

Donna Summer, "I Feel Love" (live) (1978)

Donna Summer, "Last Dance" (live) (1978)

Munich Machine, "Let Your Body Shine" (1979)

Space, "Save Your Love for Me" (1979)

Brooklyn Dreams, "Make It Last" (live) (1979)

Godz, "He's a Fool" (1979)

Meadowlark Lemon, "My Kids" (1979)

Angel, "Don't Take Your Love" (1979, unreleased)

Santa Esmeralda, "Another Cha-Cha" (1979)

Dennis Parker, "Like an Eagle" (1979)

Village People, "In the Navy" (1979)

Village People, "Go West" (1979)

KISS, "I Was Made for Lovin' You" (1979)

KISS, "Sure Know Something" (1979)

Village People, "Sleazy" (1979)

Village People, "Ready for the 80s" (1979)

Captain and Tennille, "Do That to Me One More Time" (1979)

Lipps, Inc., "Funkytown" (1980)

Skatt Brothers, "Life at the Outpost" (1980)

KISS, "Shandi" (1980)

Crazy Joe and the Variable Speed Band, "Eugene" (1981)

KISS, "A World without Heroes" (1981)

KISS, "I" (1981, montage edit)

KISS, "I" (1981, unreleased performance version)

KISS, "I Love It Loud" (1982)

Irene Cara, "Flashdance . . . What a Feeling" (1983)

Michael Sembello, "Maniac" (1983)

Index